Everybody's Guide to

Small Claims Court

Everybody's Guide to Small Claims Court

Attorney Ralph Warner

Research: David W. Brown

A NOLO PRESS BOOK

▲▼ ADDISON-WESLEY PUBLISHING COMPANY

Reading, Massachusetts • Menlo Park, California
London • Amsterdam • Don Mills, Ontario • Sydney

Library of Congress Cataloging in Publication Data

Warner, Ralph E.
  Everybody's guide to small claims court.
  Includes index.
  1.   Small claims courts–United States.
I.   Title.
KF8769.W37   347.73'28   80–455
ISBN 0-201-08304-3
ISBN 0-201-08303-5 pbk.

For Toni,
the light, the heart, and the love of my life

To Our Readers

This book can be of great help to you and your family. The advice it offers about Small Claims Court is as sound as I have been able to make it, after much study of, and experience in, the area. Many knowledgeable people have reviewed these materials and many of their suggestions for change and clarification have been included. But advice will not always work. Like well-meaning recommendations of all kinds, some of the advice I present here may not be helpful. So here are some qualifications. If you have access to a lawyer's advice and it is contrary to that given here, follow your lawyer's advice; the individual characteristics of your problem can better be considered by someone in possession of all the facts. Laws and procedures vary considerably from one state to the next and it's impossible to guarantee that every bit of information and advice contained here will be accurate. It is your responsibility to get a copy of the rules governing your local Small Claims Court and to make sure that the facts and general advice contained in this book are applicable in your state and to your situation. Please realize, too, that this book was printed in the spring of 1980. Small Claims Court rules and regulations change constantly, and you should check with your Small Claims Court clerk to make sure that information printed here is still current. And finally, please pay attention to this general disclaimer: Of necessity, neither the author nor the publisher of this book makes any guarantees regarding the outcome of the uses to which this material is put. Thank you, and good luck!

Berkeley, California　　　　　　　　　　　　　　　　　　　　R. W.
April 1980

Thank You

A number of talented friends have read the manuscript of this book and made helpful suggestions for improvement. With enough help, even a tarnished penny can be made to shine. Thanks to Dan Armistead, Leslie Ihara Armistead, Peter Honigsberg, Toni Ihara, Keija Kimura, Eileen Baris Luboff and Walter Warner. I am especially indebted to Ron Lomax of the Alameda County Law Library, who has the nose of a bloodhound and the eye of an eagle when it comes to finding esoteric bits of legal information.

Special thanks to Ellen Roddy of the Small Claims Court Clerk's Office in Berkeley, California, who patiently answered hundreds of questions during the months that I was putting this book together, and then made dozens of excellent suggestions for change after reading the manuscript. Thanks too, to Roger Dickinson of the State of California Department of Consumer Affairs, who doesn't always agree with what I write, but is, nonetheless, unfailingly helpful.

David Brown compiled the research for all material appearing in the Appendix. His thorough, patient and dedicated work have made this a better book.

Linda Allison's wonderful drawings speak for themselves. Working with her is like catching the first ray of sunshine on a clear morning.

Contents

8. Who Can Be Sued?   **63**

9. Where Can I Sue?   **71**

10. Plaintiff and Defendant's Filing Fees, Court Papers, and Court Dates   **77**

11. Serving Your Papers

12. The Defendant's Options

13. Getting Ready for Court

14. Witnesses   117

15. Presenting Your Case to the Judge   127

16. Motor Vehicle Repair Cases   135

17. Motor Vehicle Purchase Cases   141

18. Cases in Which Money Is Owed

19. Vehicle Accident Cases

20. Landlord– Tenant Cases

21. Miscellaneous Cases

Introduction

Here is a practical book on how to use Small Claims Court. It is a tool that will help you answer such questions as:

"How does Small Claims Court work?"

"Do I have a case worth pursuing or defending?"

"How do I prepare my case to maximum advantage?"

"What witnesses and other evidence should I present?"

"What do I say in court?"

"Can I appeal if I lose?"

"How do I collect my judgment?"

Proper preparation and presentation of your Small Claims Court action can often mean the difference between receiving a check and writing one. This isn't to say that I can tell you how to take a hopeless case and turn it into a blue ribbon winner. It does mean that with the information you will learn here and your own creativity and common sense, you will be able to develop your position in the best possible way. It does mean that I can show you how a case with a slight limp can be improved and set on four good legs.

Just as important as knowing when and how to bring your Small Claims Court action is knowing when not to. You don't want to waste time and energy dragging a hopeless case to court. Here we will teach you to understand the difference between winners and losers, and we hope, keep the losers at home.

The goal of this book is to give both people bringing a case and those defending one all the step-by-step information necessary to make the best possible use of Small Claims Court. From deciding whether you have a case through gathering evidence, arranging for witnesses, planning your courtroom presentation, and collecting your money, you will find everything you need here.

Certain arbitrary decisions have had to be made as to order and depth of coverage. For example, the question of whether an oral contract is valid is discussed in Chapter 2, but not again in Chapter 16 on automobile repairs, where you may need it. So please take the time to read, or at least skim, the entire book before you focus on the chapters that interest you most. You may find something on page 106 that will change what you learned on page 32. A good way to get an overview of the entire Small Claims Court process is to read carefully the Contents pages. It would be worthwhile to read them through several times before starting the text itself. Also, be sure to examine the detailed rules (in the Appendix) for the area in which you live.

Chapter 23 is the last part of this book designed to help you win your case and collect your money. Chapter 24 is devoted to a different cause—how our court system must be changed to deliver more justice and less frustration. In many ways this material is intensely personal in that it reflects my own experience with our formal, lawyer-dominated legal delivery system. It springs from my own painful realization that neither law, nor justice, nor the resolution of disputes is what our courts are presently about. We have allowed them to become instead the private fiefdom of lawyers, judges, and other professionals, and it is their selfish interests that are being served rather than the common good.

I have included this material because I believe that it will be of interest to all of you who have become involved in the resolution of your own disputes in Small Claims Court. You have had the courage to take responsibility for solving your own problems. Given the opportunity, you can do a great deal more. It is past time that you are allowed to participate in your own legal system. It is past time that you are made welcome in your own courthouses. It is past time that all of us realize that a society whose legal system is run by and for lawyers can't survive long.

In the Beginning 1

First Things

Small Claims procedures are established by state law. This means that there are differences in the operating rules of Small Claims Courts from state to state.* Differences include such things as the maximum amount for which you can sue, who can sue, and what papers must be filed where and when. In the text of this book, I will be using examples primarily from Small Claims Court in California and New York, but will indicate those situations in which the rules of other states may vary. In addition, an Appendix includes most of the information you will need no matter where you are using these materials.

The differences among Small Claims Courts from state to state tend to be of detail, not substance. The basic approaches necessary to prepare and present a case properly are remarkably similar everywhere. But details are important, and you will wish to obtain from your local Small Claims Court clerk a copy of its procedural rules to supplement what you read here. Many times in this book I will advise you to check a particular detail in your state's law. If you can't find the answer in your local rules, call the Small Claims Court

---

*There are also differences among names used for Small Claims Court (or its equivalent) in the different states. As you will see in the Appendix, "Justice of the Peace," "conciliation," "District," "Justice," "Municipal," "City," and "County" courts are among the names commonly used. Often, Small Claims Courts will be listed in the telephone directory under these "parent" courts, and not as "Small Claims Courts" as such.

clerk and ask. Remember, your tax money pays for the court system, and you have a right to be completely informed.

The purpose of Small Claims Court is to hear disputes involving modest amounts of money, without long delays and formal rules of evidence. Disputes are normally presented by the people involved. Lawyers are not prohibited in most states, but the limited dollar amounts involved usually make it uneconomical for people to hire them.* The maximum amount of money for which you can sue (in legal jargon this is called the "jurisdictional amount") is $750 in California, and $1,000 in a number of states, including New York.† These amounts are about average, although there is considerable variation. Some states allow Small Claims Court cases involving thousands of dollars, and others limit Small Claims Court to cases worth no more than two or three hundred dollars. (See Appendix.)

In recent years the maximum amount for which suits can be brought has been on the rise almost everywhere. Don't rely on your memory, or what a friend tells you, or even what you read here. Call the local Small Claims Court clerk and find out exactly how much you can sue for. You may be pleasantly surprised and find that the maximum is more than you thought.

There are three great advantages of Small Claims Court. First, you get to prepare and present your own case without having to pay a lawyer more than your claim is worth. This right to self-representation should be radically expanded to types of cases not permitted in Small Claims Court. Unfortunately, such expansion runs counter to the self-interest of lawyers, who, like the czars of old Russia or the French nobility at the time of the Revolution, will fight to the death rather than ease the way for sensible reform.

The second great advantage to bringing a dispute to Small Claims Court is simplicity. The gobbledygook of complicated legal forms and language is kept to a minimum. To start your case, you need only fill out a few lines on a simple form (e.g., "Honest Al's Used Chariots owes me $1,000 because the 1977 Chevette they sold me in supposedly 'excellent condition' died less than a mile from the car

---

*The trend, however, is to eliminate lawyers completely (see Appendix for state-by-state rules). In California, Michigan, and Oregon, for example, lawyers may appear in Small Claims Court only when they are suing (or being sued) on their own case, but may not represent others.

†Effective April 1, 1979, the maximum amount for which you can sue has been raised to $1,500 in six California judicial districts: Oakland-Piedmont, East Los Angeles, Fresno, Compton, San Bernardino (Chino Division), and West Orange County.

lot."). When you get to court, you can talk to the judge without a whole lot of "res ipsa loquiturs" and "pendente lites." If you have documents or witnesses, you may present them for what they are worth, with no requirement that you comply with the thousand years' accumulation of fusty, musty procedures, habits and so-called rules of evidence of which the legal profession is so proud.

Third, and perhaps most important, Small Claims Court doesn't take long. Most disputes are heard in court within a month or two from the time the complaint is filed. The judge makes his or her decision on the basis of what is presented in the courtroom, and normally renders a decision within a few days.

But before you decide that Small Claims Court sounds like just the place to bring your case, you will want to answer a basic question. Are the results you are likely to achieve in proportion to, or greater than, the effort you will have to expend? This question must be answered individually, and the answers at which you and your neighbor arrive may be very difficult. It is all too easy to get so emotionally involved in a dispute that you lose sight of the fact that the time, trouble, and expense of continuing are way out of balance with any likely return.

In order to think profitably about whether your case is worth the effort, you will need to understand the details of how Small Claims Court works—who can sue, where, for how much, etc. You will also want to learn a little law—are you entitled to relief, how much, and how do you compute the exact amount? Finally and most importantly comes the detail that so many people overlook to their later dismay. Assuming that you prepare and present your case brilliantly, and get a favorable judgment for everything you request, can you collect? This seems a silly thing to overlook, doesn't it? Sad to say, however, it is often done. Plaintiffs commonly go through the entire Small Claims Court procedure with no chance of collecting a dime because they have sued a person with no money.

The purpose of the first dozen chapters of this book is to help you decide whether or not you have a case worth pursuing. These are not the Perry Mason sections where grand strategies are brilliantly unrolled to baffle and confound the opposition—that comes later. Here we are more concerned with what Della Street does off camera—such mundane tasks as locating the person you want to sue, suing in the right court, filling out the various forms, and getting them served properly. Perhaps it will disappoint those of you with a dramatic turn of mind, but most cases are won or lost before anyone enters the courtroom.

Throughout this book we reproduce forms used in one or another judicial district in California and New York.* Forms in use outside of these states will sometimes look quite different from these

---

*Even within California, forms are laid out differently from one judicial district to the next. Thus if you live in Los Angeles and we reproduce a San Francisco form, you will have to make some changes.

samples, but you will find that the differences are usually more a matter of graphics than of substance. The basic information requested—who is suing whom about what—is very similar everywhere. Blank copies of all forms are available at your local Small Claims clerk's office. It's an excellent idea to look these over at home before you find yourself trying to deal with them at a noisy counter. I often get calls from people who have made silly mistakes in filling out papers and have found that they are troublesome to correct.

Checklists of Things to Think Out before Initiating or Defending Your Case

Here is a sort of preliminary checklist of things you will want to think about at this initial stage. As you read further, we will go to each of these areas in more detail. But let me remind you again, if you haven't already gotten a copy of your local Small Claims Court rules, do it now. It's silly to come to bat with two out in the ninth and the bases loaded and not know if you are supposed to run to first or third.

CHECKLIST OF QUESTIONS NEEDING ANSWERS BEFORE YOU FILE IN SMALL CLAIMS COURT

- Does the other person owe you the money, or, put another way, "is there liability"? (See Chapter 2.)
- What is the dollar amount of your claim? If it is more than the Small Claims maximum, do you wish to waive the excess and still use Small Claims? (See Chapter 4.)
- Is your suit brought within the proper time period (Statute of Limitations)? (See Chapter 5.)
- In what Small Claims Court should you bring your suit? (See Chapter 9.)
- Whom do you sue? As you will see in many cases, especially those involving businesses and automobiles, this can be a little more technical and tricky than you might have guessed. (See Chapter 8.)
- Have you made a reasonable effort to contact the other party to offer a compromise? (See Chapter 6.)
- And again, the most important question—assuming that you can win, is there a reasonable chance that you can collect? (See Chapters 3 and 2.)

CHECKLIST OF QUESTIONS NEEDING ANSWERS BEFORE DEFENDING A CASE

- Do you have a good defense to the claim of the plaintiff? (See Chapters 2 and 12.)
- Has the plaintiff sued for a reasonable or an excessive amount? (See Chapter 4.)
- Has the plaintiff brought his or her suit within the proper time limits (Statute of Limitations)? (See Chapter 5.)
- Has the plaintiff followed reasonably correct procedures in bringing suit and serving you with the court papers? (See Chapters 11, 12.)
- Have you made a reasonable effort to contact the plaintiff in order to arrive at a compromise settlement? (See Chapters 6 and 12.)

Defendant's Note: In addition to your right to defend a case, you also have the right to file your own claim (Chapters 10 and 12). You would want to do this if you believed that you suffered damage arising from the same incident or transaction that formed the basis of the plaintiff's suit against you, and that the plaintiff was responsible for your loss. If your claim is for less than the Small Claims Court maximum, you can file your claim of defendant (called a "counterclaim" in many states) in Small Claims Court. But if it is for more, you will probably wish to get the case transferred to a formal court.* Before making any decision, read your local rules carefully.

Legal Jargon Defined

Mercifully, there is not a great deal of technical language in use in Small Claims Courts. But there are a few terms that may be new to you. Don't try to learn all of these now. A quick read-through is enough—you can refer back to later if you find particular jargon confusing. Here we give you the most widely used version of most terms. In some states jargon may vary slightly, but the substance will be remarkably similar everywhere.

> **Abstract of Judgment:** An official document which you get from the Small Claims Court clerk's office that shows you that you have a money judgment against another person. This is usually needed as part of the collection process.

*A few states require that even claims over the Small Claims Court limit be first presented to a Small Claims Court judge to see if they have merit before transfer to a formal court is allowed. Some states, such as New York, Hawaii, and Washington, will refuse to accept counterclaims over the dollar limit at all, and transfer to a higher court is not allowed on this basis. In these states a defendant must initiate a new action in formal court if his or her claim is for more than the Small Claims Court maximum.

Appeals: Some states only allow a defendant to appeal; others allow appeals based only on law—not facts. Many require a bond to be posted. (See Chapter 22 and Appendix.)

Arbitration: A voluntary system under which a case is heard by arbitrators rather than in a court setting. Not available in most states, but used widely in New York City night courts. Ask your court clerk for local rules, if any.

Civil Code (C.C.) and Code of Civil Procedure (C.C.P.): Books which contain some of a state's substantive and procedural laws. They are available at all public libraries and at law libraries located at the county courthouse and open to the public in most states. Some states call their collected laws by other names, such as "Revised Statutes," "Rules of Civil Procedure" (RCP), and "Rules of Court." Ask the law librarian for help if you have trouble finding the right book.

Claim of Defendant: A claim by a defendant that the plaintiff owes him or her money. A Claim of Defendant is filed as part of the same lawsuit that the plaintiff has started.

Claim of Exemption: A procedure by which a "judgment debtor" can claim that under federal and/or state law certain of his or her money or other property is exempt from being grabbed to satisfy the debt.

Continuance: A court order that a hearing be postponed to a later date.

Counterclaim: Basically the same as a "claim of defendant" or a "cross complaint." Different states use different names.

Default Judgment: A court decision given when one person fails to show up (defaults).

Defendant: The person being sued.

Equity: That amount of a particular piece of property that you actually own. For example, if a car has a fair market value of $2,000 and you owe a bank $1,000 on it, your equity is $1,000.

Formal Court: As used here, this term refers to the regular "lawyer-dominated" state courts. The states call their trial courts by all sorts of names (municipal, superior, district, circuit, supreme, civil, etc.). All of these courts require a knowledge of confusing language and procedure, and you will want to avoid them if possible. For example, in California, claims of up to $15,000 that are not eligible for Small Claims Court are heard in Municipal Court, and claims over that amount are heard in Superior Court.

Garnishee: To attach money, usually wages or commissions, for payment of a debt the creditor has a court judgment. This is often how Small Claims Court judgments are collected.

Homestead Declaration: Many, but by no means all, states have procedures by which homeowners can protect some of the equity in their homes from creditors. In California, this protection is $40,000 in equity for families and persons 65 or over, and $25,000 for a single person.*

Judgment: The decision rendered by the court.

Judgment Creditor: A person to whom money is owed under a court decision.

Judgment Debtor: A person who owes money under a court decision.

Levy: A legal method to seize property or money for unpaid debts. For example, a sheriff could levy on (sell) your automobile if you refused to pay a judgment.

Lien: A legal right to an interest in the property of another for payment of a debt. To get a lien you first must get a court judgment and then take proper steps to have the court enter an "Abstract of Judgment." You can then take the Abstract to the County Recorder's office in a county where the judgment debtor has real property to establish the lien.

Order of Examination: A procedure allowing a creditor to question a debtor about the extent and location of his or her assets. Other states have similar procedures, but names may vary somewhat. Often they are referred to as "Supplemental Proceedings."

---

*For more information and all the forms necessary to file a Declaration of Homestead in California, see Warner, Sherman, and Ihara, 1978, Protect Your Home with a Declaration of Homestead, Nolo Press. For information on homestead amounts in other states, see Kosel, 1980, A Legal Guide to Bankruptcy, Addison-Wesley.

Plaintiff: The person who starts a lawsuit.

Recorder (Office of the County Recorder): The person employed by the county to make and record documents that relate to the ownership of real property. The County Recorder's office is usually located in the main county courthouse.

Statute of Limitations: The period of time you have to file a suit from the time that the act or omission occurs. (See Chapter 5.)

Transfer: The procedure by which the defendant can have a Small Claims case transferred to a "formal court." In most states this can be done when the defendant has a claim against the plaintiff arising out of some incident for an amount more than the Small Claims maximum. In a few states it can also be done because the defendant simply doesn't want to be in Small Claims Court. In many states a defendant who wants a jury trial can also transfer to formal court. See Appendix for details.

Writ of Execution: An order by a court to the sheriff (or marshal, constable, or other official) of a specific area (in most states, this is either a city or county) to collect a specific amount of money due.

Do You Have a Case? 2

Before you even start thinking about going to court—any court—you must answer a basic question. Do I have a good case?

Many mornings I have sat in Small Claims Court and watched people competently and carefully present hopeless cases. Why hopeless? Usually because the plaintiffs overlooked one of the most basic facts of litigation. Before you can collect for a loss you have suffered, you must show that the other party caused you to suffer the loss. Put into legal slang, this means that you must show that there is "liability." Obvious, you say. Perhaps it is to you, but apparently not to lots of others.

Here is what often seems to happen. People focus on their own loss—the amount of money that they are out as a result of whatever incident occurred. They think that because they have been damaged they must have a right of recovery against someone. But the fact that a loss has occurred isn't enough to make a winning case. You must also prove that the person you are suing is legally responsible to compensate you for the loss. Doing this is often easy and obvious, but sometimes it is neither.

How do you establish that another person owes you money? Or, put another way, how do you establish "liability"? Normally, you must establish at least one of the following three things. There are a number of technical legal defenses to all of these approaches, but for now, let's just look at the general theories.

1. That a valid contract (written, oral or implied) has been broken by the person you are suing and that, as a result, you have suffered money damages (see "How to Approach a Breach of Contract Case");

13

2. That the intentional behavior of the person you are suing has caused you to suffer money damages (see "How to Approach a Case in Which Your Property Has Been Damaged by the Negligent or Intentional Acts of Someone Else");

3. That the negligent behavior of the person you are suing has caused you to suffer money damages (see "How to Approach a Case in Which Your Property Has Been Damaged by the Negligent or Intentional Acts of Someone Else").

Before we look at each of these theories of "liability" in detail, let me tell you the story of a case I watched recently in Small Claims Court in Berkeley, California. The plaintiff (remember, the plaintiff is the person who initiates the lawsuit), a college student, who we'll call Sue, had rented a parking space in the basement garage of an apartment house owned by defendant. There was a driveway entrance door to the garage that could be shut and locked, sealing the garage from the street. However, as the tenants were unwilling to go to the trouble of opening and closing the door, it always stood open. Indeed, the door had been open night and day for years, including the six months during which plaintiff had kept her car in the garage. There was also access to the garage from inside the building, which contained 15 apartments, most of them occupied by more than one person.

One night someone entered the garage, smashed a window in Sue's car and stole a fancy AM–FM radio and tape deck worth $528.50. Upon discovery of the theft, Sue immediately got several witnesses to the fact that her car had been broken into. She took pictures and then called the police. After the police investigation was completed, Sue obtained a copy of their investigation report. She also got several estimates of the cost of repairing the damage to the car window, the lowest of which was $157. Sue then filed suit against the building owner for $685.50.

Sue overlooked only one thing. Unfortunately for her, it was an important one. In the circumstances, the building owner wasn't liable. He had never promised (orally or in writing) to keep the garage locked, had never done so, had never led Sue to believe that he would do so, and indeed could point to requests from other tenants that the garage be kept open. All the tenants were reasonably on notice that it was easy to gain access to the garage from either inside or outside the building. Put simply, the building owner was neither in violation of a contract, nor guilty of any negligent behavior in failing to lock the garage. The situation facing Sue was no different from what it would have been if her car had been damaged in the street.

Now let's take this same little drama and change a few facts. Instead of a situation in which the door was always open and no one ever expected it to be closed, let's now assume that the lease contract signed by the landlord and tenant stated that the tenant would be assigned a parking place in a "locked garage." Let's also assume that the garage had always been locked until the lock broke seven days before the theft occurred. Finally, let's assume that Sue and other tenants had asked the owner to fix the lock the day after it broke, but that he hadn't "gotten around to it."

In this situation, Sue should win. The landlord made certain promises to the tenant (to keep the garage locked) and then failed to keep them, even though he had ample opportunity to do so. The failure presumably allowed the robber access to the car.

Note: In both of the situations above, the total amount of actual damage, $685.50, was the same. In the first, there was no right of recovery (the defendant wasn't liable). But in the second, the apartment owner's failure to keep the door locked violated defendant's lease contract. In addition, the failure of the apartment owner to fix the lock within a reasonable time constituted negligence.

How to Approach a Breach of Contract Case

In broad outline, a contract is any agreement between parties in which one person agrees to do something for the other in exchange for something in return. The agreement may be written, oral, or implied from the circumstances (e.g., I deliver milk to your house and you pay for it).*

Example: "I promise to give you $750 on the first of January." This is not a contract because you have promised to do nothing for me in return. I have only indicated that I will give you a gift in the future. This sort of promise is not enforceable.†

---

*Contracts that can't be performed within a year must be in writing. However, the great majority of consumer type contracts can be performed in a year, and therefore oral contracts are normally enforceable.
†If the promise was based on an underlying loan—that is, "I promise to give you $750 on the first of January because you lent me that amount last year," it would be a valid contract.

Example: "I promise to pay you $750 on January 1 in exchange for your promise to shine my doorknob every morning before 7 o'clock." This is a valid contract. If I refuse to pay you, you can go to court and get a judgment for the $750.

Perhaps the largest number of cases coming before Small Claims Courts involve the breach of a contract. Often, the contract that has not been honored involves a failure to pay money. Hardly a day goes by when someone isn't sued for failing to pay the phone company, the milk deliverer, the local hospital, or even book fines to the public library. But sometimes a breach of contract suit stems not from failure to pay a bill but from the fact that one party has performed his or her duties under the contract badly, or not at all, and the other person has been damaged as a result. Such might be the case if an apartment owner accepted a deposit and agreed to rent an apartment to a tenant and then rented it to someone else.*

Damages resulting from a breach of contract are normally not difficult to prove. You must show that the contract existed (if it is written, it should be presented to the court, and if it's oral or implied from the circumstances, it should be stated). You must then testify as to the circumstances of the other person's breach of the contract and the amount of damages you have suffered. In many situations this involves no more than stating that a legitimate bill for X dollars has not been paid.

Example: "Joe Williams owes me $500 because he failed to pay for car repairs that he asked me to perform. I did all the repairs properly. Here is a work order signed by Joe authorizing me to do the work."

The fact that many contract cases are easy to win doesn't mean that all are won. I have seen a good number of plaintiffs lose what seemed to them open and shut cases. Why? Simply because they failed to show that defendant owed them any money. Put another way: they failed to show that a contract existed. (See the second example below.) In other situations the plaintiff is able to show that a contract existed, but not that defendant breached it.

Example: Let's go over the facts of a situation that I witnessed recently in Small Claims Court. Plaintiff sued defendant for $450, the cost of replacing a pigskin suede jacket that was ruined by defendant's cleaning establishment. Plaintiff had taken the jacket to defendant for cleaning and given him a $40 fee. Defendant, by accepting the jacket and the fee, clearly implied that he would properly clean the jacket. A contract existed.

Leases and rental agreements, whether written or oral, are contracts.

Plaintiff was very sure of his loss. He stood in the courtroom, a great bear of a man, looking as if he had just escaped from a professional football team, and slowly put the jacket on. As he wiggled into it, the whole courtroom, including the judge, who almost choked trying to keep a straight face, burst out laughing. With a little luck, the jacket would have fit a good-sized jockey. The sleeves barely covered the man's elbows and the hemline didn't reach his waist.

As I sat watching, I thought that the case was over and that the plaintiff had won easily. Certainly he had made his point more effectively by putting on the jacket than he could have with ten minutes of testimony. I was wrong. The plaintiff had overlooked two things, one obvious, and one not so obvious. The defendant, a clever man, started his testimony, and by the time he was done, the plaintiff's case had shrunk almost as much as the jacket.

The obvious thing that plaintiff overlooked in asking for the $450 replacement value of the jacket was that the jacket was two years old and had been worn a good bit. Valuation is a common problem in clothing cases, and we will discuss it in detail in Chapters 4 and 21. Let's just say here that the jacket was worth no more than $250 in its used condition and that, in any case where your property is damaged or destroyed, the amount of your recovery will be limited to the fair market value of the goods at the time the damage occurs—not their replacement value.

Now let's look at defendant's other defense. He testified that, when he saw the jacket after cleaning, he had been amazed. His cleaning shop specialized in leather goods, and the process used should have resulted in no such shrinking problem. What's more, he testified that he had examined a number of other garments in the same cleaning batch and found no shrinking problem with any of them. To find out what had happened, he sent the jacket to an "independent testing laboratory." Their report, which he presented to the court, stated that the problem was not in the cleaning but in the jacket. It was poorly made in that the leather had been severely overstretched prior to assembly. When it had been placed in the cleaning fluid, it had shrunk as a result of this poor original workmanship.

What happened? The judge was convinced by the testing lab report and felt that defendant had breached no contract as far as the cleaning was concerned.* However, he also felt that defendant, as a leather cleaning specialist, had a responsibility to notify plaintiff

*Plaintiff could still bring suit against the person who made the jacket for defective workmanship. It could be argued that, by using inferior material, they had breached an implied warranty (contract) that the goods sold were reasonably fit.

that the jacket should not have been cleaned in the first place. Therefore, the judge held mostly for the defendant, but did award the
plaintiff $50 in damages.

Example: A few weeks later I saw another contract case in which
the plaintiff had suffered an obvious loss, but failed to show that defendant was responsible for making it good. This time it was a plaintiff landlord suing the parent of a tenant for damages that the tenant
had done to her apartment. The parent was sued because he had co-
signed his daughter's lease contract. The plaintiff easily convinced
the judge that the damage had in fact occurred, and the judge
seemed disposed toward giving judgment for the $580 requested until
the parent presented his defense. He showed that the lease between
his daughter and the landlord that he had originally co-signed had
been rewritten three times without request for his signature. He
claimed that, because he had not co-signed any of the subsequent
lease contracts, he wasn't liable. The judge agreed.*

Note: We will get into individual factual situations of contracts further in Chapters 16–21. Before you decide whether or not you have a
good case, read on.

How to Approach a Case in Which Your Property Has Been Damaged by the Negligent or Intentional Acts of Someone Else

After cases involving breach of contract, the most common disputes
that come to Small Claims Court involve damage to one person's
property caused by the negligent actions of another. Less often, the
plaintiff claims that he or she suffered loss because the defendant intended to damage his or her belongings.

A technical definition of what constitutes negligence could easily fill the next few pages. Indeed, whole law texts have been written

---

*Leases, rental agreements, and the rights and responsibilities of co-signers
are discussed in more detail in Moskovitz, Warner, and Sherman, 1980, California Tenants' Handbook, Fifth Edition, Nolo Press. While this book relates
specifically to California, it contains much general information of value in all
states.*

on the subject. I remember thinking in law school that the more the scholarly professors wrote, the more mixed up they got. Like good taste or bad wine, negligence seems to be easy to recognize, but hard to define.

Here is one-sentence definition. If, as a result of another person's conduct, your property is injured and that person didn't act with reasonable care in the circumstances, you have a case based on his or her negligence.* It's as simple—or complex—as that. If you

*Sometimes negligence can occur when a person who has a duty or responsibility to act fails to do so. For example, a car mechanic who fails to check your brakes after promising to do so would be negligent.

want to get into the gory details of the subject, go to your nearest law library and get any recent text on "torts." "Torts" are wrongful acts or injuries.

Example: Jake knows the brakes on his ancient Saab are in serious need of repair, but does nothing about it. One night when the car is parked on a hill, the brakes fail and the car rolls across the sidewalk and destroys Carolyn's pomegranate tree. Carolyn sues Jake for $25, which is the reasonable value of the tree. Jake would lose because he did not act with reasonable care in the circumstances.

Another situation obviously involving negligence is one in which a car or bus swerves into your driving lane and sideswipes your fender. The driver of the offending vehicle had a duty to operate it in such as way as not to harm you and failed to do so. However, if your neighbor's tree falls on a car parked in your driveway, negligence could be difficult to show. Here you have to be ready to prove that for some reason (age, disease, an obviously bad root system, etc.) the tree was in a weakened condition, and the neighbor was negligent in failing to do something about it. If the tree had looked to be in good health, you would have a tough time proving that your neighbor was negligent in not cutting it down or propping it up.

There is no foolproof way to determine in advance if someone is or is not negligent. It's often a close question—a matter of judgment. If you are in doubt, bring your case and let the judge decide. After all, he or she gets paid (by you) to do it.

Here are a couple of questions which may help you make a decision as to whether you have a good case based on someone else's negligence.

- Did the person whose act (or failure to act) injured you behave in a reasonable way? Or to put it another way, would you have behaved differently if you were in his or her shoes?
- Was your conduct partly the cause of the injury?

If you believe that the person who caused you to suffer a monetary loss behaved in a unreasonable way (ran a red light when drunk) and that you were acting sensibly (driving at 30 mph in the proper lane), you probably have a good case. If you were a little at fault (slightly negligent), but the other fellow was much more at fault (very negligent), you can still recover in California, New Jersey, New York, Wisconsin, and most other states. If a judge finds that one person (drunk and speeding) was 80 percent at fault and that the other (slightly inattentive) was 20 percent at fault, the comparatively innocent party can recover 60 percent of his or her loss.*

How to Approach a Personal Injury Case

The considerations here are much the same as outlined in section above. You must show not only that you were injured but that someone's intentional or negligent behavior caused your injury.†

Example: Keija takes Harry, her Pekinese puppy, for a walk without a leash. Soto walks by and Harry takes an instant dislike to his purple and orange socks and shows it with a quick nip on Soto's right ankle. As Soto was on a public sidewalk where he had a right to be, we can safely assume that Keija was negligent in allowing Harry to bite him. Why? Because, as a society, we have decided that you can't let your dog run about biting people in public places, even if those people do have horrible taste in socks. If you do, you are negligent and are going to have to pay for it.

Example: Now, let's change our example and assume that, instead of biting Soto, Harry went after a burglar who was trying to sneak into Keija's garage window. Let's also assume that after the dust cleared and the cops hauled the burglar away it was discovered that he had suffered the same injury as Soto. Although the burglar's blood was just as red as Soto's, he can recover nothing. Why? Because

*There is also a concept called "strict liability." This concept is applied to such things as nuclear reactors, munitions storage, people who keep wild and potentially dangerous animals (a cheetah in the city), and other extremely hazardous activities. Anyone injured by an hazardous activity can recover without showing either negligence or intent to harm. This is so because, when a high level of danger is present, the person undertaking the activity is "strictly liable" for any and all injuries.
†A few states still follow an old-fashioned rule that says that if a person filing suit was even a little negligent, he or she can't recover. This is called the doctrine of "contributory negligence." See Chapter 3 of Heft and Heft, 1980, Comparative Negligence Manual, Callaghan. You may wish to check which system exists in your state at your local law library. Other states follow a system that mixes some concepts of comparative negligence and some of contributory negligence.

Keija is entitled to protect herself and her property and, as a society, we have decided that keeping a dog with sharp teeth is a reasonable way to do so.

Now let's change the example again. This time Harry bites Walter, Keija's next door neighbor, who had climbed over the backyard fence to get some apples from Keija's tree. Keija knew that the neighbor took apples, but never encouraged him to do so. The neighbor knew that Harry was in the yard and that Harry's slogan seemed to be "if it moves, bite it." Here again, there would be no liability. Keija had taken reasonable precautions to secure Harry in her own yard. She owed no duty of care to her apple-poaching neighbor in this situation.

I know you're getting sick of hearing about nasty little Harry, but bear with him a moment longer. Let's assume now that Harry bites a traveling salesman of carrot-peelers who knocks at the front door. Can the salesman recover? Probably. Even though Keija didn't invite him to come onto her land and never let a carrot in the house, the salesman had the right to assume that it was safe to go up the walk to the front door. But suppose Keija had a fence around the front yard with a latched gate and a "Beware of the Dog" sign, complete with a picture of Harry hanging onto someone's leg? This would be enough to satisfy Keija's duty of care to the rest of the world and if the carrot-peeler salesman entered the gate anyway, he would do so at his own risk.

Suggestion: Before you sue someone for a personal injury (or for property damage), think about whether they owed you a duty of care and whether they breached that duty. If in doubt, go ahead and sue, but be prepared to deal with this question ("liability") as well as simply showing the extent of your injury. In later chapters I will give some practical advice on how to prove your case.

Stating Your Claim on Your Court Papers

Before you get too far into theories of law, let me bring you back to earth for a minute. While it is helpful to have a good grasp of what's involved in proving a contract or negligence case (the judge, after all, is a lawyer), it is also essential that you stay grounded on the facts of your grievance. One of the joys of Small Claims Court is that you don't plead theories of law—you state facts.

Let's jump ahead and take a look at the form you will fill out when you file your case. Turn to Chapter 10 and find Exhibit 10.1 entitled "Plaintiff's Statement." Look at Line 5. As you can see, there is little space for theory. Indeed, there is barely room to set down the facts of your dispute. You should state your case like this:

"I took my coat to John's Dry Cleaners and it was returned in a damaged (shrunken) condition."

"Defendant's dog bit me on the corner of Main and Canal Streets in Dover, Pennsylvania."

"The car repairs that Joe's Garage did on my car were done wrong, resulting in my engine burning."

"Defendant refused to return the cleaning deposit for my apartment even though I left it clean."

Note: When you state your case on the court papers, your only goal is to notify the other party and the court as to the broad outlines of your dispute. You don't want to try to argue the facts of your case or the law that you believe applies to it. Your chance to do this will come later in court.

Important: Now is a good time to start organizing your materials in one place. Get a couple of manila envelopes or file folders, label them carefully, and find a safe place for storage. One folder or envelope should be used to store all documentary evidence such as receipts, letters, photographs, etc. The other is for your court papers, filing fee receipts, etc. It's no secret that more than one case has been won or lost because of good (or bad) record keeping.

Can You Collect If You Win? 3

This is the shortest chapter in the book and the most important. In it, I ask all of you who are thinking of filing a Small Claims Court suit to focus on a very simple question—can you collect if you win? Collecting from many individuals or businesses isn't a problem as they are solvent and will routinely pay any judgments entered against them. But all too often, the main problem you face in Small Claims Court is not winning your case, but collecting your money when you do win.

I am co-author with Peter Jan Honigsberg of the book published by Nolo Press in 1979 entitled *The California Debtors' Handbook—Billpayers' Rights*. It contains information for Californians who are over their heads in legal debts and don't know how they are going to keep the roof over their heads and clothes on their kids' backs. The message of the book is that, surprisingly, there are many ways for debtors to protect themselves. A creditor can't take the food from the debtor's table, or the TV from the living room, or even the car from the driveway.* And this isn't true only in California—substantial debtor protection laws exist everywhere and are set out in Kosel, 1980, *A Legal Guide to Bankruptcy*, Addison-Wesley.

What do these facts mean to you? Simply that many people who are not completely without money are nevertheless "judgment-proof." You can sue them and get judgments against them until red cows dance on the yellow moon, but you can't collect a dime. Unfortunately, just this sort of frustrating thing happens every day—peo-

---

*In California, a debtor's car is protected only if he or she has $500 or less equity in it, unless he or she uses the car as a tool of trade, in which case the car is exempt from attachment as long as the equity is $2,500 or less, C.C.P. 690.4, 690.2.

ple go to lots of trouble to win cases only to realize that the judgment is uncollectible. This, of course, compounds the misery. Not only has the person suing lost the money from the original debt or injury, but also the time, trouble and expense of the Small Claims Court suit. As my grandmother used to say, "No one ever got to live in the big house on the hill by throwing a good quarter after a bad dime."

Whenever a dispute develops, it is all too easy to get caught up in thinking and arguing about who wronged whom. So easy that perspective is lost and the problems of collection are forgotten. I emphasize this because I have so often observed people bringing cases to court in which there was never a hope of collecting. How can I tell ahead of time? I can't always, but in many situations, it's not hard. One thing I look for is whether or not the defendant is working. If a person fails to pay a judgment voluntarily, the easiest way to collect it is to garnishee his or her wages.* Thus if the person sued is working there is an excellent chance of collecting if payment is not made voluntarily. But you can't garnishee a welfare, social security, unemployment, pension, or disability check. So, if the person sued gets his or her income from one of these sources, red flags are flying.

But what about other assets? Can't a judgment be collected from sources other than wages? Yes, it can—bank accounts, motor vehicles, and real estate are other common collection sources. But before you get too enthusiastic, you should know that many states have restrictions on what you can go after—or to say the same thing in a different way, many items of property are exempt from attachment. In New York, for example, among a long list of exemptions, we find "all stoves kept for use in the judgment debtor's dwelling house," a "pew occupied by the judgment debtor in a place of public worship" and a TV set. Many states say that a portion, or all, of the equity in a debtor's home is exempt. In California a creditor can't effectively get at the equity in a family house unless it exceeds $40,000.†

*Wage garnishments are limited by federal and state law to 25 percent or less of net earnings. New Mexico, Texas, and North Carolina exempt 100 percent of wages. Several other states exempt all (or most) of the wages of low-income families.

†California also exempts a whole list of other possessions including furniture, a car with $500 or less in equity, the tools of a person's trade, etc. Each state has a list of "exempt" property. See Kosel, 1980, A Legal Guide to Bankruptcy, Addison-Wesley, for a 50-state list of exemptions. In California, property that is exempt from being taken to satisfy debts is listed in Warner and Honigsberg, 1979, The California Debtor's Handbook—Billpayers' Rights, Nolo Press. The Debtors' Handbook contains forms and instructions necessary for a debtor to take advantage of his or her rights.

So before you go down and file your papers, ask yourself these questions:

1. Does the person you wish to sue voluntarily pay debts—or are you dealing with a person who will make it as difficult as possible to collect if you win?

2. Does he or she have a job?

3. If this person doesn't have a job, does he or she have some other means of support or assets that convince you that you can collect?

4. If you have your doubts about voluntary payment and the person you are suing doesn't have a job, can you identify some nonexempt assets that you can attach, such as a bank account, or real property other than the place where the person lives?

5. If a business is involved, is it solvent and does it have a good reputation for paying debts?

Note: If a person or a business declares bankruptcy and lists you as a creditor, your right to recover is normally cut off. In theory, you have a right to share in any assets the bankrupt has at the time of the bankruptcy but, as a practical matter, this usually doesn't amount to much, if anything. If you are owed money on a secured debt (there was a security agreement as in the case of a car or major appliance), you are entitled to recover your security as part of the bankruptcy proceeding if the debt was incurred as part of the purchase of the secured item.

In Chapter 23, we deal in detail with the mechanics of collecting after you get your judgment. If you think that this may pose a problem, you will wish to read this chapter now. But remember what my canny, old grandmother said about bad dimes and good quarters and don't waste your time chasing people who have no money.

How Much Can You Sue For? 4

The maximum amount for which you can sue in Small Claims Court varies from state to state. It's $750 in Connecticut, and $1,000 in many states, including Illinois, New York, and Wisconsin. It's $2,000 in Alaska, but only $200 in Wyoming* (see the Appendix for other states, Washington, D.C., and Puerto Rico). As suggested in Chapter 1, you should get a copy of the rules that affect you by calling your local Small Claims Court clerk. With some exceptions, Small Claims Court does not hear cases unless they are for money damages. This means that you can't use Small Claims Court to get a divorce, stop (enjoin) the city from cutting down your favorite oak tree, change your name, or do any of the thousands of other things that require some solution other than the payment of money.†

Note: In a step in the right direction California has joined Alabama, Nebraska, and a number of other states, and now allows the judge to grant equitable relief in the form of recission, restitution, reformation, and specific performance instead of, or in addition to, money damages (C.C.P. Section 116.2). See "Equitable Relief" in this chapter for details.

*In a number of states, you can use Small Claims Court to handle certain types of eviction. See Chapter 20 and the Appendix.
†A few states, such as Massachusetts, have different maximum amounts depending on the type of claim. In Massachusetts, an individual can sue a business for as much as $2,250.

The fact that you have a claim that is less than the Small Claims Court maximum doesn't mean that you must sue in Small Claims Court. In California and most states you can sue in formal court for a $200 claim if you wish, but if you do, you must follow all their technical rules and pay filing fees that will average $25—$75. A few states, however, restrict cases involving less than a few hundred dollars to Small Claims Court.

Why is Small Claims Court limited to such small amounts and to cases involving money? Well, the traditional assumption has been that people aren't very competent to deal with their own legal affairs. Only lawyers, it was thought, were clever enough to handle anything but the most inconsequential claims. Who made these assumptions? We all have, but we have been encouraged to do so by lawyers themselves, who have long dominated our state legislatures in which our court rules are made. Somehow, as a society, we have allowed lawyers to metamorphose from dry, little men in English villages, with little more going for them than an ability to read and write and a fireproof box in which to store papers, to self-proclaimed superpeople who seem convinced they have been given a mandate to run the world. Small Claims Courts have been tolerated in part as a direct result of this growth in lawyers' egos. Lawyers have become so important in their own eyes that it is somehow beneath their dignity to become involved in disputes over piddling amounts.

But times are starting to change. All sorts of people are beginning to realize that our legal system is staggering under a heavy load of favoritism, waste, and archaic and often nonsensical rules designed primarily by and for lawyers. One result of this realization is a growing interest in expanding Small Claims Courts. In some states Small Claims Court jurisdiction has already been substantially increased. As you might guess, lawyers regard this expansion much as they would a 500-pound bear stepping slowly on their toes.

Knowing the "dollar limit" or the largest amount for which you can sue is important, but it is only one of many facts that you will have to deal with in deciding how much you wish to demand when you fill out your papers. Here are some other things to think about.

Cutting Down a Claim That's Over the Limit to Fit It into Small Claims Court

It is legal to reduce an excessive claim so that it will fit into Small Claims Court. For example, you could take a $1,350 debt in New York (where the dollar limit is $1,000) and bring it into Small Claims Court, claiming only $1,000.* But if you do this, you forever waive the $350 difference between $1,000 and $1,350. In legal parlance, this is called "waiving the excess." Why wouldn't this be a silly thing to do? It would be if it wasn't for the insanity of our court system where the alternative to Small Claims Court involves filing your suit in a formal court with dozens of complicated rules and the considerable expense involved in having a lawyer draw up papers, etc. A lawyer would probably charge considerably more than $600 to represent you. It is possible to represent yourself in a formal court, but doing so requires a good bit of homework and the guts to walk into an unfamiliar and sometimes hostile arena. I don't mean to discourage you. Lots of people have successfully handled their cases in our formal courts, but you should be aware before you start that your path may be lonely and frustrating. If you wish to take your case to a formal court yourself, you might start by looking at the legal form books which are available for most states. These encyclopedia-like books show you how to prepare most of the papers that you will ever need to file.†

Splitting Small Claims Court Cases

It is not legal to split an over-the-limit claim into two or more pieces to fit each into Small Claims Court. Taking the $1,350 figure we used above, this means that you couldn't sue the same person separately for $700 and $650. As with most rules, however, a little creative thought will take you a long way. While you can't split a case that's too big to get it into Small Claims Court, you can bring multiple suits against the same person as long as they are based on different claims. This is where the creativity comes in. There is often a large gray area in which it is genuinely difficult to differentiate between one divided claim and several independent ones. If you can reasonably argue that a $1,350 case actually involves two or more separate contracts, or injuries to your person or property, you may as well try dividing it. The worst that will happen is that a judge will disagree

---

*Cost, such as filing fees, serving of process, fees where witnesses are subpoenaed, etc., are recoverable in addition to the dollar limit in California and most states.

†You will find these books, as well as many others that may be helpful to you, at your county law library. Law libraries exist in most major courthouses and are open to the public. Law librarians are usually very helpful in assisting you to find materials. The best book on how to decipher the code of the law library and really understand how to use it is Peter Jan Honigsberg, 1979, Cluing into Legal Research, Golden Rain Press.

and tell you to make a choice between taking the entire claim to a formal court, or waiving any claim for money in excess of the dollar limit and staying in Small Claims.

Example: Recently I watched a man in the private telephone business come into Small Claims Court with three separate lawsuits against the same defendant for a combined total of $2,000 in a state where the Small Claims Court maximum is $750. One claim, he said, was for failure to pay for phone installation, another was for failure to pay for phone maintenance, and the third was for failure to pay for moving several phones to a different location. The man claimed that each suit was based on the breach of a separate contract. The judge, after asking a few questions, told the man that he was on the border-line between one divided (no good) and several separate (OK) claims, but decided to give him the benefit of the doubt and allowed him to present each case. The man won all three and got two judgments for $700 and a third for $600.

Example: Another morning in the same state, a women alleged that she had lent a business acquaintance $750 twice and was there-fore bringing two separate suits, each for $750. The defendent said that this wasn't true. She claimed that she had borrowed $1,500 on two installments. A different judge, after listening to each person briefly, told the plaintiff that only one claim was involved and that, if she didn't want to waive all money over $750, she should go to formal court.

Suggestion: If you wish to sue someone on two related claims that you believe can be viewed as separate, you may be better off to file your actions a few days apart. This will result in their being heard on different days, and in most metropolitan areas, by different judges. Unless the defendant shows up and argues that you have split one claim, you will likely get your judgments without difficulty. There is, however, one possible drawback to this approach. If you bring your claims in on the same day and the judge rules that they are one claim, he or she will give you a choice as to whether to waive the excess over the small claims maximum in your state, or go to a formal court. However, if you go to court on different days and the question of split claims is raised on the second or third day, you may have a problem. If the judge decides that your action in splitting the claims was im-proper, he or she has no choice but to throw the second and third claims out of court with no opportunity to refile in a formal court. The reason for this is that you have already sued and won, and you are not entitled to sue the same person twice for the same claim.

How to Compute the Exact Amount of Your Claim

Sometimes it's easy to understand exactly what dollar amount to sue for, but often it's tricky. Before we get to the tricky part, let's go over the basic rule. When in doubt, always bring your suit a little on the high side. Why? Because the court has the power to award you less than you request, but can't give you more, even if the judge feels that you are entitled to it. But don't go overboard—if you sue for $1,000 on a $300 claim, you are likely to spur your opponent to furious opposition, ruin any chance for an out-of-court compromise, and lose the respect of the judge.

COMPUTING THE EXACT AMOUNT— CONTRACT CASES

To arrive at the exact figure to sue on in contract cases, compute the difference between the amount you were supposed to receive under the contract and what you actually received. For example, if Jeannie Goodday agrees to pay Homer Brightspot $1,200 to paint her house to look like a rainbow, but then only gives him $600, Homer has a claim for $600 plus the cost of filing suit and serving Jeannie with the papers (costs are discussed in more detail in Chapter 15). The fact that Jeannie and Homer made their agreement orally does not bar Homer from suing. Oral contracts are OK as long as they can be carried out in a year. Of course, people tend to remember oral contracts differently, and this can lead to serious proof problems once you get to court. It is always wise to reduce agreements to writing, even if only to a note or letter agreement dated and signed by both parties.

Where the contract involves lending money in exchange for interest, don't forget to include the interest due in the amount for which you sue. * I have seen several disappointed people sue for the

*As a general rule, you can only recover interest when it is called for in a written or oral contract. If you loaned a friend $100 but never mentioned interest, you can sue only for the return of the $100.

exact amount of the debt (say $900) and not include interest (say $100), thinking that they could have the judge add the interest when they got to court. This can't be done—the judge doesn't have the power to make an award larger than the amount you request. Of course, you can't sue for interest if the interest amount would make your claim larger than the Small Claims Court maximum.*

Unfortunately, not all claims based on breach of contract are easy to reduce to a money amount. This is often due to a legal doctrine known as "mitigation of damages." Don't let the fancy term throw you. As with so much of our law, the concept behind the "mumbo jumbo" is simple. "Mitigation of damages" means simply that the person bringing suit for breach of contract must take all reasonable steps to limit the amount of damages he or she suffers. Let's take an example from the landlord-tenant field. Tillie the tenant moves out three months before the end of her lease (remember a lease is a contract). Her monthly rent is $500. Can Lothar the landlord recover the full $1,500 ($500 × 3 months) from Tillie in Small Claims Court, assuming that the Small Claims Court limit in the state in which Tillie and Lothar live is at least that high? Probably not. Why? Because Lothar has control of the empty apartment and must take reasonable steps to attempt to find a new tenant. If Lothar can re-rent the apartment to someone else for $500 or more per month, he has suffered no damage. Put another way, if Lothar re-rents the apartment, he has fulfilled his responsibility to "mitigate damages." In a typical situation it might take Lothar several weeks (unless he had plenty of advance notice, or Tillie herself found a new tenant) to find a suitable new tenant. If it took three weeks and $50 worth of newspaper ads, Lothar could recover approximately $425 from Tillie.

The "mitigation of damages" concept isn't applicable only to landlord-tenant situations, but applies to every contract case in which the person damaged can take reasonable steps to protect himself or herself. In the earlier example, if Jeannie Goodday had agreed to pay Homer Brightspot $200 per day for six days to paint her house and then had canceled after the first day, Homer could sue her for the remaining $1,000 but, if he did, he would surely be asked whether he had earned any other money during the six days. If he had, it would be subtracted from the $1,000. But what if Homer re-

*This is the general rule. In some states you may collect interest in situations where your underlying claim equals the Small Claims maximum and the interest brings the total over the maximum. Check your local rules.

fused other work and slept in his hammock all week? If Jeannie could show that he had turned down other jobs, or had refused to make reasonable efforts to seek available work, this too would be used to reduce Homer's recovery.

Suggestion: Sue only for the amount of money you are out. Don't try to collect money in court that you have already recovered from someone else.

COMPUTING THE EXACT AMOUNT— PROPERTY DAMAGE CASES

When your property has been damaged by the negligent or intentional act of someone else, you have a right to recover for your loss.* This amount is often, but not always, the amount of money that it would take to fix the damaged item.

Example: John Quickstop bashes into Melissa Caretaker's new Dodge, smashing in the left rear fender. How much can Melissa recover? The amount that it would cost to fix or, if necessary, replace the damaged part of her car. Melissa should get several estimates from responsible body and fender shops and sue for the amount of the lowest one, if John won't pay voluntarily. (See Chapter 19.)

There is, however, a big exception to the rule that a person who has had property damaged can recover the cost of fixing the damaged item. This occurs when the cost to fix the item exceeds its actual cash market value. You are not entitled to a new or better object—only to have your loss made good. Had Melissa Caretaker been driving a 1969 Dodge, the cost to fix the fender might well have exceeded the value of the car. If this were the case, she would be entitled to the value of the car, not the value of the fender repair.

Think of it this way. In any situation in which the value of repair exceeds the value of the object, you are limited to the fair market value of the object (what you could have sold it for) a minute before the damage occurred. From this figure, you have to subtract the value, if any, of the object after the injury. Of course, in deciding how much to claim, you should give yourself the benefit of the doubt as to

*If you haven't already done so, read Chapter 2. It is important to remember that you have to establish not only the amount of your damage but that the person you are suing is legally responsible ("liable") to pay your damages.

how much a piece of property is worth, but don't be ridiculous. A $500 motor scooter might conceivably be worth $650 or $700 but it's not worth $1,250.

Example: Let's return to Melissa. If her 1969 Dodge was worth $900 and the fender would cost $1,000 to replace, she would be limited to a $900 recovery, less what the car could be sold for in its damaged state. If this was $100 for scrap, she would be entitled to $800. However, if Melissa had just gotten a new engine and transmission and her car was worth $1,500, she would legally be entitled to recover and sue for the entire $1,000 needed to get her Dodge fixed.

Note: Many people insist on believing that they can recover the cost of getting a replacement object when theirs has been totaled. As you should now understand, this isn't necessarily true. If Melissa's $900 car was totaled and she claimed that she simply couldn't get another decent car for less than $1,500, she would still be limited to recovering $900. To get $1,500 she would have to show that her car had a sale value of that much just before the accident. This rule can cause you a real hardship when an older object that is in great shape is destroyed. The fair market value may be low, while the cost of replacement high.

Knowing what something is worth and proving it are quite different. A car that you are sure is worth $1,800 may look like it's worth only $1,200 to someone else. In court you will want to be prepared to show that your piece of property is worth every bit of the $1,800. Perhaps the best way to do this is to get some estimates (opinions) from experts in the field (e.g., a car dealer if your car was ruined). This is best done by having the expert come to court and testify, but can also be done in writing. You will also want to check newspaper and flea market ads for the prices asked for comparable goods and creatively explore any other approaches that make sense, given the type of damage you have suffered. We talk more about proving your case in court in Chapters 16–21.

COMPUTING THE EXACT AMOUNT— CASES INVOLVING DAMAGE TO CLOTHING

Clothing is property, so why am I separating it out for special treatment? For two reasons. Cases involving clothing are extremely common in Small Claims Court, and judges seem to apply a logic to them that they apply to no other property damage cases. The reason for this is that clothing is personal to its owner and often has small or little value to anyone else even though it may be in good condition. If the rules that we just learned (i.e., you can recover the repair cost of a damaged item unless this would be more than its market value before the damage occurred, in which case you are limited to recovering its total value) were strictly applied to clothing, there would often be little or no recovery because there is not much market for used clothing.

When suing for damage to new or almost new clothing, sue for its cost. If it is older, sue for that percentage of the value of the clothing that reflects how worn it was when the damage occurred. For example, if your two-year-old suit which cost $400 new was destroyed, sue for $250 if you feel the suit would have lasted another two years. In clothing cases most judges want answers to these questions: How much did the clothing cost originally? How much of its useful life was consumed at the time the damage occurred? Does the damaged item still have some value to the owner, or has it been ruined?

Example: Angeles took her new $200 coat to Salvador, a tailor, to have alterations made. Salvador cut part of the back of the coat in the wrong place and ruined it. How much should Angeles sue for? $200, as the coat was almost new. She could probably expect to recover close to this amount.

Example: The same facts as just above but the coat was two years old and had been well worn. Here Angeles would be wise to sue for $125 and hope to recover $100.

Example: Again, Angeles and the coat. This time we will return it to its almost new condition, but have Salvador slightly deface the back, instead of completely destroying it. I would still advise Angeles to sue for the full $200. Whether she could recover that much would depend on the judge. Most would probably award her a little less on the theory that the coat retained some value. Were I Angeles, however, I would strongly argue that I didn't buy the coat with the expectation that I could wear it only in a closet and that, as far as I was concerned, the coat was ruined. (See Chapter 21 for more details.)

COMPUTING THE EXACT AMOUNT—
PERSONAL INJURY CASES

Lawyers quickly take over the great majority of cases in which someone is injured. These claims are routinely inflated (a sprained back might be worth $4,000–$6,000 or more), because it is in everyone's selfish interest to do so. The insurance adjusters and insurance company lawyers are as much a part of this something-for-nothing syndrome as are the ambulance-chasing plaintiff's attorneys. If there aren't lots of claims, lots of lawsuits, lots of depositions and negotiations, it wouldn't take lots of people making lots of moeny to run the system. Even in states with so-called no-fault automobile insurance, the dispute resolution bureaucracy has managed to protect itself very well.

Some small personal injury cases do get to Small Claims Court, however. Dog-bite cases are one common example, and there are others. Here is how you figure the amount to sue for:

Out-of-pocket medical costs,
including medical
transportation   _____

Loss of pay or vacation time
for missing work   _____

Pain and suffering*   _____
Total†   _____

In more serious cases you would also have to figure the monetary value of any permanent injury. These cases do not, however, get to Small Claims Court.

†Often a personal injury is accompanied by injury to property. Thus, a dog bite might also ruin your pants. You add all of your damages together as part of the same suit. You can't sue separately for your pants and your behind.*

Medical and hospital bills, including transportation to and from the doctor, are routinely recoverable as long as you have established that the person you are suing is at fault. However, if you are covered by health insurance and the insurance company has already paid your medical costs, you will find that your policy says that any money that you recover for these costs must be turned over to the company. Often, insurance companies don't make much effort to keep track of, or recover, Small Claims Court judgments as the amounts of money involved don't make it worthwhile. Knowing this, many judges are reluctant to grant judgments for medical bills unless the individual can show that they are personally out-of-pocket the money.

Loss of pay or vacation time is viewed in a similar way. If the cocker spaniel down the block lies in wait for you behind a hedge and grabs a piece of your derriére for breakfast, and as a result you miss a day of work getting yourself patched up, you are entitled to recover the loss of any pay, commissions, or vacation time. However, if you are on a job with unlimited paid sick time, so that you suffer no loss for missing work, you have nothing to recover.

The third area of recovery is for what is euphemistically known as "pain and suffering." This is a catch-all phrase that simultaneously means a great deal and nothing at all. Generations of lawyers have made a good living mumbling it. Their idea is often to take a minor injury (sprained ankle) and inflate its value as much as possible by claiming that the injured party underwent great "pain and suffering." "How much is every single minute that my poor client suffered an unbearably painful ankle worth—one dollar, five dollars, ten thousand dollars?" etc. When you read about million-dollar settlements, a good chunk of the recovery routinely falls in the "pain and suffering" category. I don't mean to suggest that recovery for "pain and suffering" is always wrong—just that it is often abused.

But back to the case of the nasty cocker spaniel. If you received a painful bite, spent the morning getting your rump attended to, had to take several painkillers and then make sure that the dog was free of rabies, you would very likely feel that you were entitled to some recovery. One judge I know doesn't pay much attention to the evidence in this type of case. He simply awards $300 for a bite by a medium-sized dog, adds $100 for anything the size of a lion, and subtracts $100 if the dog looks more like a hamster.

Suggestion: In thinking about how much you wish to sue for, be aware that lawyers often bring suit for three to four times the amount of the out-of-pocket damages (medical bills and loss of work). Therefore, if you were out-of-pocket $150, you might wish to ask for

$500, the extra $350 being for "pain and suffering." If you have no medical bills (there is no blood, or at least x-rays), you will find it difficult to recover anything for "pain and suffering." This is why lawyers routinely encourage their clients to get as much medical attention as possible. Or, as my friend Anne-Therese says, "The squeaky cat gets the most tuna fish."

Example: Mary Tendertummy is drinking a bottle of pop when a mouse foot floats to the surface. She is greatly nauseated, loses her lunch and goes to the doctor for medication. As a result, she loses an afternoon's pay. She sues the pop company for $700. This is reasonable. She will probably recover most of this amount.

Example: The same thing happens to Roy Toughguy. He just throws the pop away in disgust and goes back to work. A few weeks later he hears about Mary's recovery and decides that he too could use $700. How much is he likely to recover? Probably not much more than the price of the soda—he apparently suffered little or no injury.

Note: Certain costs of suit such as filing fees, subpoenaed witness fees, costs of serving papers, etc., can be recovered, but many, such as compensation for time off from work to go to court, transportation to and from court, etc., cannot. See Chapter 15 for more information. You do not add these costs to the amount of your suit. The judge does this when the case is decided.

Equitable Relief (or Money Can't Always Solve the Problem)

Nearly half the states* (including California) allow judges to grant relief (provided you ask for it) in ways that do not involve the payment of money if equity (fairness) demands it. "Equitable relief"† is

---

*If you think you may want to sue "in equity," where the payment of money just isn't enough, go to your local library and check the Small Claims statute section number referred to in the Appendix. If your state allows equitable relief, then the law will usually either refer to recission, restitution, specific performance, etc., or it may just state that Small Claims "jurisdiction" is the same (with a lower dollar limit) as that of the format court of which Small Claims is a department or branch. But if your state's law limits recovery to "payment of money only," or some such words, equitable relief is probably not allowed in Small Claims Court.

†This discussion of equitable remedies is, of necessity, short and simplistic. For more information, see Rutter, 1962, Equity, Gilbert Law Summaries, Gardena, California.

usually limited to one or more of four categories: "recission," "restitution," "reformation," and "specific performance." Let's translate these into English.

Recission: This is a remedy that is used when a grossly unfair or fraudulent contract is discovered, or when a contract was based on a mistake concerning an important fact. Thus, if a merchant sued you for failure to pay for aluminum siding that you contended had been misrepresented and was a total rip-off, you could ask that the contract be rescinded.

Restitution: This is an important remedy. It gives a judge the power to order that a particular piece of property be transferred to its original owner when fairness requires that the contracting parties be restored to their original positions. It could be used in the common situation in which one person sells another a piece of property (say a motor scooter) and the other fails to pay. Instead of simply giving the seller a money judgment which might be hard to collect, the judge now has the power to order the scooter restored to its original owner.

Reformation: This remedy is somewhat unusual. It has to do with changing (reforming) a contract to meet the original intent of the parties in a situation in which some term or condition agreed to by the parties has been left out and fairness dictates that this be done. Thus, if Arthur the Author and Peter the Publisher orally agree that Peter will publish Arthur's 200-page book, and then they write a contract inadvertently leaving out the number of pages, a court would, at Peter's request, very likely "reform" the contract to include this provision if Arthur showed up with a 750-page manuscript. Reformation is most commonly used when an oral agreement is written down wrong.

Specific Performance: This is an important remedy that comes into play where a contract involving an unusual or "one-of-a-kind" object has not been carried out. Say you agree to buy for your mother's birthday an antique jade ring that is exactly like one she lost years before, and then the seller refused to go through with the deal. A court could cite the doctrine of "specific performance" to order that the ring be turned over to you. "Specific performance" will be ordered only in situations in which the payment of money will not make a party to a contract whole.

Note: In filling out your court papers you will still be required to indicate that the value of the item for which you want equitable relief is under the Small Claims maximum (see Appendix). Thus, you might describe the nature of your claim (Chapter 10, Step 1) as follows: "I want the delivery of a 'one-of-a-kind' antique jade ring worth approximately $700 according to my contract with defendant."

Is the Suit Brought within the Proper Time Limits (Statute of Limitations)? 5

Each state sets up time limits within which lawsuits must be filed. These are called Statutes of Limitations. Time limits are different for different types of cases. If you wait too long, your right to sue will be barred by these statutes. Why have a Statute of Limitations? Because it has been found that disputes are best settled soon after they develop. Unlike wine, lawsuits don't improve with age. Memories fade and witnesses die or move away, and once-clear details tend to blur together. As a general rule, it is wise to sue as soon after your dispute arises as is reasonably possible. Statutes of Limitations are almost never less than one year, so if you file promptly,you should have little to worry about. Often suits against governments can't be brought unless the government is notified almost immediately of your claim. So, if your dispute is with a city, county, or state, check the rules as quickly as possible.

Almost all disputes brought to Small Claims Court are brought promptly, so the question of whether the person suing has waited too long usually doesn't come up. If your case is one of the rare ones in which the statute of limitations is, or may be, an issue (this will almost never occur unless *at least* one year has passed since the dispute arose), you will want to check out the statute of limitations for your state. Check your state's laws under the headings "Limitations" or "Statute of Limitations." Read the material carefully—the time periods in which a suit must be brought will vary depending on the type of suit (e.g., oral contract, written contract, personal injury, etc.).

Statute of Limitations Periods— California and Texas

I include here Statute of Limitation periods for two of our largest states. As stated above, time limits for starting legal actions in other states will vary and you should check the rules that apply to you. But don't get so bogged down with the Statute of Limitations that you miss the major point, which is to sue as promptly as possible after you have suffered a loss. You will find a set of your state's laws at a public library or a law library, which, in most states, will be located at the local courthouse. Check the index under "Statute of Limitations" or just "Limitations." If you have trouble finding what you need, ask the librarian for help. Librarians positively enjoy finding things.

CALIFORNIA

Personal Injury: One year from the injury, or, if the injury was not immediately discovered, one year from the date it was discovered.

Oral Contracts: Two years from the day the contract was broken.

Written Contracts: Four years from the date of breach of contract.

Damage to Personal or Real Property: Three years from the date the damage occurs.

Fraud: Three years from the date of the discovery of the fraud.

Suits against Public Agencies: Before you can sue a city, county, or state government, you must file an administrative claim form. The time period in which this must be done is normally 100 days. This is not precisely a Statute of Limitations, but it has the same effect. (See Chapter 8 for a more complete discussion of how to sue governments in Small Claims Court.)

TEXAS

Libel and Slander: One year from the date of the libel or slander.

Evictions (Forcible Entry and Detainer): Two years.

Oral Contracts (Debts): Two years from the day the contract was broken.

Personal Injuries: Two years from the injury or, if the injury was not immediately discovered, two years from the date of discovery.

Written Contracts (Debts): Four years from the day the contract was broken (but limitation period for actions upon stated or open accounts is only two years).

Note: Some contracts which you may assume to be oral may actually be written. People often forget that they signed papers when they first arranged for goods or services. For example, your charge accounts, telephone service, and insurance policies, as well as most major purchases of goods and services, involve a written contract, even though you haven't signed any papers for years. And another thing—to have a written contract you need not have signed a document full of whereases and therefores. Any signed writing can be a contract, even if it's written on toilet paper with lipstick. When you go to a car repair shop and they make out a work order and you sign it—that's a contract. (See Chapter 2 for more about contracts.)

Computing the Statute of Limitations

OK, now let's assume that you have found out what the relevant limitations period is. How do you know what date to start your counting from? That's easy. Start with the day the injury to your person or property occurred or, if a contract is involved, start with the day that the failure to perform under the terms of the contract occurred. Where a contract to pay in installments is involved, start with the day that the first payment was missed.

Example: Doolittle owes Crabapple $500, payable in five monthly installments of $100. Both live in San Jose, California. They never wrote down any of the terms of their agreement. Doolittle misses his third monthly payment which was due on July 1, 1980. Crabapple should compute his Statute of Limitations period from July 2, 1980, assuming, of course, that Doolittle doesn't later catch up on his payments. Since the Statute of Limitations period for oral contracts is two years, this means that Crabapple has until July 1, 1982 to file his suit. If a written contract had been involved, Crabapple could file until July 1, 1984, as the Statute of Limitations on written contracts is four years in California.

I am frequently asked to explain the legal implications of the following situation. After the Statute of Limitations runs out (say two years on an oral contract to pay for having a fence painted), the debtor commences voluntarily to make payments. Does the voluntary payment have the effect of creating a new two-year Statute of Limitations period, allowing the person who is owed the money to sue if the debtor again stops paying? In most states including California, simply starting to pay on an obligation barred by the Statute of Limitations doesn't create a new period for suit.* All the creditor can do is to keep his toes crossed and hope that the debtor's belated streak of honesty continues. However, if the debtor signs a written agreement to make the payments, this does create a new Statute of Limitations period. In legal slang this is called "reaffirming a debt."

Example: Back to the drama of Doolittle and Crabapple. Let's assume that in February, 1983, Doolittle experiences a burst of energy, gets a job, and decides to pay off all of his debts. He sends Crabapple $50. A week later, suffering terrible strain from getting up before noon, he quits his job and reverts to his old ways of sleeping in the sun when not reading the racing form. Is the Statute of Limitations allowing Crabapple to sue reinstated? No. As we learned above, once the limitation period of two years has run out, it can't be revived by simply making a payment. However, if Doolittle had sent

*See *California Code of Civil Procedure Section 360. If you live outside California, check your state laws to see if they are the same.

Crabapple the $50 and had also included a letter saying that he would pay the remainder of the debt, Crabapple would again be able to sue and get a judgment if Doolittle failed to pay. Why? because a written promise to pay a debt barred by the Statute of Limitations has the legal effect of reestablishing the debt.

Telling the Judge That the Statute of Limitations Has Run Out

What should a defendant do if he believes that the Statute of Limitations period has run out? Tell the judge.* Sometimes a judge will figure this out without a reminder, but sometimes he won't. If you are a defendant, don't ever assume that because the clerk has filed the papers and you have been properly served, this means that the plaintiff has started his or her suit on time. Clerks never get involved in Statute of Limitations questions. They will cheerfully file a suit brought on a breach of contract occurring in 1916. It's up to you to protect yourself.

---

*If your state is one of the few that requires a defendant to file a written request prior to the hearing date (see Appendix), you should also mention any statute of limitations problem in that response.

How to Settle Your Dispute 6

Litigation should be a last, not a first, resort. Suing is not as bad as shooting, but neither is it as much fun as a good back rub. Rarely does anyone have a high time in court. In addition to being time consuming and emotionally draining, lawsuits tend to polarize disagreements into win-all or lose-all propositions in which face-saving (and pocketbook saving) compromise is difficult. Most of us are terrified of making fools of ourselves in front of strangers. When forced to defend our actions in a public forum, we tend rather regularly to adopt a most self-righteous view of our own conduct, and to attribute the vilest of motives to our opponents. Many of us are willing to admit that we have been a bit of a fool in private—especially if the other person does, too—but in public, we will stonewall all the way, even when it would be to our advantage to appear a little more fallible.

I have witnessed dozens of otherwise sensible people litigate the most appalling trivia, including one case in which the parties effectively tied up over $2,000 of each other's property (and had a fist fight) over a fishing pole worth $15. This doesnt mean that I don't think you should pursue your case to court if necessary. What I am suggesting is this: before you file your case, ask yourself whether you have done everything reasonably possible (and then a little more) to try to settle the case.

Try to Talk Your Dispute Out

Making an attempt to settle your case isn't a waste of time. Indeed, you are required to make the attempt. The law in many states, including California, requires that a "demand" for payment be made prior to filing a court action. Increasingly the "demand" requirement is be-ing interpreted to mean that the "demand" be in the form of a letter.*

But first things first. Before you reach for pen and paper, try to talk to the person with whom you are having the dispute. I can't count how many times clients have consulted me about supposedly insurmountable disputes without having even once tried to talk it out with the other person. Just before making final revisions on this chap-ter, I sat as judge *pro tem* in a case in which one man sued another for $500 resulting from a car accident. The defendant "was willing to pay," he said. "Why haven't you paid before?" I asked. "No one asked me to," he replied.

Apparently, many of us have a strong psychological barrier against talking to people we are upset with, especially if we have al-ready exchanged heated words. Sometimes we seem to think that a willingness to compromise shows weakness. But it was a wise man who said, "I would rather jaw, jaw, jaw than war, war, war."

Important: An offer of compromise, made either orally or in writ-ing, does not bind the person making the offer to that amount if the compromise is not accepted. Thus, you could make an original de-mand for $800, then offer to compromise for $550, and, if your com-promise offer was turned down, still sue for $800.

If you take my advice and again try to talk things out with your opponent and are successful, write down your agreement. Oral understandings, especially between people who have small confi-dence in one another, are often not worth the breath used to speak them. Exhibit 6.1 shows two sample compromise forms that you may be able to adapt to your uses.

Write a "Demand" Letter

If your efforts to talk your problems out fail (or despite my urging you refuse to try), your next step is to send your adversary a letter. As noted above, many courts require that a "demand" letter be sent. But even if there is no such requirement, it is almost essential that you send one. Why? Simple. The "demand" letter is not only useful in trying to settle your case but it is also your best opportunity to lay your case before the judge in a carefully organized way. In a sense, it allows you to manufacture evidence that you will be permitted to use

---

In Massachusetts, for example, under the Consumer Protection Act (Mass. Gen. Law, Ch. 93A), a person can sue a business for up to $2,250, but only if a written demand for what is owed is made at least 30 days prior to filing suit.

SAMPLE AGREEMENT 1

Dusty Rider and Bigshot Owner agree as follows:

1. Dusty was to exercise Bigshot's horses every morning for two weeks from October 1 to October 15 at Churchill Downs Racetrack in Louisville, Kentucky, and was to be paid $25 per horse exercised each morning;

2. Bigshot's horses got sick on September 29 and there was no need for Dusty's services;

3. Dusty gave up other employment to make herself available to ride Bigshot's horses, and she couldn't find another riding job at short notice;

4. Dusty and Bigshot agree that $800 is fair compensation for her loss of work and Dusty agrees to accept this amount as a complete settlement of all of her claims.

_____   _____
Date   Dusty Rider

_____   _____
Date   Bigshot Owner

SAMPLE AGREEMENT 2

Walter Spottedhound and Nellie Neighbor agrees that Walter's "mixed breed" black dog Clem sneaked onto Nellie's patio and bit her behind the right knee. After taking into consideration Nellie's medical bills, the fact that she had to miss two hours' work while at the doctor's office, and the pain and discomfort she has suffered, it is agreed that Walter will pay her $350 in full settlement of all her claims. The money will be paid in five equal monthly installments. The first installment is hereby paid this date and the next four will be paid on the first day of February, March, April, and May 1980.

It is also agreed that Walter will commence at once to construct a fence to keep Clem out of Nellie's yard.

_____   _____
Date   Walter Spottedhound

_____   _____
Date   Nellie Neighbor

Exhibit 6.1

in court if the case isn't settled. Either way, you can't lose, so take the time to write a good letter.

Your letter should be reasonably short, directly to the point, and, above all, polite. (You catch more flies with honey than by hitting them over the head with a mallet.) Use a typewriter, and keep a carbon or photocopy. Limit your remarks to a page or, at most, a page and a half. Remember, if the case doesn't settle, you will want to show the letter to the judge—and what's more important, you will want the judge to read it. It's my experience that aside from letters of the heart, no one ever reads much more than a page with anything like attention.

Remember, the judge doesn't know anything about how your problem started and developed. This means that you will want to write the letter so that it briefly reviews the entire dispute. It may seem a little odd, writing all the facts for your opponent who well knows them, and it may result in a formal sounding letter. So what? You want to produce a result that the judge can understand.

Let's consider a case I watched the other morning. The facts (with a little editorial license) were simple. Jennifer moved into Peter's house in August, agreeing to pay $250 per month rent. The house had four bedrooms, each occupied by one person. The kitchen and other common areas were shared. Things went well enough until one chilly evening in October when Jennifer turned on the heat. Peter was right behind her to turn it off, explaining that the heat inflamed his allergies.

As the days passed and fall deepened, heat became more and more of an issue until one cold, late November night when Jennifer returned home from her waitress job to find her room "about the same temperature as the inside of an icicle." After a short cry, she started packing and moved out the next morning. She refused to pay Peter any additional rent, claiming that she was within her rights to terminate her month-to-month tenancy without giving notice because the house was uninhabitable.* It took Peter one month to find a suitable tenant and to have that person move in. Therefore, he was without a tenant for one month and lost rent in the amount of $250.

After calling Jennifer several times and asking her to make good the $250 only to have her slam down the phone in disgust, Peter wrote her the letter in Exhibit 6.2.

*In many states, including California, tenants do have the right to simply leave or, as an alternative, to stay and cease paying rent if conditions in their rented home become uninhabitable due to lack of heat, water, electricity, etc. See the 1980 California Tenants' Handbook, Moskovitz, Warner, and Sherman, Nolo Press.

```
                                 61 Spring St.
                                 Detroit, MI

                                 January 1, 1979

Jennifer Tenant
111 Lake St.
Detroit, MI

Dear Jennifer:

     You are a real idiot.  Actually you're worse than that; you're mali-
cious--walking out on me before Christmas and leaving me with no tenant when
you know that I needed the money to pay my child support.  You know that I
promised to get you an electric room heater.  Don't think I don't know that
the real reason you moved out was to live with your boyfriend.

     Please send me the $250 I lost because you didn't give me a month's
notice like the law says you are supposed to.  If you don't, I will sue you.



                         In aggravation,


                         Peter Landperson
```

Exhibit 6.2

To which Jennifer replied in the letter shown in Exhibit 6.3.


```
                                 111 Lake St.
                                 Detroit, MI

                                 January 4, 1979

Peter Landperson
61 Spring St.
Detroit, MI

Dear Mr. Landperson:

     You nearly froze me to death, you cheap bastard.  I am surprised it
only took a month to rent that iceberg of a room--you must have found a
rich polar bear (ha ha).  People like you should be locked up.

     I hope you choke on an ice cube.


                         Jennifer Tenant
```

Exhibit 6.3

As you no doubt have guessed, both Peter and Jennifer made similar mistakes. Instead of being businesslike, each deliberately set out to annoy the other, reducing any possible chance of compromise. In addition, they each assumed that they were writing only to the other, forgetting about the judge. Thus, both lost a valuable chance to present the judge with a coherent summary of the facts as they saw them. As evidence in a subsequent court proceeding, both letters were worthless.

Now let's interrupt these proceedings and give Peter and Jennifer another chance to write sensible letters. (Exhibits 6.4 and 6.5.)

---

61 Spring St.
Detroit, MI

January 1, 1979

Jennifer Tenant
111 Lake St.
Detroit, MI

Dear Jennifer:

As you will recall, you moved into my house at 61 Spring St. on August 1, 1978, agreeing to pay me $250 per month rent of the first of each month. On November 29 you suddenly moved out, having given me no advance notice whatsoever.

I realize that you were unhappy about the fact that the house was a little on the cool side, but I don't believe that this was a serious problem as the temperature was at all times over 60° and I had agreed to get you an electric heater for your room by December.

I was unable to get a tenant to replace you (although I tried every way I could and asked you for help) until January 1, 1979. This means that I am short $250 rent for the room you occupied. If necessary, I will take this dispute to court because, as you know, I am on a very tight budget. I hope that this isn't necessary and that we can arrive at a sensible compromise. I have tried to call you with no success. Perhaps you can give me a call in the next week to talk this over.

Sincerely,

Peter Landperson

Exhibit 6.4

To which our now enlightened Jennifer promptly replied:

```
                                        111 Lake St.
                                        Detroit, MI

                                        January 4, 1979


        Peter Landperson
        61 Spring St.
        Detroit, MI

        Dear Peter:

            I just received your letter concerning the rent at 61 Spring St. and
        am sorry to say that I don't agree either with the facts as you have pre-
        sented them, or with your demand for back rent.

            When I moved in August 1, 1978, you never told me that you had an al-
        lergy and that there would be a problem keeping the house at a normal
        temperature.  I would not have moved in had you informed me of this.

            From early October when we had the first cool evenings, all through
        November (almost 2 months), I asked that you provide heat.  You didn't.
        Finally it became unbearable to return from work in the middle of the
        night to a cold house which was often below 60°.  It is true that I moved
        out suddenly, but I felt that I was within my rights because the living
        space was uninhabitable.

            Since you mentioned the nonexistent electric heater in your letter,
        let me respond to that.  You first promised to get the heater over a
        month before I moved out and you never did.  Also, as I pointed out to
        you on several occasions, the heater was not a complete solution to the
        problem as it would have heated only my room and not the kitchen, living
        room, dining area, etc.  You repeatedly told me that it would be impos-
        sible to heat these areas.

            Peter, I sincerely regret the fact that you feel wronged, but I be-
        lieve that I have been very fair with you.  I am sure that you would
        have been able to re-rent the room promptly if the house had been warm.
        I regret that I don't believe that any compromise is possible and that
        you will just have to go to court if that's what you wish to do.


                                        Sincerely,



                                        Jennifer Tenant
```

Exhibit 6.5

As you can see, while the second two letters are less fun to read, they are far more informative. Both Peter and Jennifer have clearly set forth their positions. The goal of reaching an acceptable compromise was not met, but both have prepared a good statement of their positions for the judge. Of course, in court, both Peter and Jennifer will testify, present witnesses, etc. in addition to their letters, but court proceedings are often rushed and confused and it's nice to have something for the judge to fall back on. Be sure to bring the carbon copy (or Xerox) of your demand letter to court when your case is to be heard. Be sure, too, that the judge is given the copy as part of your case. The judge won't be able to guess that you have it; you will have to let him or her know and hand it to the clerk. (For more about what happens in court, see Chapters 13–15.)

Important: If you compromise your case after you have filed it in court, but before the court hearing, be sure to do so in writing. Also let the court know that you won't be appearing . Some courts will ask that the plaintiff sign a "Request for Dismissal" form. Never do this unless your compromise agreement has already been reduced to writing. Also, it is not wise to have a case dismissed unless you have been paid in full because once the case is dismissed, you can't refile it. Thus if the compromise settlement involves installment payments, it would be wise to go to court and present it to the judge. He or she can then enter a judgment in the same terms as the compromise. If this is done and then the judgment is not paid, it can be collected using the techniques discussed in Chapter 23.

Settlement in Court

Sometimes cases are settled in court while you are waiting for your case to be heard. It is perfectly proper to ask the other person if he or she wishes to step into the hall for a moment to talk the matter over.

If you can agree on a compromise, wait until the case is called and tell the judge the amount you have agreed upon and whether the amount is to be paid all at once, or over time. The judge can either order the case dismissed if one person pays the other on the spot, or can enter a judgment for the amount that you have compromised upon, if payment is to be made later.

A few states, particularly New York (but not California and most others), strongly encourage informal arbitration before a lawyer who is volunteering his or her time as an arbitrator. The lawyer and the parties involved just sit down at a table and talk things over. It's often faster to see an arbitrator right away than it is to wait for the 16 cases ahead of yours in the regular Small Claims Court. Some states provide arbitration as an option (you don't *have* to do it) but make the parties agree that the arbitrator's decision will be final without a right of appeal by anyone, if they do choose arbitration. Other states require, or make available, nonbinding arbitration before going to court, but if the parties still can't agree on a settlement, the Small Claims judge will hear the case.

Who Can Sue? 7

In most situations, the question of who can sue in Small Claims Court is easy to answer. Anyone of legal age in his or her state (18 in New York, California, and most other states) who has not been declared mentally incompetent in a judicial proceeding and (usually) is suing on his or her own behalf. Sometimes, however, listing yourself as the party bringing suit isn't quite so easy.

Here are the general rules in force in all states. Your state's rules may vary slightly, however, and you will wish to check the Appendix and your local rules.

1. If you are suing for yourself alone, simply list your full name where it says "Plaintiff" on the "Plaintiff's Statement" and sign the "declaration under penalty of perjury" on the "Claim of Plaintiff" form (see sample forms in Chapter 10).

2. If more than one person is bringing suit, list all the names on the "Plaintiff's Statement." Only one person need sign the "declaration under penalty of perjury" stating that all the information given is true and correct (see Chapter 10).

3. If you are filing a claim on behalf of an individually owned business, the owner of the business must do the suing. He or she should list his or her name and the business name as plaintiffs on the "Plaintiff's Statement." The "declaration under penalty of perjury" should be signed by the business owner. (See Chapter 10).

4. If you are filing a claim on behalf of a partnership, list the partnership name as plaintiff. Only one of the partners need sign the "declaration under penalty of perjury." (See Chapter 10.)

5. If you are filing a claim on behalf of a corporation, whether profit or nonprofit, list the corporation as plaintiff.* The "declaration under penalty of perjury" must be signed by either:
   a) an officer of the corporation
      or
   b) a person authorized to file claims on behalf of the corporation by the Board of Directors of the corporation.
   If a nonofficer of a corporation is involved, the court clerk will want to see some documentation that the person suing is properly authorized. Exhibit 7.1 shows a sample authorization statement that you can use. If you use a particular Small Claims Court regularly, you can file a copy of the authorization in its permanent file.†

6. When a claim arises out of damage to a motor vehicle, the registered owner(s) of the vehicle must file in Small Claims Court. This means that if you are driving someone else's car and get hit by a third party, you can't sue for damage done to the car. The registered owner must do the suing.

7. If you are suing on behalf of a public entity, such as a public library, city tax assessor's office, or county hospital, you must show the court clerk proper authorization to sue.

Participation by Attorneys

Attorneys, or other people acting as representatives, cannot normally appear in Small Claims Court in California, Colorado, Idaho, Kansas, Michigan, Nebraska, Oregon, and Washington. In the majority of states, however, attorneys are permitted. (See Appendix.)‡

---

*In a few states, including Arizona, Illinois, and Wisconsin, a corporation is required to be represented by an attorney in Small Claims Court. This is also the rule in the City of Chicago "pro se" Court. Refer to Appendix for Illinois.
†Local rules differ as to requirements for filing on behalf of a corporation. Some courts no longer require an authorization adopted by the Board of Directors. Call your Small Claims Court clerk.
‡Allowing attorneys to represent people in Small Claims Court is a serious mistake. The whole idea of Small Claims Court is to allow people to settle small claims themselves without a lot of legal mumbo jumbo and expense.

```
                    RESOLUTION - SMALL CLAIMS

              APPOINTING A CORPORATION REPRESENTATIVE

     It appears to the Board of Directors of ____Acme Illusions, Inc._____

_____.

a corporation, qualified to do business in the State of California, that it is ne-

cessary to appoint an agent for this corporation to act for and in its behalf in the

Small Claims Court of ____Oakland-Piedmont_____Judicial District,

County of _Alameda_____, State of California, that ___KEIJA SOTO_____

is a suitable individual for such appointment.

     It is therefore resolved that ____KEIJA SOTO_____

be and ___he is appointed to represent and appear for said corporation in the lawful

process of any and all claims filed in the above named court, and ___he is further

authorized to accept service of process issued by said court, for and on behalf of

said corporation.

     I certify that foregoing resolution was adopted by the Board of Directors of this

corporation, at a regular meeting of said board, held on ____(Date)_____ .

                                            Tom  Jake
                                            _____
                                                  Secretary

(SEAL)
                                            Acme Illusions, Inc.
The local business address of this corporation is:  100 Primrose Path
                                                    Oakland, CA
     Keija  Soto
_____
(Signature of agent so appointed)

  41 Mandrake, Oakland, CA.
_____
(Address of agent)
```

Exhibit 7.1

Even in states such as California in which attorneys are not allowed
to represent others, they are commonly allowed to sue or defend
their own personal claims. In California this includes appearing for
law firms of which they are a part (C.C.P. 117.4).

Suits by Minors

If you are a minor (under the age of legal adulthood, usually 18), your parent or legal guardian must sue for you. To do this, a form must be filled out and signed by the judge appointing the person in question as your "Guardian Ad Litem." This simply means guardian for the purposes of the lawsuit. Ask the court clerk for a "Petition for Appointment of Guardian Ad Litem" form.

In some states problems can develop for unincorporated small business trying to use Small Claims Court efficiently. This occurs because the law states that the owner of the business must do the suing personally and must show up in court. Thus a dentist who wished to sue on an overdue bill would have to appear in court himself or herself. But California and a number of other states are more understanding of business time pressures and allow both incorporated and unincorporated businesses to send employees to court when the case involves unpaid bills. Thus in California it would be proper for the dentist (or dressmaker) to send the person who keeps the books to court when a bill isn't paid (C.C.P. 117.4).*

Note: Many states, including California, Michigan Missouri, Nebraska, New Jersey, New York, and Ohio, forbid the use of Small Claims Court by "assignees" (a fancy term that usually refers to collection agencies). The majority of states, including Pennsylvania, Massachusetts, Maine, and Oregon still allow suits by collection agencies. Texas and Kentucky seem to be unique in barring lenders of money at interest from using Small Claims Court. See the Appendix under "Notes" for information about your state.

---

*Remember, as I discuss earlier in this chapter, in California an incorporated business (whether profit or nonprofit) can appoint a representative to appear on its behalf in Small Claims Court for all types of claims.

Who Can Be Sued? 8

You can sue just about anybody (person, partnership, corporation, government, etc.) in Small Claims Court in most states. Indeed, it is more often the "Where can I sue?" problem (see Chapter 9) than the "Who can I sue?" problem that causes difficulties. For example, you can sue the Chase Manhattan Bank, but you will find it very difficult to have the case heard in Billings, Montana, or Emporia, Kansas, unless you can show that the bank has an office or actively does business there, or entered into or agreed to carry out a contract with you there. This doesn't mean that you have a problem with suing the bank—you don't. The problem is only with suing in Billings or Emporia. If you go to New York, where the bank has its headquarters, you can bring your suit with no difficulty.

Here are some hints that may prove helpful when it comes to filling out your papers. Again, the information I give here is general, but it does not differ much from state to state. See the Appendix and your local rules.

Suing One Person

If you are suing an individual, simply name him or her, using the most complete name that you have for that person. If the person calls himself J. R. Smith and you don't know what the initials stand for, simply sue him as J. R. Smith.

Suing Two or More People

If you are suing more than one person on a claim arising from the same incident or contract, you must list and serve (see Chapter 11) each to bring them properly before the court. In cases involving a husband and wife, you must list each separately.*

Example: J. R. and June Smith, who are married, borrow $200 from you to start an avocado pit polishing business. Unfortunately, in the middle of the polishing, the seeds begin to sprout. J. R. and June get so furious that they refuse to repay you. If you wish to sue them and get a judgment, you should list them as J. R. Smith and June Smith—not Mr. and Mrs. Smith. But now suppose that J. R. borrowed $500 for the avocado pit business in January, June borrowed $200 to fix her motorcycle a month later, and neither loan was repaid. In this situation, you would sue each in separate Small Claims Court actions.

Suing an Individually Owned Business

Here you list the name of the owner and the name of the business (e.g., J. R. Smith—doing business as [d.b.a.] Smith's Texaco). Don't assume that the name of the business is in fact the same as the name of the owner. Often it is not. Jim's Garage may be owned by Pablo García Motors, Inc. (See "Suing a Corporation" below.) If you get a judgment against Jim's Garage and there is no Jim, you will find that it's worthless in most states—you can't collect from a nonexistent person. Take the trouble to be sure you know who the owner of the business is before you sue.

New York has joined several other states and now allows a plaintiff to sue a defendant under any name used in conducting business if it is impossible to find out the defendant's true name. This is a

---

*A problem may arise in some states in which you can sue a person only in the county or district where he or she lives. What happens when you sue two people who live in different counties or districts? In most states, including California, this type of situation is handled by allowing the person suing to sue in either place. But a few states don't make even this exception, so that it might actually be impossible to sue both these people in the same court. This possibility is noted in the Appendix where applicable.

valuable reform, but it has not yet been adopted in most states that still follow the general rule explained above.

California requires that all people doing business in a name other than their own file a Fictitious Business Name Statement with the county clerk in the county or counties in which the business operates.* This is public information and you can get it from the court clerk. Another way to figure out who owns a business is to check with the Business Tax and License Office in the city in which the business is located. If the business is not in an incorporated area, try the county. The tax and license office will have a list of the owners of all businesses paying taxes in the city. They should be able to tell you, for example, that the Garden of Exotic Delights is owned by Rufus Clod. Once you find this out, you sue Rufus Clod, d.b.a. the Garden of Exotic Delights.

If for some reason the tax and license office and the county clerk can't help, you may want to check with the state. Millions of people, from exterminators to embalmers, must register with one or another state office. So, if your beef is with a teacher, architect, smog control device installer, or holder of a beer or wine license, you will very likely be able to learn who and where they are with a letter or phone call. Check the phone book for the capital city of your state (usually available at public libraries or the telephone company) and look under the listings of state offices.†

Suing Partnerships

List the names of all the business partners even if your dispute is only with one (Patricia Sun and Farah Moon, d.b.a. Sacramento Gardens). If a business has a lot of partners, or if some partners are not in the area, you will have to do the best you can, suing and serving the ones that are available. A judgment against the partner you sue and serve is valid even if you don't sue everyone. See the preceding section for information on how to learn just who owns what. Never assume that you know who owns a business without checking. All partners to a business are individually liable for all the acts of the business.

*All states have similar requirements. Call your Small Claims Court clerk or city or county offices for more information.
†The best information on skip-tracing, including complete information on who the state keeps track of and how to get the information is found in Part 2 of Luboff and Posner, 1977, How To Collect Your Child Support and Alimony, Nolo Press.

Example: You go to a local cleaners with your new, sky blue suit. They put too much cleaning fluid on it with the result that a small grey cloud settles on the rear right shoulder. After unsuccessfully trying to get the cleaners to take responsibility for improving the weather on the back of your suit, you start thinking about a different kind of suit. When you start filling out your court papers (see Chapter 10), you realize that you know only that the store says "Perfection Cleaners" on the front, and that the guy who has been so unpleasant to you is named Bob. You call the city business tax and license people and they tell you that Perfection Cleaners is owned by Robert Johnson and Sal De Benno. You should sue both and also list the name of the business.

Note: It is wise to get a judgment against more than one person if possible. When it comes to trying to collect, it's always nice to have someone in reserve if one defendant turns out to be an artful dodger.

Suing a Corporation

Corporations are legal people. This means that you can sue, and enforce a judgment against, a corporation itself. You should not sue the owners of the corporation or its officer or managers as individuals unless you have a personal claim against them that is separate from their role as part of the corporation. In most situations the real people who own or operate the corporation aren't themselves liable to pay the corporation's debts. This is called "limited liability" and is part of the reason that many people choose to incorporate.

Be sure to list the full name of the corporation when you file suit (John's Liquors, Inc., a Corporation). Here again, the name on the door or on the stationery may not be the real name. Corporations too sometimes do business using fictitious names. Check with business license people in the city or county in which the corporation does business. Information is also available from either the Secretary of State or the Corporations Commissioner's office, which you will find located in your state capital.

Suing on a Motor Vehicle Accident

Here there are some special rules. In most states, if your claim arises from an accident with an automobile, motorcycle, truck or R.V., you must name both the driver of the vehicle and the registered owner as part of your suit. Most times you will have obtained this information at the time of the accident. If a police accident report was made, it will also contain this information. You can get a copy of any police report from the police department for a modest fee. If there was no police report, contact the Department of Motor Vehicles. In most states, including California, they will tell you who owns any vehicle for which you have a license number.*

Remember, when you sue more than one person (in this case the driver and the owner if they are different), you serve papers on both. When a business owns a vehicle, sue both the driver and the owners of the business.

*In California and a number of other states, the Department of Motor Vehicles will ask you why you want this information. Simply tell them "to file a lawsuit based on a motor vehicle accident that occurred in (name of city or county) on (date) at (time), involving myself and a car with a license number_____ ." This is a legitimate reason in most states, and you will get the information you need. However, in many states, the owner of the car will be notified of your request.

Special Procedures for Suits against Minors

It is very difficult to sue a minor for a breach of contract in most states because minors can disavow (back out of) any contract they sign as long as they do it before they become adults, unless the contract was for a necessity of life, e.g., food, in which case the parents are responsible. You can sue minors for damage to your person or property. If you wish to do so, you must also list a parent or legal guardian on the court papers. You could do it like this:

"John Jefferey, a minor, and William Jefferey, his father." It is very difficult to collect from minors themselves, as most don't have money or income. Of course, there are exceptions to this rule, but most minors are, almost by definition, broke. Thus, it doesn't usually pay to bother with suits against minors unless you can collect from the minor's parents. Normally a parent is not legally responsible to pay for damages done by his or her children but there are some exceptions to this rule. In California, when a child is guilty of "willful misconduct," a parent can be liable up to $2,000 per act ($30,000 if a gun is involved). Californian parents are also liable for damage done by their minor children in auto accidents when they authorized the child to drive.*

Example: John Johnson, age 17, trips over his shoelace while delivering your newspaper and crashes through your glass door. Can you recover from John's parents? Probably not, as John is not guilty of "willful misconduct."

Example: John shoots out the same glass door with a slingshot after you have repeatedly asked his parents to disarm him. Can you recover from the parents? Probably.

Rules for Suits against City, County, and State

Many states have special rules and procedures that must be followed before a suit can be brought against a government entity. Often, you have to act very quickly or you lose your right to sue. The Small

*Check the index to your state's laws under "Minors" or "Children" or "Parent and Child" for your rules.

Claims Court clerk will be able to advise you as to the procedures you must follow and the time limits you must meet.

Let's look at the rules of a state we will call "typical." Before you can sue a city because your car was illegally towed away or a city employee caused you damage, or for any other reason involving personal injury or property damage, you must first file a claim with the city and have it denied. Get a claim form from the city clerk. Your claim must be filed within 100 days of the date of the incident. The city attorney will review your claim and make a recommendation to the City Council. Sometimes the recommendation will be to pay you—most often it will be to deny your claim. Once the City Council acts, you will receive a letter. If it's a denial, take it with you when you file your Small Claims action. The clerk will want to see it.

The rules for suits against counties are basically the same. Get your complaint form from the clerk of the governing legislative body for the county (e.g., County Commissions, Board of Supervisors, etc.). Complete and file it within 100 days of the incident. Within a month or so after filing, you will be told whether your claim is approved or denied. If your claim is denied, you can then proceed to file in Small Claims Court. Claims against the state must also be filed within 100 days for personal injury and property damage.

Where Can I Sue? 9

Small Claims Courts are local. This makes sense because the amounts involved aren't large enough to make it worthwhile to require people to travel great distances. A Small Claims Court district covers all or part of a city, several cities, or a county. The next city or county will have its own similar, but separate, Small Claims Court. Normally, your dispute will be with a person or business located nearby. You can sue in the judicial district in which the defendant resides, or, if a corporation is involved, the area in which its main place of business is located. Sometimes though, it is not so easy to understand where to file your suit. This might be the case if the person you wish to sue lives 100 (or 500) miles away, or has moved since the dispute arose.

Of all the aspects of Small Claims Court that differ from state to state, the rule on where to sue seems to be the most variable. Some states let you sue another person only in the district or county where he or she resides. Others also allow you to choose the place in which an accident occurred, a contract was broken or originally signed, merchandise was purchased, a corporation does business, and so on.

On the first page of the first chapter we asked you to get a copy of the rules for your local Small Claims Court.* Refer to them and to the listing for your state in the Appendix under "Where to Sue." The

---

*If your dispute arose at an area some distance from your home and the person you wish to sue also lives there, you will want the rules for that district.

first thing you will wish to understand are the types of political subdivisions (judicial districts, precincts, cities, counties, etc; for brevity we will refer to them from here on out as "judicial districts") that your state uses to mark off the territory of one Small Claims Court from another. Next, you will want to study carefully your local rules in order to understand the geographical boundaries of the Small Claims Court judicial district or districts that are relevant to you. If this information is not set out in the information sheet, call the clerk of the court and ask. You may be able to sue in more than one judicial district. If this is the case, choose the one that is most convenient to you. In a few states, such as California, Georgia, Illinois, and Washington, this can be very important because suits can be brought for different amounts in different parts of each of these states. (The rules for all states are set out in the Appendix.)

SUMMARY OF GENERAL RULES REGARDING WHERE YOU CAN SUE

Depending on the specific rules of your state, you can generally sue in any one of the following counties:

1. In all states you can sue in the county in which defendant resides or has a place of business at the commencement of the action.

2. In about half of the states you can also sue in the county in which the obligation on which the suit is based was contracted to be performed.

3. In about half of the states you can also sue in the county in which an injury to persons or personal property occurred.

4. In a very few states, including California and Colorado, you can also sue in the county in which the defendant resided or did business at the time a contract was entered into.

Note: As a general rule, it is not possible to bring into court a person who lives outside of the state in which you bring suit, unless that person shows up voluntarily.

Now let's consider in more detail the rules concerning where you can sue.

You Can Sue a Person or Business Where He, She, or It Resides/Does Business*

Every state allows suits to be brought where the defendant lives or maintains a business headquarters. (See Appendix.) This rule makes good sense, doesn't it? If a suit is brought where the defendant is located, he or she can't complain that it is unduly burdensome to appear. Books have been written about the technical definition of residence. Indeed, I remember with horror trying to sort out a law school exam in which the professor had given a person with numerous homes and businesses "contact" with six different judicial districts. The point of the examination was for us students to figure out where he could be sued. You can be thankful that you don't have to worry about this sort of nonsense. If you believe a business or individual to be sufficiently present within a particular judicial area so that it would not be a hardship for the business owner to appear in court there, go ahead and file your suit. The worst that can happen—and this is highly unlikely—is that the judge will tell you to start over someplace else.

Example: Downhill Skier lives in the city, but also owns a mountain cabin at which he spends several months a year. Late one snowy afternoon, Downhill drives his new Porsche from the ski slopes to his ultra-modern, rustic cabin. Turning into his driveway, he skids and does a bad slalom turn right into Woodsey Carpenter's 1957 International Harvester Pickup. Where can Woodsey sue? He can sue in the city in which Downhill has his permanent address. He can probably also sue in the county in which the cabin is located, on the theory that Downhill also lives there. But read on—it might not be necessary for Woodsey even to get into the residence question because as many states would allow Woodsey to sue in the mountain county on the theory that the injury occurred there.

This rule can sometimes cause problems if you wish to sue a corporation or other business that operates in your area but has its headquarters elsewhere. Most states solve the problem by allowing you to sue in any judicial district in which the business operates and/or where the act or omission that gave rise to your lawsuit occurred. See Appendix and your state rules.

Note: In California, Illinois, Minnesota, New Jersey, and the great majority of states, you can sue multiple defendants in any county in which one resides, even though the other(s) live in another part of the state. But in a few states, including New York, Florida, and Massachusetts, you can sue only in the place in which the the defendant resides or does business and thus can't bring one lawsuit against defendants who reside in different judicial districts. (See Appendix; if the listing says that you must sue where "a defendant resides," you can sue them all in the same place, but if it says that you must sue where "the defendant resides," you can't sue them in the same place unless you can find another valid reason to do so (such as where the act or omission occurred).

In Most (But Not All) States You Can Sue Where the Facts Regarding the Dispute Occurred

California, Illinois, Indiana, and many other states allow you to sue in the district in which the "act or omission occurred" (See Appendix.) "Act or omission" is a shorthand way of lumping together things like automobile accidents, warranty disputes, and landlord–tenant disputes for the purpose of deciding where you're allowed to sue. If you are in a car accident, a dog bites you, the roofer botches repair of your roof, a tree falls on your noggin, or a neighbor floods your cactus garden, etc., you may sue in the judicial district where the "act" or injury occurred, even if this is a different district from the one in which the defendant resides.

Example: Downhill is returning to his home in San Francisco. He is driving his Porsche carefully, still thankful that no one was injured when he hit Woodsey. At the same time, John Gravenstein is rushing to the city from his home in Sonoma County, 100 miles north of San Francisco, to try to get spare parts for his broken apple picker. John jumps a red light and crumples Downhill's other fender. The accident occurs in Marin county, a county in which neither John nor Downhill lives. After parking his car and taking a taxi home, Downhill tries to figure out where he can sue if he can't work out a fair settlement with John. Unfortunately for him, he can't sue in San Francisco, as John doesn't reside there and the accident occurred in Marin. Downhill would have to sue either in Marin County, where his property was damaged, or in Sonoma County, where John lives. Luckily for Downhill, Marin County adjoins San Francisco. However, had the accident occurred in Los Angeles County, which is over 400 miles away, Downhill would have been put to a lot more trouble if he wished to sue.

An "omission" can refer to an accident, but often it means that someone promised to pay money or deliver goods and then didn't do as promised. The "omission" occurred wherever it was that the person promised to do whatever it was that he or she didn't do. You could, therefore, sue at the place where an obligation (contract) was to be carried out. This, too, is good common sense, as the law assumes that if people agree to carry out a contract at a certain location, it is probably reasonably convenient to both. If, for example, Downhill gets a telephone installed in his cabin, or has the fender on his Porsche fixed, or has a cesspool put in, or agrees to sit for a portrait in the mountain county, he can be sued there if he fails to keep his part of the bargain. Of course, as we learned above, Downhill may also be sued in the city in which he resides permanently.

Example: John Gravenstein lives in Sonoma County, California, where he owns an apple orchard. He calls the Acme Mechanical Apple Picker Co., an international corporation with offices in San Francisco, New York, Paris, and Guatemala City, and orders spare parts for his Acme apple picker. John deals with the San Francisco office. The parts are sent to John from San Francisco via UPS and turn out to be defective. After trying and failing to reach a settlement with Acme, John wants to know if he can sue them in Sonoma County. No. Acme doesn't reside in Sonoma County, and they performed no action there in connection with their agreement to sell John the spare parts.* John would have to bring his claim in Small Claims Court in San Francisco. But now let's assume that John dealt with Acme's Sonoma County representative, who came to his orchard to take the order and who later installed the defective machinery. In this case John can sue locally because the contract was to be performed in Sonoma County.

Reminder: You should realize by now that there may be several reasons why it can be OK to bring a suit in a particular place. You need only one reason, but it never hurts to have several. Also, as you should now understand, there may be two, three, or more judicial districts in which you can file your case. In this situation, simply choose the one most convenient to you, or at least the one in which it's per-

The fact that John spoke to Acme while John was on the phone at his home in Sonoma County makes no difference. Acme "accepted the offer to make a contract" while in its office elsewhere.

missible to bring all the defendants (if there are more than one) into court. But check the Appendix and your local rules to make sure which places are appropriate in your case.

In California and a Few Other States You Can Sue Where a Contract Was Signed or Was to Be Carried Out

Most states assume that a written contract is signed and will be carried out at the same location. Thus they assume that the place where the contract was signed is the place in which "the act or omission occurred" if a problem develops.

Arizona, California, Indiana, and a few other states are more thorough. (See Appendix.) In these states, a suit can be brought either where the contract was signed or where it was to be carried out. Suppose now that John comes to Acme's office in San Francisco and signs the apple picker contract, and that the equipment purchased is to be installed at John's farm by Acme's local employee in Sonoma County. Assume that this time Acme keeps its part of the bargain, but John fails to pay. Where can Acme sue? Either in San Francisco where the contract was signed, or in Sonoma County where the contract was to be carried out. Also, as we learned above, Acme has another reason for being able to sue in Sonoma County—it's the place of John's residence.

Some large retailers used to put a clause in all of their contracts saying that, no matter where the contract was actually signed, the signature of the company didn't take effect until it was approved at the home office (often on the other side of the state). This was a gimmick which allowed the company to sue everyone at the location of the company's home office. People often couldn't defend themselves because it was impractical to show up in a court at the other end of the state. This practice is no longer legal in California and in most other states. Now, the legal action must be brought where the contract was actually signed by the defendant. If you feel that you are being cheated by this old hustle, call your Attorney General's office and report the violators.

Note: In California, if the person or corporation you wish to sue resided or did business in the judicial district at the time a contract was signed, you can sue them there even though they moved later and no longer reside in the judicial district at the time of the suit. This is an unusual provision not in force in most states.

Plaintiff and Defendant's Filing Fees, Court Papers, and Court Dates 10

How Much Does It Cost?

Fees for filing a case in Small Claims Court are very moderate. It's rare to find a state that charges as much as ten dollars, and many charge less than five. Normally, a defendant is not charged at all unless he or she files an independent claim. There is usually an additional fee for serving papers on the opposing party, unless you are in a state that allows personal service to be carried out by a nonprofessional process server and you have a friend who will do it for you without charge. (See Chapter 11.) Most states allow service by certified or registered mail, so service costs are usually low. In a few situations you may have to hire a professional process server. This will normally cost between ten and twenty dollars, but may be higher if the person you are suing is a pro at evading service. You can get your filing fees and service costs added to the court judgment if you win. (See Chapter 15.)

Filling Out Your Court Papers and Getting Your Court Date

Now let's look at the initial court papers themselves to be sure that you don't trip over a detail. Again, I refer specifically to forms in use in California and also include some New York forms, but you will find that your local forms will require similar information. You should have little trouble filling out your papers by following the examples printed here but, if you do have trouble, simply ask the clerk for help. Small Claims Court clerks are required by law in most states to give you as much help as possible short of practicing law (whatever that

77

is). A friendly, courteous approach to the clerk can often result in securing much helpful information and advice. In a very few Small Claims Courts, such as those in New York City, trained legal assistants will be available to help you.

SMALL CLAIMS COURT OF CALIFORNIA, COUNTY OF ALAMEDA

Andrew Printer,
         Plaintiff(s) vs.

Acme Illusions, Inc.,
        Defendant(s)

SMALL CLAIMS CASE NUMBER

PLAINTIFF'S STATEMENT

1. Please read carefully the instructions appearing below before filling out this form:
   a. If you are suing one or more individuals, give full name of each.
   b. If you are suing a business owned by an individual, give the name of the owner and the name of the business he owns.
   c. If you are suing a partnership, give the names of the partners and the name of the partnership.
   d. If you are suing a corporation, give its full name.
   e. If your claim arises out of a vehicle accident, the driver of the other vehicle must be named, and the registered owner of the other vehicle should also be named.
2. State your name and residence address, and the name and address of any other person joining with you in this action. If this claim arises from a business transaction, give the name and address of your business.

see ch. 7
a. Name **Andrew Printer**
   Address *1800 Marilee St., Fremont, CA.* Phone No. *827-7000*
b. Name _____
   Address _____ Phone No. _____

3. State the name and address of each person or business firm you are suing:

see ch. 8
a. Name *Acme Illusions, Inc.*
   Address *100 Primrose Path, Oakland, CA.*
b. Name _____
   Address _____
c. Name _____
   Address _____

see ch. 4
4. State the amount you are claiming. $ *600.00*

see ch. 2
5. Describe briefly the nature of your claim:
Failure to pay for printing and typesetting.

6. If your claim does **not** arise out of a vehicle accident, give address below where obligation was entered into or was to be performed or where injury was incurred.
1800 Marilee St., (street address) *Fremont, CA* (city or locality)

7. Fill out this section **if your claim arises out of a vehicle accident:**

see ch. 9
a. Date on which accident occurred: _____ , 19____.
b. Street or intersection and city or locality where accident occurred:
_____

c. If you are claiming damages to a vehicle, were you on the date of the accident the registered owner of that vehicle? _____ (yes or no)

8. I have received and read the form entitled ''Information to Plaintiff''
Andrew Printer
Signature

Exhibit 10.1

STEP 1: The Plaintiff's Statement

(In some states, slightly different terminology, such as "General Claim" or "Plaintiff's Claim," is used.)

To start your case in Small Claims Court, go to the Small Claims Court clerk's office and fill out the form entitled "Plaintiff's Statement." If you have read carefully the first nine chapters of this book, this should be easy. Be particularly careful that you are suing in the right judicial district (Chapter 9) and that you are naming the defendant properly (Chapter 8). Exhibits 10.1 and 10.2 show the forms in use in California and New York, respectively.

CIVIL COURT OF THE CITY OF NEW YORK
SMALL CLAIMS PART
REQUEST FOR INFORMATION

MAXIMUM: $1,000.00
TIME OF TRIAL: 6:30 P.M.
FILING FEE: $ —NO CHECKS

NAME AND ADDRESS OF PARTY BEING SUED: {See Ch. 8}

Lester Landlord

127 E. 89th St.

New York, New York

NAME AND ADDRESS OF PARTY SUING: {See Ch. 7}

Theresa Tenant

1234 Park Avenue

New York, New York

AMOUNT: $ 200.00   {See Ch. 4}

STATE YOUR CLAIM HERE: Failure of landlord to return residential rental security deposit after I moved out of apartment.

{See Ch. 2}

Exhibit 10.2

STEP 2: The Claim of Plaintiff

When you have completed your "Plaintiff's Statement," give it to the court clerk. In some states the clerk will file your form, but often, as in California, he or she will retype it and then assign you a case number. You will be asked to sign this form under penalty of perjury. One

```
                                              MUNICIPAL COURT
                                              SMALL CLAIMS DIVISION
BERKELEY - ALBANY                             COUNTY OF ALAMEDA, CALIF.
2000  CENTER ST.
BERKELEY, CALIF. 94704      (415) 644-6303              NO S C
            PLAINTIFF (Name and address)               DEFENDANT (Name and address of each)

          Andrew Printer                          Acme Illusions, Inc.
          1800 Marilee Street                     100 Primrose Path
          Berkeley, CA  94704                     Berkeley, CA  94704
```

CLAIM OF PLAINTIFF   CLAIM OF PLAINTIFF
AND ORDER

1. Defendant is indebted to plaintiff in the sum of: $ __600.00_____ not including court costs, for: __failure to pay__
   __for printing and typesetting.__

2. Plaintiff has demanded that defendant pay this sum and it has not been paid.

3. This court is the proper court for the hearing because
   a. ____ At least one defendant now resides or a corporate defendant does business in this judicial district;
   b. ____ Injury to person or damage to personal property occurred in this judicial district;
   c. _X_ Defendant entered into or signed in this judicial district a contract not involving a retail installment account or an auto finance sale;
   d. _X_ The obligation was to be performed in this judicial district on a contract not involving a retail installment account, an auto finance sale, or the furnishing of goods, services, or loans intended primarily for personal, family, or household use;
   e. ____ Defendant resided or a corporate defendant did business in this judicial district at the time the contract was entered into for the furnishing of goods, services or loans intended primarily for personal, family, or household use, and not involving a retail installment account or an auto finance sale.
   f. ____ This action is on a retail installment account or contract (CC 1812.10); specify:
   g. ____ This action is on a motor vehicle finance sale (CC 2984.4); specify:

4. I have not previously filed this claim against the above named defendant(s).

5. I understand that
   a. Although I may consult an attorney, I cannot be represented by an attorney at the trial in the small claims division;
   b. I must appear at the time and place for trial and have with me witnesses and evidence (Such as books, papers, receipts, and exhibits) to prove my claim;
   c. I have no right of appeal from a judgment on my claim.
   I declare (Certify) under penalty of perjury that the foregoing is true and correct and that this declaration is executed on

(Date): _____ at (Place): __Berkeley_____ , California

                              ORDER   Andrew Printer
                                                 Signature of declarant

TO DEFENDANT: If you wish to oppose plaintiff's claim, you are directed to appear in the above entitled court in:
Department _____ at _____ on _____
You should have with you any witnesses and evidence (Such as books, papers, receipts and exhibits) to establish your defense.

IF YOU DO NOT APPEAR, THE COURT MAY AWARD PLAINTIFF THE AMOUNT FOUND TO BE DUE UPON PLAINTIFF'S CLAIM AND ALSO COSTS OF THE ACTION INCLUDING COST OF SERVICE OF THIS ORDER, WHICH COULD RESULT IN GARNISHMENT OF YOUR WAGES AND TAKING OF YOUR MONEY OR PROPERTY.

Dated_____   Clerk, By_____
Date_____ Hearing reset for CHARLES E. McCAIN ____at_____M., Dept._____
Date_____ Hearing reset for_____at_____M., Dept._____
Date_____ Hearing reset for_____at_____M., Dept._____
Date_____ Hearing reset for_____at_____M., Dept._____

Date of Proceeding	Proceedings (applicable only when dated and/or checked in box)	FEES, COSTS, ETC.	
		AMOUNT	RECEIPT NO.
	Claim of Plaintiff: Fees paid, order issued		
	Delivered to Plaintiff for personal service		
	Order and copy of declaration: Mailed to defendant(s) by certified mail.		

The declaration under penalty of perjury must be signed in California, or in a state that authorizes use of a declaration in place of an affidavit; otherwise an affidavit is required.

Exhibit 10.3

(Refer to this Number)

S. C. N.Y.   34567 -   **1979**

Civil Court of the City of New York
111 Centre Street, New York, N. Y. 10013
Small Claims Part, County of New York
Telephone: 374-8403

To.... LESTER LANDLORD, Defendant

127 E. 89th ST.
NEW YORK, NEW YORK

THERESA TENANT,

Plaintiff,

ask judgment in this Court against you for $.....200.00.....together with costs upon the following claim:

Failure to return residential rental security deposit following termination of tenancy.

There will be a hearing upon this claim on ....September 5, 1981...................., **at 6:30 P.M.**, **in the Small Claims Part Courtroom, Ground Floor, 111 Centre Street, County of New York.**

You must appear at the time and place above indicated and present your defense and any counterclaim you may desire to assert at the hearing. Unless you do, judgment will be entered against you by default. If your defense or counterclaim, if any, is supported by witnesses, account books, receipts, or other documents, you should produce them at the hearing. Before the hearing you may request the clerk to issue subpoenas without fee.

If you admit the claim, but desire time to pay, you must appear personally on the day set for the hearing, state to the court that you desire time to pay and show your reasons for desiring time to pay.

☛ **Corporation defendants may appear by an officer or major stockholder, but Voluntary Associations must appear by attorney. See Section 321A—C.P.L.&R.**

IN WITNESS WHEREOF, I have hereunto subscribed my name and affixed the seal of the Court this ....10th.... day of ....August, 1981....................,

PHOENIX INGRAHAM
Chief Clerk

Claimant .....Theresa Tenant...

Address and Telephone .....1234 Park Avenue, New York, New York..... (202) 555-1234

If you desire a jury trial, you must, at least one day before the day upon which you have been notified to appear, file with the clerk of the court, a demand for a trial by jury. At that time you will have to make an affidavit specifying the issues of fact which you desire to have tried by a jury, and stating that such trial is desired, and demanded in good faith. To obtain a jury trial you will have to pay a jury fee of Twenty Five Dollars, and you will have to file an undertaking in the sum of $50.00 in cash, to secure the payment of any costs that may be awarded against you. Under the law, the Court may award $25.00 additional cost to the plaintiff if a jury trial is demanded, and a verdict is rendered against you.

BRING THIS NOTICE WITH YOU AT ALL TIMES

Exhibit 10.4

copy of the "Claim of Plaintiff" will go to the judge, and another must be served on the defendant. (See Chapter 11). Exhibit 10.3 shows a sample of the "Claim of Plaintiff" in use in Berkeley, California. Exhibit 10.4 shows a sample of the "Claim of Plaintiff" form in use in New York City.

STEP 3: Supplying Documentary Evidence

In most Small Claims Courts, no written evidence need be provided until you get to court, but others, such as Washington D.C., require that certain types of evidence (e.g., copies of unpaid bills) be provided at the time that you file your first papers.

Whether your local rules require written documentation of certain types of claims or not, it is wise to spend a little time thinking about how you will prove your case. We discuss this in detail in the later chapters of this book. You should read ahead and figure out exactly what proof you will need and how you will present it, before you file your first court papers. Being right is one thing—proving it is another.

STEP 4: Getting a Hearing Date

One of the great advantages of Small Claims Court is that disputes are settled quickly. All states have strict rules as to how long a case can last. This is important. Many people avoid lawyers and the regular courts primarily because they take forever to settle a dispute. Business people, for example, rely increasingly on private arbitration, caring more that a dispute be resolved promptly than that they win a complete victory. Anyone who has had to wait two years for a case to be heard in some constipated state trial court knows through bitter experience that the old cliché, "justice delayed is justice denied," is all too true.

In New York and many other states, an "early" hearing is required, but no maximum number of days is set. Other states, such as California, require that the case be set for trial within a certain number of days.

When you file your papers, you should also arrange with the clerk for a court date. Get a date that is convenient for you. You need not take the first date the clerk suggests. Be sure to leave yourself enough time to get a copy of the "Claim of Plaintiff" or "Notice of Claim" form served on the defendant(s). (See Chapter 11 for service information.) If you fail to serve your papers on the defendant properly and in time, there is no big hassle—just notify the clerk, get a new court date, and try again.

Small Claims Courts are most often held at 9:00 A.M. on working days. Some judicial districts are beginning to hold evening and Saturday sessions. (New York City's sessions are held only in the evenings.) Ask the clerk for a schedule. If evening and Saturday sessions aren't available, ask why not.

The Defendant's Forms

In most states, no papers need be filed to defend a case in Small Claims Court.* You must show up on the date and at the time indicated, ready to tell your side of the story. If you need to get the hearing delayed, see "Changing a Court Date" below. It is proper, and advisable, for a defendant to call or write the plaintiff and see if a fair settlement can be reached without going to court. (See Chapter 6.)

Sometimes, someone you were planning to sue sues you (i.e., over a traffic accident in which you each believe the other is at fault). As long as your grievance stems from the same incident, you can file a "Claim of Defendant" or "Counterclaim" for up to the Small Claims Court maximum and have it heard by a judge at the same time that the plaintiff's claim against you is considered.† However, if you believe that plaintiff owes you money as the result of a different injury or breach of contract, you may have to file your own separate case.

But what happens if your claim (on facts arising out of the same incident) is over the Small Claims Court maximum? First, reread Chapter 4 and decide whether you want to scale down your claim to fit into Small Claims Court. If you don't, you can have the whole case transferred to a formal court in most states. The defendant does this either by initiating an action in formal court prior to the time of the Small Claims Court hearing data and by notifying the Small Claims Court that this has been done, or by filing the over-the-limit claim in Small Claims Court. In California, the defendant must prepare an affidavit setting out the facts of the commencement of his or her action and file it with the Small Claims Court clerk along with a copy of the formal court "complaint." These papers must be served on the plaintiff by personal service prior to the Small Claims Court hearing. The clerk does the rest.

In New York, filing a counterclaim over the Small Claims Court dollar limit will not cause a transfer to formal court. Transfer is allowed only if the defendant demands a jury trial and posts jury fees.

Important: In some states a judge will check to see if a counterclaim is filed in bad faith (i.e., if there is no reasonable chance that it will succeed) and won't transfer the case if this is so.

*In a few states, including Alabama, Iowa, and Oregon, a defendant must respond in writing. This is unusual—see Appendix. In several states, including California, transfer is possible only if the defendant's claim is over the Small Claims Court dollar limit.

†Many states call a "Claim of Defendant" either a "cross-complaint" or a "counterclaim."

Note: If you have a claim against a plaintiff arising out of the same transaction or situation that forms the basis for his or her suit against you, you are required in many states to file it prior to the time when the plaintiff's case is to be heard. If you fail to file and let the case be decided, you may find that you will not be permitted to file at a later time.

In essence, filing a claim against the defendant simply means that you and the other party are suing each other. The judge can

---

170-133 Name, Address and Telephone No. of Defendant(s)

Acme Illusions, Inc.
100 Primrose Path
Oakland, California 94602

Space Below for use of Court Clerk Only

SMALL CLAIMS COURT OF CALIFORNIA, COUNTY OF ALAMEDA

Andrew Printer
_____
Plaintiff(s)

vs.

Acme Illusions, Inc.
_____
Defendant(s)
(abbreviated title)

No. SC

CLAIM OF DEFENDANT

I, the undersigned, defendant and claimant in the above-entitled action say that the plaintiff is indebted to me in the sum of $ 300.00 for delays and poor workmanship in printing job

which amount I pray be allowed against the plaintiff herein.

Executed on _____(Date)_____ at _____Oakland_____, California.
(date)

I declare under penalty of perjury that the foregoing is true and correct.

Waldo Fergus, President
Signature of defendant

DECLARATION OF SERVICE

I served the within Claim by delivering to and leaving with the person or persons personally, hereinafter named, a copy thereof, at the address and on the date set forth opposite each name of said person or persons, in the County of Alameda , State of California, to wit:

Name of Person Served*	Street Address and City where Served	Date of Service
Andrew Printer	1800 Marilee St., Fremont, CA.	(Date)

Fee for Service $ 8.00 , Mileage $, Total $ 8.00

Executed on _____(Date)_____ , at _____Oakland_____, California.
(date)   (place)

I declare under penalty of perjury that the foregoing is true and correct.

Robert Rooter
Signature of Declarant

*If service is upon a corporation, partnership, or association, state its name and the name and official title of person to whom copy is delivered.

JUDGEMENT ON CLAIM OF DEFENDANT
Judgment for Claimant $
Stay _____ days   Costs $
Dated:

Exhibit 10.5

make a decision in favor of either of you, or decide that no one gets anything.* Your claim should be on file with the Small Claims Court clerk as early as possible after you're served with the plaintiff's claim (see Chapter 11 for information on serving a "Claim of Defendant" and what to do if you can't get it served).

Jury Trials

Jury trials are not available in Small Claims Court in the great majority of states, including California, Colorado, and Michigan. Some states allow a defendant to transfer a case to a formal court in order to be eligible for a jury trial no matter how small his or her claim, while the majority, including California and Ohio, allow transfer when the "Claim of Defendant" is over the Small Claims Court maxi-

---

*When you file a "Claim of Defendant" you become a plaintiff as far as this claim is concerned. In a few states, such as California, this means that if you lose, you can't appeal because plaintiffs can't appeal. Of course, if you lose on the original plaintiff's claim, you can normally appeal that portion of the judgment. Appeal rules vary a great deal from state to state and can be complicated. See Chapter 22 and the Appendix.

mum. Normally, a jury trial must be requested as soon as notice of the case is received, and "jury fees" (which often reach $50–150) must be paid in advance. Fees are normally recoverable if you win. Asking for a jury trial tends to delay proceedings, and some people will make the request for this reason. The trend across the country is to eliminate jury trials in Small Claims Court. I believe that this is a good idea—it is simply too expensive to round up a large group of people to decide a small claim.

Changing a Court Date

It is sometimes impossible for a defendant to be present on the day ordered by the court for the hearing. It can also happen that the plaintiff will pick out a court date and get the defendant served only to find that an unexpected emergency makes it impossible for the defendant to be present.

It is normally not difficult to get a case delayed. To arrange this, call the other party and see if you can agree on a mutually convenient date. Don't call the clerk first—they don't know what days the other party has free. Sometimes it is difficult to face talking to someone you are opposing in a lawsuit, but you will just have to swallow your pride and start dialing. Once all parties have agreed to a new date, send the court clerk a notice in writing signed by both parties.*
Exhibit 10.6 shows a sample.

```
                                    11 South Street
                                    Denver, CO

                                    January 10, 19--


Clerk of the Small Claims Court
Denver, CO                          Re:  SC 4117 Rodriguez v. McNally

Dear Clerk:

Mr. Rodrigeuz and I agree to request that you postpone this case to a
date after March 1, 19--.



                                    _____
                                    JOHN McNALLY
```

Exhibit 10.6

Check your local Small Claims Court rules and contact the court clerk if you have any questions.

If you speak to the other party(ies) and find that he or she is completely uncooperative, put your request for a delay (continuance) in writing, along with the circumstances that make it impossible for you to keep the first date. Send your letter to the judge of the Small Claims Court. Exhibit 10.7 shows a sample letter.

```
                                  37 Birdwalk Blvd.
                                  Occidental, CA

                                  January 10, 19--


Judge John Justice
Small Claims Court
City Hall
San Francisco, CA          Re:  Small Claims No. 374-628

Dear Judge Justice:

     I have been served with a complaint (No. 374-628) by John's Laundry,
Inc.  The date set for a hearing, February 15, falls on the day of my
son's graduation from Nursing School in Oscaloosa, Oklahoma, which my
husband and I plan to attend.

     I called John's Laundry and asked to have the case delayed one week.
They just laughed and said that they would not give me any cooperation.

     I feel that I have a good defense to this suit.  Please delay this
case until any day after February 22, except March 13, which is my day
for a medical check-up.



                                  Thank you,



                                  Sally Wren
```

Exhibit 10.7

If One Party Doesn't Show Up

If one party to a case doesn't appear in court on the proper day at the proper time, the case is normally decided in favor of the other. Depending on whether it is the plaintiff or defendant who fails to show up, the terms used by the judge to make his decision are different. If the plaintiff appears but the defendant doesn't, a "default judgment" is normally entered in favor of the plaintiff. (See Chapters 12 and 15 for more information on defaults.) Occasionally, although it happens far less frequently, it is the plaintiff who fails to show up. In this situation, the judge will probably dismiss the case.

In some states, if neither party appears, a judge may simply take the case "off calendar," meaning that the plaintiff will get another chance to schedule it for a hearing.

If you are the person who failed to show up (whether defendant or plaintiff) and you still want a chance to argue the case on its merits, you must act immediately or forever hold your piece.

SETTING ASIDE A DEFAULT (DEFENDANT'S REMEDY)

Courts are not very sympathetic to setting aside default judgments to allow a defense to be made unless you can show that the original papers weren't properly served on you and that you didn't know about the hearing. This can happen if someone signs your name for the certified letter and then doesn't give it to you, or because a dis-

honest process server doesn't serve you but tells the court he did, or for some other reason. As soon as you find out that a default judgment has been entered against you, call the court clerk. It doesn't make any difference if the hearing you missed took place months before as long as you move to set it aside immediately upon learning about it.

If you have had a default judgment entered against you after you were properly served, you will face an uphill struggle to get it set aside. Some judges will accept excuses such as "I forgot," "I was sick," "I got called out of town," etc., and some will not. Generally, judges assume that you could have at least called, or had a friend call, no matter what the emergency. However, if you act promptly (this means within 30 days after the default), and if you have a good excuse, you stand a reasonable chance of getting the judge to set the default aside.

Note: In most states, you can't appeal a default judgment even if you have a great case, and you must try to get the default set aside or the judgment will be final. To try to set aside a default, go to the Small Claims Court clerk's office and ask for the proper form. Exhibit 10.8 shows an example.

VACATING A JUDGMENT OF DISMISSAL (PLAINTIFF'S REMEDY)

The plaintiff who fails to show up and then requests that the judge vacate his or her decision to dismiss the case will encounter even more difficulty than a no-show defendant who tries to persuade the judge to set aside a default. Why? Because the plaintiff is the one who started the case and arranged for the court date. The judge assumes that the plaintiff should be able to show up for his or her own case, or at least call the court clerk prior to the court date and explain why he or she can't appear.

However, now and then emergencies happen, or someone simply makes a mistake about the day. Judges can, and do, vacate dismissals if both of the following circumstances exist. One, the plaintiff moves to have the judgment vacated "immediately" upon learning of his mistake. "Immediately" is never interpreted to be more than a few weeks, at most, after the day the dismissal was entered, and is thought by most judges to be a much shorter time. Two, the plaintiff has a good explanation as to why he or she was unable to be present or call on the day the case was regularly scheduled. A judge might accept something like this: "I had a flu with a high fever and simply lost track of a couple of days. As soon as I felt better, which was two days after my case was dismissed, I came to the clerk's office to try to get the case rescheduled."

To get a dismissal vacated (when allowed), you must fill out a form similar to the one shown in Exhibit 10.8.

211-147

COUNTY OF ALAMEDA, STATE OF CALIFORNIA

Andrew Printer   vs   Acme Illusions, Inc.
        Plaintiff(s)   Defendant(s)

ACTION NO. (Fill in)

DECLARATION AND NOTICE OF MOTION TO VACATE JUDGMENT

I, the undersigned, say: I am the President of Defendant Corp in the above entitled action: that judgment was entered on (Fill in date) , 19...... against Acme Illusions, Inc. ,

I was not present at the trial and did not notify the court before trial that I could not be present because ....

A death in the family made it impossible to do so

I believe I can prove the following facts to support my case, to wit: that Acme Illusions is not

indebted to Andrew Printer because the printing work was improperly done

WHEREFORE, I request that said judgment be vacated and the case be tried on its merits.

I declare under penalty of perjury that the foregoing is true and correct.

Executed on (Date) , at Oakland, California.

Waldo Fergus
Signature of Declarant

NOTICE OF MOTION

(To be filled in by the clerk)

To................................ , ... (address)

Please take notice that on..., 19......... , at........................... M., in Dept. Two

of the above entitled court, 2120 Grove Street, Berkeley, California, ...

will move the court for an order vacating the judgment heretofore entered in this case and for trial forthwith.

Dated... , 19......... .

....
Deputy Clerk

Exhibit 10.8

Serving Your Papers 11

After you have filed your "Claim of Plaintiff" form with the clerk, following the instructions in Chapter 10 under "Filling Out Your Court Papers and Getting Your Court Date," a copy must be served on the person, persons, or corporation you are suing. This is called "service of process." Your lawsuit is not complete without it. The reason that you must serve the other side is simple—the person(s) you are suing are entitled to be notified of the general nature of your claim and the day, time, and place of the hearing so that they can show up to defend themselves. The general rules of all states are similar, but details do differ. Refer to your local rules and to the Appendix of this book.

Who Must Be Served?

All defendants that you list on your "Claim of Plaintiff" or "Notice of Claim" should be served. It is not enough to serve one defendant and assume that he or she will tell the other(s). This is true even if the defendants are married or living together. If you don't serve a particular defendant, the court can't enter a judgment against that person. If you sue more than one person and can serve only one, a judge can enter a judgment against the person served, in effect dropping your action against the other defendant(s).

Where Can Papers Be Served?

Normally papers must be served within the state in which your action is brought. Thus you can't sue someone in a Massachusetts court and serve papers on them in Oklahoma. The one exception involves suits having to do with motor vehicle accidents. Many states have a procedure for out-of-state service on this type of claim. Your Small Claims Court clerk will show you how this is handled in your state.

Now let's assume that the person you want to sue resides or does business in your state. In most states, papers can be served anyplace in the state as long as the suit is brought in the correct judicial district. (See Chapter 9, "Where Can I Sue?") But a few states, including New York, New Jersey, and New Mexico, require with some exceptions that a defendant be served in the same county or judicial district where the suit was filed. (See the Appendix).

How to Serve Your Papers*

There are several approved ways to serve papers. All depend on your knowing where the defendant is. If you can't find the defendant, you can't serve him or her and it makes little sense to file a lawsuit.

METHOD 1: Personal Service

Sheriff, Marshal, or Constable: All states allow personal service to be made by law officers. This is often good for its sobering effect, but can cost a few dollars. Ten to twenty dollars is the average fee, but you can get it added to your judgment if you win. Many states, including California, also allow service by professional process servers, whom you will find listed in the Yellow Pages. (See Appendix.)

Service by Disinterested Adult: California, Colorado, Ohio, and a number of other states (but by no means all—see Appendix) allow service by any person who is eighteen years of age or older, except the person bringing a suit or a person who will appear as a witness. Any person means just that—a relative or a friend is fine.

---

*In a few states, including Alaska and Colorado, service is accomplished even though a certified letter is rejected.

The "Claim of Plaintiff" or "Notice of Claim" must be handed to the defendant personally. You can't simply leave the paper at his or her job, or home, or in the mailbox. A person making a service who doesn't know the person involved should make sure that he or she is serving the right person. If a defendant refuses to take the paper, acts hostile, or attempts to run away, the process server should simply put the paper down and leave. Valid service has been accomplished. The process server should never try to use force to get a defendant to take any papers.

METHOD 2: By Certified or Registered Mail

In California, New York, and the majority of states, you can also serve papers by certified mail. In some states service by certified (or registered) mail is an option of the plaintiff, while others require that it be tried before any other method of service is attempted. (See Appendix.) Normally, the court clerk does the mailing for you and charges a fee of three dollars per defendant. The mail method is both cheap and easy, but depends for its success on the defendant signing for the letter. Most businesses and many individuals routinely sign to accept their mail. However, some people never do, knowing instinctively, or perhaps from past experience, that nothing good ever comes by certified mail. Clerks estimate that about 50 percent of certified mail services are accepted.

Note: Never assume that your certified mail service has been accomplished and show up in court on the day of the court hearing. If the defendant didn't sign for the paper, you will be wasting your time in all but a few states. Call the clerk a couple of days in advance and find out if the service of process has been completed.

METHOD 3: Substituted Service (or "Nail and Mail")

Often it is hard to serve particular individuals. Some people have developed avoiding the process server into a high (but silly) art. In California and some other states, this no longer works, as there is now a procedure that allows "substituted service."

Important: If you live outside of California and are having trouble with service, ask your local Small Claims Court clerk if "substituted service" exists in your state. Often the slang for this type of service is

"Nail and Mail," because in several states, if you are unable to serve the defendant personally, you do not have to leave the summons with a person at his or her home or business, but can simply tack one copy to his or her door and mail the second copy.

In California, substituted service works like this. If a person can't be served with "reasonable diligence," which is normally interpreted to mean three unsuccessful tries at personal service, the papers may be served by leaving a copy of the summons and complaint at the person's dwelling in the presence of a competent member of the household who is at least 18 years of age and who must be told what the papers are about *and* thereafter mailing a copy of the summons and complaint by first-class mail to the person served. Service is complete ten days after mailing. Be sure that all steps are carried out by a disinterested adult. Because some Small Claims Court clerks interpret the requirement for "due diligence" differently, you should discuss the procedure with your local clerk before trying it. If your suit is against a corporation, the substituted service procedure is easier. There is no requirement in this case that you try personal service three times before using substituted service. Papers may be served by leaving a copy of the summons and complaint at the defendant's office with a person apparently in charge of the office during normal business hours, and then sending another copy of the summons and complaint by first-class mail to the person to be served at the same address. Service is accomplished ten days after mailing.

After service is accomplished, you must return an affidavit to the court clerk that all proper steps have been accomplished. (See "Serving a Business," below).

METHOD 4: For Serving Subpoenas Only

In Chapter 14 we discuss subpoenaing witnesses and documents. Subpoenas can't be served by mail. They must be served by personal service. The rules as to who can do the serving, etc., are the same as those set forth above in Method 1, however, in California and many other states, there is an important added requirement. The person making the service must be ready to pay the person subpoenaed a witness fee (usually $12–$20) on the spot if it is requested. If you hire a sheriff or marshal to do the service, he or she will ask you to pay this fee, plus a service fee, in advance. In many states, if the witness doesn't ask for the fee, it will be returned to you.

Costs of Personal Service

Professional process servers commonly charge between ten and twenty dollars per service, depending on the time and mileage involved.* You can usually get your costs of service added to your judgment if you win, but be sure to remind the judge to do this when you conclude your court presentation. However, a few courts will not give the successful party an award of costs for a process server unless he or she tried first to have the papers served by the cheaper certified mail approach (Method 2 above). Other judicial districts prefer that you don't use the mail approach at all because they feel that, too often, the mail isn't accepted. Ask the Small Claims Court clerk in your district how he or she prefers that you accomplish service and how much the judge will allow as a service of process fee before you pay anyone to accomplish service for you.

Time Limits in Which Papers Must Be Served

All states have a rule that the defendant is entitled to receive service of the "Claim of Plaintiff" or "Notice of Claim" form before the date of the court hearing. Rules as to how many days in advance of the hearing papers must be served vary considerably, with some states requiring as little as five and others requiring as many as 30. Check your local rules for details.

If the defendant is served fewer than the required number of days before the trial date, he or she can either go ahead with the trial anyway, or request that the case be delayed (continued). If a delay is granted, it is normally in the range between two weeks and a month. If it is impossible to show up in person to ask for a delay, call the court clerk (telegraph if you can't call) and point out that you weren't

---

*County officials such as sheriffs and marshals will serve papers only in the county in which they are located. Call them to ask about fees. Be sure to authorize them to serve papers by either personal or substituted service if the latter exists in your state. If you don't authorize substituted service, they probably will not use it.

served in the proper time and that you want the case put over. The clerk will see that a default judgment is not entered against you. (See Chapter 10, "Changing a Court Date.)

To count the days to see if service has been accomplished in the correct time, you do not count the day the service is accomplished or the day of the court appearance in most states (check your local rules). Do count weekends and holidays. Thus, if Jack served Julie on

July 11 in Los Angeles County (where the limit is five days) with a "Declaration and Order" listing a July 17 court date in the same county, service would be proper. This is true even if Saturday and Sunday fell on July 14 and 15. To determine the number of days you would not count July 11, the day of service, or July 17, the court date, but you would count July 12, 13, 14, 15, and 16, for a total of five days. If you are unable to serve the defendant(s) within the proper time, simply ask the court clerk for a new court date and try again.

Defendant's Note: If you were improperly served because you were not given adequate time, or the papers weren't handed to you personally, or a certified letter wasn't signed for by you, you would still be wise to call the court clerk or show up in court on the day in question. Why should you have to do this if service was improper? Because the plaintiff may succeed in getting the case heard as a default if you fail to show up. It's more trouble to get a default set aside than to protect yourself from the start. But isn't this a Catch-22? You are entitled to proper service, but if you don't get it, you have to show up in court anyway? Perhaps, but as Catch-22s go, this one is mild. You can call the clerk or show up in court and request that the judge grant you a continuance to prepare your case. If the original service was in fact improper, your request will be honored. Of course, if you were improperly served and simply want to get the hearing out of the way, you can show up and go ahead with your case.

Serving a Business

If you are suing someone who owns his or her own business, or is a partner in the business, you must serve the person individually using the rules set out above. However, if you are suing a corporation, the rules are a little different.

Although a corporation is a legal person for purposes of lawsuits, you still must have your papers served on someone who lives and breathes. This is true whether you have the papers served personally or use certified mail. The flesh-and-blood person should be an officer of the corporation (president, vice president, secretary or treasurer). Simply call the corporation and ask who, and where, they are. If they won't tell you, the city or county business tax and license people should be able to, at least for local corporations. (See Chapter 8.) If you have trouble getting someone at a large national corporation to accept service, call or write your Secretary of State or Commissioner of Corporations. Their office will be located in your state capital.

Notifying the Court That Service Has Been Accomplished ("Proof of Service")

Where certified or registered mail is involved, you need do nothing. The court clerk sends out the certified mail for you, and the signed post office receipt comes back directly to the clerk if service is accomplished. It's as simple as that.

However, a court has no way of knowing whether or not papers have been successfully served by personal service unless you tell them. This is done by filing a piece of paper known as a "Proof of Service" with the court clerk after the service has been made. The "Proof of Service" is a small, perforated, tear-off form (Exhibit 11.1) that is part of the "Declaration and Order" package that must be signed by the person actually making the service. A "Proof of Service" is used both by the plaintiff and by the defendant if he or she files a counterclaim. It must be returned to the clerk's office before the trial. A "Proof of Service" is used when any legal documents are served by personal service. If the papers are served by a law enforcement officer, he or she will prepare and file the "Proof of Service" automatically. Check your local rules for specific filing requirements in your area.

Sample Proof of Service

Note: If you serve by substituted service (Method 3, above), the person making the service should fill out a "proof of service" form specifically designed for this method. Forms are available at Small Claims Court offices in all states that recognize "substituted service." In California, if service is on an individual, the person making the service must submit to the court clerk an affidavit that establishes that he or she tried with "reasonable diligence" to serve the defendant personally before resorting to substituted service. No affidavit is required when substituted service is used to serve a business.

S. C. No..

CIVIL COURT OF THE CITY OF NEW YORK
SMALL CLAIMS PART
COUNTY OF...

State of New York

County of.......................................⎬ *ss.:*

----

being duly sworn, deposes and says, I am over

18 years of age and not a party to this action.

On.., 19........,

at...

in the County of.......................................

City of New York, I served the NOTICE OF

CLAIM herein on..

----

known to me to be the defendant mentioned and

described as defendant therein, by delivering the

said NOTICE to and leaving the same with............

....known to me to

be the..of the said

defendant corporation.

(Signed)...

Sworn to before me this ....⎬

day of............................, 19....⎬

43-2094C-3M-707591(75) 346

Exhibit 11.1

Serving a "Claim of Defendant" (or "Counterclaim")

A "Claim of Defendant" must be filed with the Small Claims Court clerk and served on the plaintiff. Time limits vary from state to state, as do the technical requirements for service. In California, a "Claim of Defendant" should be filed and served at least five days prior to the date that the court has set for the hearing on the plaintiff's claim. In New York, the time limit is seven days. Check your local rules if you wish to file a defendant's claim in your state. If you file a claim of defendant and can't find the plaintiff to serve the papers, all is not lost. Explain your problem to the court clerk. In most states, the clerk will either arrange to have the hearing date delayed or will tell you to show up for the first hearing with your papers. You can serve them on the plaintiff in the hallway (not the courtroom). Then explain to the judge why it was impossible to locate the plaintiff earlier. The judge will either put the whole case over for a few days or allow you to proceed with your claim that day. Either way, he or she will accept your "Claim of Defendant" as validly served.

Serving Someone in the Military— Declaration of Nonmilitary Service

It is proper to serve someone who is on active duty in the armed forces. If he or she shows up, fine. If he or she doesn't, you have a problem. We learned in Chapter 10 that, as a general rule, if a properly served defendant doesn't show up, you can get a "default judgment" against him or her. This is not true if the person you are suing is in the military (the reserves don't count).

Default judgments cannot normally be taken against people in the armed forces because Congress has given our military personnel special protections. To get a default judgment in California against any defendant, a statement must be filed under penalty of perjury that he or she is not in the military. The "Declaration of Nonmilitary Service" is part of your "Claim of Plaintiff" package and is routinely filled out and signed as part of every case, unless, of course, the defendant is in the military. Clerks accept "Declaration of Nonmilitary Service" signed by the plaintiff, as long as the plaintiff reasonably believes that the defendant is not on active duty. This constitutes a lenient interpretation of the law by clerks, but no one seems to be complaining. Exhibit 11.2 shows a form currently used in California. Other states use similar ones.

```
                          CLAIM OF PLAINTIFF


DECLARATION OF NONMILITARY SERVICE
Defendant(s)_____
                              (name(s))
and each of them, if more than one is named herein, is not now a person in
the military service of the United States as defined in Section 101, and
subdivisions thereof, of the Soldiers' and Sailors' Relief Act of 1940, as
amended, and not entitled to the benefits of said Act as amended.

     I declare under penalty of perjury that the foregoing is true and
correct.

Executed on_____, at Berkeley, CA



                           _____
                           SIGNATURE OF PLAINTIFF
```

Exhibit 11.2

The 12 Defendant's Options

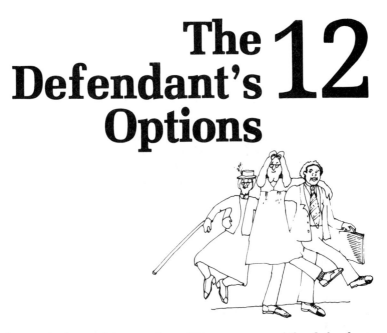

This chapter is devoted to a review of the concerns of the defendant. Most of this material has already been discussed in the first eleven chapters, but I think it would be helpful to pull it all together in one place. Let's start by assuming that you are the person being sued. How do you approach what's happening to you? When you receive the plaintiff's papers, you have to make one of several decisions. There is no one correct course of action—it all depends on your circumstances.

Improper Service

You may conclude that the service was not proper. (See Chapter 11.) Perhaps the "Claim of Plaintiff" was left with your neighbors, or maybe you didn't have the correct number of days in which to respond. You may be tempted not to show up in court, figuring that since you weren't served properly, the case can't be heard. As noted, this is not a smart idea if you wish to defend the case. The judge can easily be unaware of, or overlook, the service problem and issue a default judgment against you. If this happens, you will have to go to the trouble of requesting that the default be set aside. You are better off to contact the clerk, explain the problem with the service, and ask that the case be continued to a date that is convenient to you. If the clerk can't help, write the judge or show up on the day in question and request a continuance.

No Defense

Now let's assume that the service was OK, but you have no real defense, or don't have the time to defend yourself, or for some other reason don't feel like going to court. A decision not to show up will very likely result in a default judgment being entered against you. It will probably be for the dollar amount demanded by the plaintiff, plus his or her filing fee and costs to serve you. We discuss default judgments in more detail in Chapter 10 and 15. Basically, a default judgment has the same effect as if you had showed up, argued your case, and lost.

Many people are tempted not to show up and defend a case in Small Claims Court because they have no money and figure that even if they lose, the plaintiff can't collect. This is "grasshopper thinking." The sun may be shining today and the judgment may cause you no immediate problem. But remember, judgments are good for 10 to 20 years, depending on the state, and can usually be "renewed" for a longer period of time if necessary. You may put a few nickels together sometime in the future, and you probably won't want them taken away by an industrious little ant holding a Small Claims Court judgment in its mouth. So, wake up and defend yourself while you can!

Try to Compromise

If you feel that perhaps the plaintiff has some right on his or her side, but that you are being sued for too much, contact the plaintiff and try to work out a compromise settlement. Any settlement you make should be set down in writing along the lines outlined in Chapter 6. It should also include a specific statement that the plaintiff will forever drop his pending lawsuit. Simply add a clause like the following to the sample agreement outlined in Chapter 6.

As part of this settlement, _____ (name of plaintiff) _____
hereby agrees to drop the lawsuit, number ____ (insert number) ____
filed in Small Claims Court in the _____
judicial district on _____ (date) _____
against _____ (name of defendant) _____
and that no further court action(s) will be filed regarding the subject matter of this agreement.

As a practical matter, any lawsuit that is not actively prosecuted will be dropped by the clerk. The reason why you want to have a settlement agreement written out is to cover the unlikely possibility that the other party will accept money from you and then try to go ahead with his or her suit, too. If this happens, you need only show your written settlement agreement to the judge.

A few states prefer that both parties prepare and file a written settlement agreement with the Small Claims Court clerk. Exhibit 12.1 shows a sample form in use in New York.

CIVIL COURT OF THE CITY OF NEW YORK

COUNTY OF

SMALL CLAIMS PART

Claimant	Index No.
—against—	**STIPULATION OF SETTLEMENT**
Defendant(s)	

It is hereby agreed by and between the parties hereto that this claim is settled for the sum of

$, to be paid, on or before   to claimant, at

or as follows:

Upon such payment, parties hereto shall be released from liability as to each other covering the matters in the within dispute.

In the event of default in payment by defendant(s), for fifteen (15) days, claimant, upon presenting an affidavit setting forth such default, shall be entitled to enter judgment without further notice to the defendant, for the amount sued for, together with interest, costs and disbursements.

....
Claimant

Dated:

....
Defendant(s)

Exhibit 12.1

Fight Back

Now we get to those of you who feel that you don't owe the plaintiff a dime. You will want to fight actively. This means that you must show up in court on the date stated in the papers served on you, unless you get the case continued. (See Chapter 10.) In the great majority of states, a defendant need not file any papers with the court clerk; showing up ready to defend yourself is enough.* The strategies to argue a case properly, including the presentation of witnesses, estimates, diagrams etc., are discussed in Chapters 13–21 and apply equally to defendants and plaintiffs. You will wish to study this information carefully and develop a strategy for your case. You will also want to check whether the plaintiff has brought the case within the time allowed by the Statute of Limitations (Chapter 5) and whether he or she has asked for a reasonable amount of money (Chapter 4). If you simply show up without thinking out a coherent presentation, you are likely to lose.

File a "Claim of Defendant" or "Counterclaim"

Finally, there are those of you who not only want to dispute the plaintiff's claim, but also want to sue him or her. This involves either promptly filing a "Claim of Defendant" (often called a cross-complaint or counterclaim) in Small Claims Court for up to the Small Claims Court maximum, or having the case transferred to a formal court where you can sue for more. See Chapter 10 under "How to Serve Your Papers" and Chapter 11 under "Notifying the Court that Service Has Been Accomplished" for more details.†

*This is not true in a few states where a written response must be filed. States where a response is necessary include Alabama, Alaska, Arizona (oral OK), Colorado, Oregon, South Carolina (oral OK), South Dakota, Vermont, Virginia, and West Virginia.

†In most states, filing a "claim of defendant" or "counterclaim" or "cross-complaint" results in your case staying in Small Claims Court, unless your claim is over the Small Claims limit, in which case it will usually be transferred to a formal court. In a few states, a defendant has the right to have a case transferred to a formal court even without filing a claim in excess of the Small Claims Court limit, although this often can be done only by demanding a jury trial, which is almost always silly if the claim is small. A few states, such as New York, will not automatically allow transfer by reason of an over-the-limit counterclaim. (See Appendix.)

Getting Ready for Court 13

Once you have your papers on file and the defendant(s) served, the preliminaries are over and you are ready for the main event—your day in court. Movies, and especially TV, have had much negative impact on court proceedings. Ask yourself what a trial was like *before* lawyers fancied themselves to be Raymond Burr or Charles Laughton and judges acted "fatherly," or "stern," or "indignantly outraged."

Some of the people whose lives revolve around the courthouses have been playing movie parts for so long that they have become caricatures of one screen star or another. Lawyers are particularly susceptible to this virus. All too often they substitute posturing and theatrics for good, hard preparation. We can be thankful, though, that most people who work in our courts recover quickly from movie-itis and realize that the majestic courtroom is, in truth, a large, drafty hall with a raised platform at one end; that His Honor is only a lawyer dressed in a black shroud, who knew the right politician; and that they themselves are not bit players in "Witness for the Prosecution," "Inherit the Wind," or "Twelve Angry Men."

I mention movieitis because it's a common ailment in Small Claims Court. Cases that should be won easily are often lost because somebody goes marching around the courtroom antagonizing everyone with comic opera imitations of E. G. Marshall. And don't just assume that you are immune. Movieitis is a subtle disease, and people often don't realize they have it. Ask yourself a few self-diagnostic questions. Have you watched courtroom scenes on TV or in the movies? Have you ever imagined that you were one of the actor-law-years? How does the number of times you have been in a real court-room compare to the number of movie-set courtrooms you have seen?

My purpose here is not to lecture you on how to present yourself in court. But perhaps I can get you to remember something that you already know—you don't need to be false to yourself to succeed in Small Claims Court. You don't need to put on fancy clothes or airs, or try to appear more polished, intelligent, or sophisticated than you are. Be yourself and you will do just fine. If you have a chance, go to the court a few days before your case is heard and watch for an hour or two. You may not learn a great deal that will be helpful in your case, but you will be a lot more relaxed and comfortable when your turn comes. Watching a few cases is a particularly good thing to do if you feel anxious about your court appearance. For those of you who love to act, who simply can't pass up an opportunity to perform, at least act real. That's right, go ahead and act if you must, but make your performance that of a person—not a personality.

Movieitis aside, most people I have watched in Small Claims Court have done extremely well. Many mornings I have been in-spired, feeling that for the first time in years I have seen honesty and truth put in an appearance before the Bar of Justice. This truly sur-prised me, as I had hardly ever taken the time to watch a Small Claims case before doing research for this book. I stopped taking on clients several years ago, in part because I hated the dishonest sham that goes on in the courtroom—hated the endless natterings between lawyers about logic-chopping technicalities while clients paid, and paid, and paid. It was wonderful to see that, once the lawyers were removed and people began communicating directly, there was much about our court system that made sense.

Commonly, a judge must decide a case, at least in part, on the basis of who seems to be the most believable. This happens when there isn't enough hard evidence to be conclusive either way. Differ-ent judges have varying prejudices, hunches, feelings, etc., about who is, or isn't, telling the truth. Often, they themselves can't explain the many intangibles that go into making this sort of decision, but most agree that the more honestly a person presents himself or her-self, the more likely he or she is to be believed. For example, a house painter who shows up in his overalls and puts his lunchbox under the chair will probably be much more convincing (and comfortable) than he would be if he came painfully squeezed into his blue wedding and funeral suit. As one judge told me, "A pimp being a pimp has as good a chance as anyone else in my courtroom, but a pimp who tries to act like Saint Paul better watch out."

Interpreter Services

In California and a few other states, Small Claims Courts are required to make an effort to have interpreter services available for those who need them. Notify the court clerk well in advance if you or one of your witnesses will need an interpreter. In most areas interpreters are not routinely made available by the court. It is normally permissible to bring your own, however. Many ethnic and cultural organizations offer interpreter services to low-income persons free of charge.

Legal Advisors

A few Small Claims Courts are experimenting with legal advisor programs. In Harlem and Manhattan, New York, and several areas of California, including San Francisco, free legal advisor programs have met with some success, especially in low-income areas, where people are sometimes intimidated by court proceedings. While there is no set approach, most court-sponsored legal advisor programs make it possible for people involved in Small Claims Court actions, either as plaintiffs or defendants, to meet with a lawyer or a person with paralegal training before going to court. The idea is that the legal advisor will help the person using Small Claims Court to understand and prepare his or her case properly. You may wish to inquire if a legal advisor program is available in your area, but don't be disappointed if you don't find one. For most people, most of the time, it is not difficult to prepare a case properly for Small Claims Court without professional help. Indeed, a study prepared for the National Center for State Courts concluded that people whose education stopped before eleventh grade did just as well as those who had completed graduate school.*

Lawyers

As noted several times, many states have quite sensibly banned lawyers from appearing in Small Claims Court on behalf of either plaintiff or defendant. Unfortunately, however, most states still allow representation by an attorney. (See Appendix.) This is a mistake—it is past time that the lawyers that we have elected to our state legisla-

---

*Small Claims Court, A National Examination, Ruhnka et al., National Center for State Courts, 1978.

tures pass laws to ban their brethren in private practice from appearing in what should be the people's court.

Let's suppose that you live in a state that allows lawyers to appear in Small Claims Court, and that your case is against a lawyer, or someone represented by a lawyer. Should you hire one too? No! I think that, ordinarily, you will be better off to handle the case yourself. As you will have gathered from this book, Small Claims Court rules and procedures are quite simple—with a little study, you should be able to do a fine job of presenting your case. And you may actually have a psychological advantage—as a person without legal training, you can play David to the lawyer's Goliath. You may also be reassured to know that the National Center for State Courts found that, broadly speaking, having an attorney represent (or advise) a person in Small Claims Court did not statistically enhance that person's chances of winning. Or, put another way, people who spoke for themselves did just as well as those who hired a mouthpiece.

If you are worried about some aspect of the law that applies to your case, it is sensible to get legal advice on that particular point. This should not be expensive as long as you don't hire the attorney to handle the entire case. If no legal advisor program is available through your Small Claims Court and you are not a low-income person eligible for free legal assistance through a federally sponsored "legal aid" (often called "legal services") program, simply hire a lawyer for a short consultation. For $25–50 you should be able to find one who will review your entire case and advise you on any tricky points. Also, you may wish to spend a few hours doing some of your own research in your local law library. If you don't understand how law materials are catalogued and organized, see Honigsberg, 1979 (*Cluing into Legal Research*), Golden Rain Press.

Pretrial Settlement Conferences, Mediation, and Arbitration

Several states, most notably New York, have set up optional arbitration procedures. You can still go to court and have a hearing before a judge if you insist, but you are given the alternative choice to have your dispute decided by a lawyer-arbitrator. In New York, it is much quicker to have your case go to the arbitrator, but there is no right of appeal from his or her decision.

Several other states, including California, are experimenting with either mediation or arbitration techniques, but as yet their use is not widespread. While systems vary, most arbitration and mediation programs work something like this: The plaintiff and defendant are given a chance to get together with a local lawyer to see if the dispute can be compromised. If this is not possible, plaintiff and defendant are given a chance to present their arguments to a lawyer-arbitrator. He or she hears the dispute in a proceeding that is considerably less formal and intimidating than a normal courtroom proceeding. (Normally the parties and witnesses sit at a table and discuss the facts of the case.)

It is too early to say for sure how well these programs are working, but preliminary evidence indicates that holding hearings in a relatively informal setting (without a godlike figure in a black robe presiding from on high) produces excellent results.

However, I am extemely worried and cynical about the massive introduction of more lawyers into the Small Claims Court process. One of the main advantages of Small Claims Court has been the relative absence of lawyers, and every time I think of their increasing involvement, whether as mediators or arbitrators or advisors, I think of what eventually happened when the Arab let the camel put his nose into the tent. As an alternative, I would like to see nonlawyers trained to act as mediators and arbitrators.

Getting to the Courthouse

Before you get to the right courtroom, you have to get to the right building. Small Claims Courts are often not in the main courthouse, but are housed like a half-forgotten stepsister, wherever there's an empty room. Don't assume that you know where to go if you haven't been there before. Plaintiffs have already had to find the clerk's office, so they probably know where the courtroom is, but defendants should check this out. Be sure, too, that your witnesses know exactly where and when to show up. And do plan to be on time—people who rush in flustered and late start with a strike against them. Most Small Claims Courts begin sessions at 9:00 A.M., but there is a slow movement toward night and Saturday sessions. Check to see if night and Saturday sessions exist in your area. If not, why not?

Note: Courts in many areas of the country use a "hurry-up-and-wait" technique that would make the Army blush. San Francisco, California, is a typical example of a county using this "public-be-damned" approach. People are asked to show up at 8:15 A.M. and gather in one large room. At this time, the judges are still home having coffee. Court is supposed to start at 9:00, although 9:15 is normal, and 9:30 all too common. Can you imagine the court making lawyers show up an hour early for no good reason? Washington, D.C., has another terribly inefficient court in which everyone is asked to show up at one time only to wait and wait. How much more sensible is the approach followed in Minneapolis, Minnesota, where flexible scheduling of cases throughout the day (9:00, 10:00, 11:00, etc.) results in far less public inconvenience. But wherever you are, be warned—courts almost never start before 9:00 in the morning; if the clerk tells you to appear at an earlier time, call up and ask what time the judge *really* gets there.

Understanding the Courtroom

Most Small Claims court proceedings are conducted in standard courthouses that are also used for other purposes. Indeed, sometimes you will have to sit through a few minutes of some other type of court proceeding before the Small Claims Court calendar is called.

Most judges still sit on high in their little, wooden throne boxes, and most still wear those depressing black judicial robes that trace their history back over a thousand years to an England in which

THE JUDGE: IDENTIFIES THE PEOPLE INVOLVED. HEARS TESTIMONY. LOOKS AT DOCUMENTS AND DECIDES THE CASE.

THE ROBE: HIGH FASHION IN THE MIDDLE AGES. PERHAPS A BIT SILLY TODAY, BUT SEEMS TO MAKE THE JUDGE FEEL IMPORTANT.

THE CLERK: ANNOUNCES THE CASE. COLLECTS AND MARKS THE DOCUMENTARY EVIDENCE.

THE BAILIFF: GENERALLY DOES NOTHING, BUT IS PRESENT TO PRESERVE ORDER.

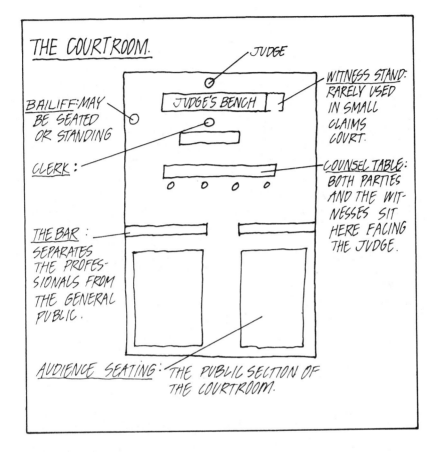

THE COURTROOM.

JUDGE

JUDGE'S BENCH

WITNESS STAND: RARELY USED IN SMALL CLAIMS COURT.

BAILIFF: MAY BE SEATED OR STANDING

CLERK:

COUNSEL TABLE: BOTH PARTIES AND THE WITNESSES SIT HERE FACING THE JUDGE.

THE BAR: SEPARATES THE PROFESSIONALS FROM THE GENERAL PUBLIC.

AUDIENCE SEATING: THE PUBLIC SECTION OF THE COURTROOM.

courts were largely controlled by king, nobility, and clergy. There are often no laws requiring these out-of-date traditions, and a few judges prefer to conduct their court more informally. In addition to the judge, a clerk and a bailiff will normally be present. They sit at tables immediately in front of the judge. The clerk's job is to keep the judge supplied with necessary files and papers, and to make sure that proceedings flow smoothly. A clerk is not the same as a court reporter, who keeps a word-by-word record of proceedings. No such record is kept in Small Claims Court, and no court reporter is present.*

Courtrooms are divided about two-thirds of the way toward the front by a little fence. This fence is known to initiates as the "bar."

*This is the rule in the vast majority of states, but there are exceptions.

The public must stay on the opposite side of the bar from the judge, clerk, bailiff, attorneys, etc., unless invited to cross. This invitation occurs when your case is called by the clerk. At this point you come forward and sit at the long table (known as the counsel table) just inside the fence. You and your witnesses sit facing the judge with your backs to the rest of the courtroom. In most Small Claims Courts, you will have been sworn (or affirmed if you wish) to tell the truth before the judge arrives. If this has not already been done, the oath will be administered at this time. In the great majority of Small Claims Courts you, your opponent, and your witnesses will present the entire case from the long table. This means that you do not sit in the witness box next to the judge. Many people (and judges) feel that it is polite to stand when addressing the judge, but in most courts it is, permissible to sit if it feels most comfortable to you.

When your case is called and you come forward to take your turn at the counsel table, have all your papers with you ready to present to the judge. This can include bills, receipts, estimates, photographs, contracts, letters to or from your opponent, etc. When the time comes to show these to the judge, you simply hand them to the clerk who will pass them to the judge. As I have said before, documentation is a great aid to your case, but don't go overboard and demand that the judge examine all sorts of irrelevant papers. Judges are a little like donkeys—load them too heavily and they are likely to lie down and go to sleep.

Dealing with Your Opponent

Before you get to the courtroom, you should do a little thinking about your opponent. Perhaps you can guess what sort of presentation he or she will make. If so, ask yourself how you can best deal with these arguments. This is a good way to take the negative energy you may feel (frustration, annoyance, anger) and turn it into creative planning and preparation. In court, be polite. You will gain nothing, and may lose the respect of the judge, if you are obviously hostile or sarcastic. Don't interrupt your opponent when he or she is speaking—you will get your chance. When you present your case, lay out the facts to the judge; don't conduct an argument with the other side.

Dealing with the Judge

It is hard to generalize about judges—each is an individual. I have seen more good than bad, but that doesn't help if your case comes up before an idiot. No great intellectual ability is required to be a good

Small Claims Court judge—indeed, most of the judges sitting on the United States Supreme Court would probably be lousy at it.* What is required is a liking for people, an open mind and, above all, patience. All those who come to Small Claims Court should have the feeling that they got a fair chance to have their say.

Most Small Claims Court judges are judges in the formal, lawyer-dominated courts who also hear the Small Claims Court calendar. This is a mistake. The last thing that is needed in Small Claims Court is the "me judge, you peasant" philosophy of our formal court system. It is my hope that, as Small Claims Court expands in the future, it will be staffed by people (not necessarily lawyers) specifically trained to meet its needs. (See Chapter 24.)

In California and many other states, lawyers are often appointed as temporary judges when a judge is ill or on vacation. The legal slang for a temporary judge is "Judge, pro tem." If your case comes up on a day when there is a "Judge, pro tem," you have one small advantage. You can choose whether or not to have your case heard by that particular person. How does this work? Under the law of most states you are not required to have your case heard by a "pro tem" judge—you can ask that the hearing be delayed until a regular judge is available. Simply sit and watch the cases that are heard before yours. If the judge seems OK to you, go ahead when your turn comes. But, if for some reason you don't like the "pro tem" judge, ask that your case be delayed until another day. You don't have to state a reason—this is your right.

When thinking about presenting your case to a judge, there is one constructive thing that you can do. Imagine yourself in the judge's shoes. What would you value most from the people appearing before you? Before I ever sat as judge, my answer was politeness, good organization of the material to be presented, and reasonable brevity. After experiencing Small Claims Court from the judge's chair, I would add only—documented evidence. By this, I mean evidence that is supported by more than the word of the person bringing, or defending, the case. Witnesses, written statements, contracts, leases, sales slips, rental agreements, police accident reports, photographs—all these give the judge a chance to make a decision based on something more than who tells the best story. And one final thing. Remember, the judge has heard thousand of stories very much like yours, and will either cease paying attention or get annoyed if you try repeating your story three times.

*Many people act as if I am nuts when I suggest nonlawyer judges. But why not? Vermont has used them with success in parts of its court system for generations.

Witnesses 14

It is often helpful to have someone in court with you who has a firsthand knowledge of the facts of your case and who can support your point of view. In many types of cases, such as car accidents, or disputes concerning whether or not a tenant left an apartment clean, witnesses are particularly valuable. In other factual situations, they aren't as necessary. For example, if a friend borrowed $500 and didn't pay it back, you don't need a witness to prove that your friend's (ex-friend's?) signature on the promissory note is genuine unless you expect him to base his defense on the theory that his signature was forged.

To arrange for a witness, simply talk to people you believe have something helpful to say and see if they will come down to the court and say it. You should do this even though subpoena forms are available from the Small Claims clerk's office to require a person's presence (see the next section for details). Subpoenas are helpful when a person would otherwise have difficulty getting out of work or school, but should almost never be used to drag someone in who doesn't want to come. Some courts have interpreter services available if there is a language difficulty, but you should let them know well in advance if an interpreter will be needed and be ready to arrange for your own interpreter if they can't supply one.

A good witness should have firsthand knowledge of the facts in dispute. This means that he or she saw the car accident, or the dog bite, or the dirty apartment, etc. The judge will not be interested in the testimony of a person who is repeating secondhand or generalized information, such as "I know Joe is a good, safe driver and would

never have done anything reckless," or "I didn't see Joe's apartment before he moved out, but both Joe and his mother, who couldn't be here today, told me that they worked for two days cleaning it up."

A good witness is believable. This isn't always a quality of easy definition—the police may be symbols of honesty to some people, while others regard them with hostility and fear. But remember, it is the judge you are trying to convince and judges tend in general to be establishment folk. (They make comfortable salaries, own their own homes, and generally tend to like the existing order of things.) Most judges I know would tend to believe a police officer.

In many types of cases, such as a car accident, you won't have much choice as to witnesses. You will be lucky to have one. But in other disputes (was the house properly painted, or the work on the car engine completed?), you have an opportunity to plan ahead. When you do, try to get a witness who is particularly knowledgeable about the dispute in question. Thus in a dispute over whether car repairs were properly done, bring a working car mechanic rather than your neighbor "who knows a lot about cars." Close friends and family are often your only witnesses. There is no rule that says that you can't have these people testify for you. Indeed, I have often seen a person's spouse, or the friend that he or she lives with, give very convincing testimony. But, given a choice, it is better to have a witness who is not your close friend or kin. A judge may discount testimony of people to whom you are close on the theory that they would naturally be biased in your favor.

I will talk more about witnesses as I go through the various case examples (Chapters 16–21), but let's outline a few basic dos and don'ts here:

- Never bring a witness to court who is hostile to you or hostile to the idea of testifying.
- Never bring a witness to court unless you know exactly what he or she will say. This sounds basic, but I have seen people lose cases because their witnesses supported the other side or got mixed up.
- Never pay, or offer to pay, a witness. It is a crime to do so. A subpoenaed witness is entitled to a small witness fee (see "Subpoenaing Witness" below), but no other money.*
- Never use a subpoena form to require a witness to be present unless you have made sure that it is OK with the witness (more in "Subpoenaing Witnesses" below);
- Prepare your witness thoroughly regarding what your position is, what your opponent is likely to say, and what you want the witness to say. In court, the witness will be on his or her own, and you want to be sure that the story comes out right. It is completely legal to discuss the case thoroughly with the witness beforehand.

*Traditionally, it has been legal to pay expert witnesses. These are not people who personally witnessed anything to do with your case. They are likely to be scientists, physicians, or others who have specific technical information about some point in dispute. Expert witnesses are almost never used in Small Claims Court. If you wish to hire one, check with the court clerk or, better yet, the judge in advance to see if it is OK to do so. You will not be able to recover expert witness fees if you win.

Important: In court a witness will be pretty much on his or her own. The witness will sit with you at the table facing the judge. Normally, a witness doesn't take the witness stand in Small Claims Court. Most judges prefer that you don't pretend to be a lawyer and ask the witness a lot of questions. Simply let the witness explain what happened as he or she saw it. The judge may ask the witness questions. If you feel that the witness has left something out, you should ask a question designed to produce the information that you want.

Subpoenaing Witnesses

In most states, you can require that a witness be present if that person resides within a certain distance from the courthouse (the distance varies from state to state, but it is often about 150 miles).* To do this, go to the clerk's office and get a "subpoena" form. Fill it out and have it served on the person you wish to have present. But remember, you never want to subpoena a person unless you have talked to him or her first and gotten an OK. The very act of dragging someone to court who doesn't want to come may set him or her against you. A subpoenaed witness is normally entitled to a fee of $10–$20 upon demand. The person serving the subpoena must have this money ready to pay if it is requested. If you win your case, you will probably be able to recover your witness fees from the othe side. The judge has discretion as to whether to grant you your witness fees. Some judges are strict about this, making the loser pay the winner's witness fees only if he or she finds that the subpoenaed witness was essential to the presentation of the case. This means that if your case is so strong that you don't need a witness but you subpoena one anyway, you may well have to pay the witness even though you win the case.

Exhibit 14.1 shows the standard California subpoena form. You must prepare an original and two copies. Once you have prepared them, take the subpoena form to the Small Claims Court clerk who will issue it. Service must be made personally, and the "Proof of Service," which is on the back of the subpoena, must be returned to the clerk's office. Rules for service are discussed in Chapter 11.

Testimony by Telephone

A surprising number of Small Claims Court judges will take testimony over the phone if a witness cannot be present because he or she is ill, disabled, out-of-state, or can't take time off from work. While proce-

In some states subpoenas reach only within county boundaries.

Name, Address and Telephone No. of Attorney(s) John O'Gara 15 Scenic St. Los Angeles, California 90011 IN PRO PER Attorney(s) for	This space for court clerk only

MUNICIPAL COURT OF CALIFORNIA, COUNTY OF LOS ANGELES

JUDICIAL DISTRICT

Public Library Plaintiff(s) vs. John O'Gara Defendant(s) (Abbreviated Title)	CASE NUMBER (Fill in number) **SUBPENA** (Civil)

THE PEOPLE OF THE STATE OF CALIFORNIA,

To   (Name of witness you wish to subpena)

You are ordered to appear in this court, located at

(Street Address of Court and City)

on _____ at _____ .m., _____ , to testify as a witness in this action.
(Date)   (Time)   (Department, Division or Room No., if any)

You must appear at that time unless you make a special agreement to appear at another time, etc., with:

John O'Gara _____ at 548-1921
(Name of Attorney or Party Requesting This Subpena)   (Telephone Number)

Disobedience of this subpena may be punished as contempt by this court. You will also be liable for the sum of one hundred dollars and all damages to such party resulting from your failure to attend.

(To be completed when subpena is directed to a California highway patrolman, sheriff, marshal or policeman, etc.)
This subpena is directed to a member of _____
(Name of Employing Agency)
I certify that the fees required by law are deposited with this court:
Receipt No.: _____   Amount Deposited $ _____

Dated _____ , Clerk

(SEAL)   By _____ , Deputy

(See reverse side for Proof of Service)

Form Approved by the
Judicial Council of California
Effective Nov. 10, 1969   **SUBPENA (Civil)**   C.C.P. §§ 1985-1997;
Gov. C. §§ 68097.1-68097.4; etc.

765803C Ci 58 (9)· PS 4 76

Exhibit 14.1

dures vary, some courts will set up conference calls so that the opposing party has the opportunity to hear what is being said and to respond.

Don't just assume that your local court will allow telephone testimony. Ask the clerk. If you get a negative response, don't give up—ask the judge when you get into the courtroom. It is also an ex-

```
                                        37 Ogden Court
                                        Minneapolis, MN
                                        September 30, 19--

Presiding Judge
Small Claims Court
Minneapolis, MN                 RE:  John Swift vs.
                                     Peter Patrakos
                                     Case # 11478
Your Honor:

    On September 15, 19--, I witnessed an auto accident at the corner
of Hennepin and Eighth in Minneapolis, involving John Swift and Peter
Patrakos.  I clearly saw Mr. Patrakos' car, which was heading east on
Eighth, go through a red light and hit Mr. Swift's blue van which was
proceeding south on Hennepin well inside the 30 MPH speed limit.

    Mr. Swift has asked me to testify on his behalf, and normally I
would be happy to do so.  However, I will be in New York City on busi-
ness during the months of October, November and December 19-- and
cannot be present.

    I have asked Mr. Swift to let me know the day and approximate time
of the court hearing and have told him that I will give him a phone
number where I can be reached.  If you think it desirable, I will be
pleased to give my testimony by phone.

                                Sincerely,


                                Victor Van Cleve
```

Exhibit 14.2

tremely good idea to have a letter from the witness who you want to
reach by phone, explaining what he or she will testify (e.g., your
opponent's car ran a red light and broadsided you), and explaining
why it is impossible for him or her to be in court. Such a letter might
look like the one in Exhibit 14.2.

Subpoenaing Police Officers

You have probably already noticed that on the California subpoena
form there is a special box to use if you wish to subpoena a police
officer. This box is easy to fill out, but expensive to pay for in most
states. The deposit to subpoena a police office is at least $75. This
money must be paid to the clerk at the time the subpoena is issued.
Depending on the amount of the officer's time that is used, you may
eventually get a refund of some of your $75. Be sure to check your lo-
cal rules.

Subpoenaing Documents

In addition to witnesses, you can also subpoena documents. It is rare that this is done in Small Claims Court but it may occasionally be helpful. Someone (police department, phone company, hospital, corporation) may have certain books, ledgers, papers, or other documents that can help your case. To get them, you must prepare a form entitled "Subpoena Duces Tecum." This is very similar to the standard subpoena form, except that there is a space to describe the papers or other documents that you want brought to court. To get a "Subpoena Duces Tecum" issued, you must attach an affidavit stating why you need the written material. Prepare three copies of all papers and, after you get the clerk to issue the subpoena, serve it on the witness, using personal service as described in Chapter 11. As with a regular subpoena, the witness is entitled to ask for the regular fee. The "Proof of Service" is on the back of the subpoena form and must be filled out and returned to the clerk.*

A Subpoena Duces Tecum must be directed to the person who is in charge of the documents, books, or records that you want. It may take you a few phone calls to find out who this is. Be sure you get this information accurately. If you list someone on the "Subpoena Duces Tecum" who has nothing to do with the documents, you won't get them. When dealing with a large corporation, public utility, municipal government, etc., it is wise to list the person who is in overall charge of the department where the records are kept. Thus if you want records from a public library having to do with library fines, or from the city tax and license department having to do with business license fees, you should not list the city manager or the mayor, but should list the head librarian or the director of the tax and license office.

Example: Let's take a hypothetical case. You are being sued by the city on behalf of the public library for $300 for eight rare books which the library officials state you failed to return. You know that you did return the books, but can't seem to get that across to the library officials who insist on treating you like a thief. You learn that each April the librarians take a yearly inventory of all books on their shelves. You believe that, if you can get access to that inventory, you may be able to figure out where the library misplaced the books.

Technical rules on filing and serving papers, as well as paying witness fees, vary from state to state. Before subpoenaing documents, be sure to ask if the other side will bring them voluntarily or give you photocopies.

Your first step is to ask the library officials to open the inventory to you voluntarily. If they refuse, you may well want to subpoena them. Exhibit 14.3 shows how to do it.

- Fill in the box on the form where you are asked to describe the books and records you want as follows: "All book inventory information collected by the main branch of the public library

Name, address and telephone no. of attorney(s)	This space for court clerk only
John O'Gara 15 Scenic St. Los Angeles, CA. 90011	
Attorney(s) for IN PRO PER	

MUNICIPAL COURT OF CALIFORNIA, COUNTY OF LOS ANGELES

JUDICIAL DISTRICT

Public Library Plaintiff(s) vs. John O'Gara Defendant(s) (Abbreviated Title)	CASE NUMBER (Fill in number) **SUBPENA DUCES TECUM** (Civil)

THE PEOPLE OF THE STATE OF CALIFORNIA, to   Robert Ringle, Head Librarian

You are ordered to appear in this court, located at _____
_____ (Street Address of Court and City)

on _____ at _____ .m., _____ , to testify as a witness in this action.
(Date) (Time) (Department, Division or Room No. if any)

You must appear at that time unless you make a special agreement to appear at another time, etc., with:

John O'Gara   at   584-1921
(Name of Attorney or Party Requesting This Subpena Duces Tecum)   (Telephone Number)

You are also ordered to bring with you the books, papers and documents or other things in your possession or under your control, described in the attached declaration or affidavit as follows: (Type or Print)

All book inventory information collected by the main branch of the Public Library during the calendar year 1979 which is more particularly described in the attached declaration.

Disobedience of this subpena may be punished as contempt by this court. You will also be liable for the sum of one hundred dollars and all damages to such party resulting from your failure to attend or to bring the books, etc., described above.

(To be completed when subpena is directed to a California highway patrolman, sheriff, marshal or policeman, etc.)
This subpena is directed to a member of _____
(Name of Employing Agency)
I certify that the fees required by law are deposited with this court:
Receipt No.: _____   Amount Deposited $ _____

Dated _____   , Clerk

(SEAL)   By   , Deputy

Note: The original declaration or affidavit must be filed with the court clerk and a copy served with this subpena duces tecum

| Form Approved by the
Judicial Council of California
Effective Nov. 10, 1969

76S809L C: 30 (9) Cdb 8-74 | (See reverse side for Proof of Service)
SUBPENA DUCES TECUM (Civil) | C.C.P. §§ 1985-1997; Evid. C. §§ 1560
1566, Gov. C. §§ 68097.1-68097.4, etc. |

Exhibit 14.3

during the calendar year 1979—more particularly described
in the attached declaration."
* Prepare your declaration., It should be brief. There is no pre-
  printed form for this. Get a piece of 8½" × 11" legal paper
  from a stationery store (the kind with numbers on the side).
  Type the heading just as it appears on the subpoena form.
  Then identify the documents that you want brought to court
  and why you want them. Don't argue the merits of your case.

1	JOHN O'GARA
	15 Scenic Street
2	Los Angeles, California
	849-1921
3	
4	IN PROPRIA PERSONA
5	
6	SMALL CLAIMS COURT OF CALIFORNIA, COUNTY OF LOS ANGELES
7	LOS ANGELES JUDICIAL DISTRICT
8	
9	Public Library, Plaintiff) Case Number ___(fill-in)___
10	vs.) DECLARATION OF JOHN O'GARA
11	John O'Gara, Defendant)
12	
13	I, John O'Gara, hereby declare that during the spring of 1979 I returned
14	six books to the Public Library. On July 1, 1979, the Public Library sued me
15	for the value of these books, claiming that I hadn't returned them. On July 5,
16	1979 I asked to see any and all book inventory records that the library main-
17	tained. I learned that during the week of May 20, 1979 an inventory had been
18	taken (this was after I returned the books), but I was told that it was not a
19	public document and that it would take too long to go through it to see if
20	the books that are the subject of this dispute had been misplaced. I believe
21	that, if I can get access to the library inventory, I can show that the books
22	were returned.
23	This declaration is made under penalty of perjury at ___Los Angeles___
	City
24	California on ___July 15, 1979___ .
	Date
25	
26	_____(signature)_____
	JOHN O'GARA
27	
28	(Notarization is not necessary)

Exhibit 14.4

• Staple your declaration to the Subpoena Duces Tecum form and have the subpoena issued by the Small Claims Court clerk. Then have the subpoena served, being sure that the "Proof of Service" (see Chapter 11, "Serving a Business") is properly filled out and return to the clerk.

Note: On the day of the hearing, the person you have subpoenaed will show up with the documents in question. The documents will be presented to the court—not to you. If you need an opportunity to examine the documents, request it from the judge. He or she may well let you do your examining right there in the courtroom while other cases go ahead or, if necessary, he or she may continue the case for a few days and arrange to have you make your examination at the place of business of the owner of the records.

Judges as Witnesses

Using a judge as a witness is a valuable technique in many situations. This is done routinely in many types of disputes, such as clothing cases in which you bring the damaged garment into court for the judge's examination. As I have said repeatedly in this book, always bring into court any physical evidence that will help your case and fit through the door.

But what if your evidence won't fit through the door (a car with a poor paint job) or can't be brought into the building (a supposedly pedigreed puppy that grew up looking as if Lassie were the mother and Rin Tin Tin the father)? Why not ask the judge to accompany you outside of the building to examine the car, or the dog, or whatever else is important to your case? Why not indeed? Most Small Claims Courts allow judges to leave the bench to examine evidence, and many (but not all) judges are willing to do so if they feel that it is necessary to a better understanding of the case and won't take too long. But never ask a judge to take time to leave his or her court to view evidence if you can prove your case just as well by other means, such as witnesses and pictures. A good approach is to do as well as you can in court, and to ask the judge to view evidence outside of court only if it is essential.

Presenting Your Case to 15 the Judge

Uncontested Cases— Getting a Judgment by Default

Surprisingly often, presenting your case will be easy—your opponent simply will not show up.* If this occurs, you will not have to make a formal presentation. The judge may check to see that your opponent was properly served and may ask you a question or two to make sure that there is no obvious flaw in your case, such as the Statute of Limitations having run out two years ago. He or she may ask you to present the basic facts of your case briefly, but will not want a long argument and lots of evidence. It's as if you were scheduled to play a ballgame and the other team failed to show up. You win by default—you don't need to hit the ball over the fence and run around the bases. And often there is no way to appeal a default judgment. A defendant who doesn't show up to argue his or her case usually can't appeal to a formal court (see Chapter 22).

Note: In some Small Claims Courts, such as those in Washington, D.C., a court clerk will enter the default if the case is for unpaid bills or some other amount of money and the person bringing suit has good documentation, such as statements, ledgers, etc. This means that you will not appear before a judge at all. If you are a plaintiff and you

---

*In the few states that require an answer to be filed (see Appendix), you should know before the court date whether the other side will appear. Check with the court clerk to see what, if anything, you must do to get your default judgment.

127

know that the defendant will not show up, you still must bring the evidence necessary to establish your case.

On rare occasions, a person who has defaulted will show up in court a few days later with a super excuse. The judge does have the discretion to set aside a default in this situation and reopen the case. This is rarely done, and in no case will it be done if the defaulting party delays in requesting that the judgment be set aside. For example, the defaulting party who shows up a month after a default judgment was entered to request that it be set aside will have the burden of explaining to the judge why he or she didn't show up or phone earlier. As you might guess, not many people can lift a burden this heavy. (We discuss the mechanics of setting aside a default in Chapter 10, "If One Party Doesn't Show Up.")

Contested Cases*

Assuming now that both sides show up and step forward when the case is called by the clerk, what happens next? First, the judge will establish everyone's identity. Next, he or she will ask the plaintiff to state his or her case briefly.

The plaintiff should tell the judge what is in dispute and then briefly outline his or her position. It is critical that the judge know what the case is about before you start arguing it. For example, if your case involves a car accident, you might start by saying, "This case involves a car accident at Cedar and Rose streets in which my car suffered $672 worth of damage," not "It all started when I was driving down Rose Street after having two eggs and a danish for breakfast." Only occasionally have I seen a case in which the plaintiff's initial presentation required more than five minutes. As part of his or her statement the plaintiff should present any papers, photos, or other documentary evidence. These should be handed to the clerk and explained. The plaintiff should also be sure to indicate to the judge the presence of any witnesses.

When the plaintiff is finished, the judge may wish to ask questions. Some judges will interrupt so often that they will pretty much take over the case. Others will simply sit back and let the plaintiff

---

*In a few states, including California, when a suit is brought by or against an unincorporated business, it is permissible for someone other than the business owner to appear in court. Thus a dentist or store owner could send a bookkeeper to establish that a bill wasn't paid. As noted in Chapter 7, corporations can routinely appoint representatives. And some states require corporations to appear through an attorney. See Appendix.

have his or her say. The judge may or may not wish to hear from the plaintiff's witnesses before the defendant speaks. Each judge will control the flow of evidence differently. It's best to go with the judge's energy, not against it. Just be sure that, at one time or another, you have made all of your points. If you feel rushed, say so. The judge will normally slow things down a little. If you appear before a lawyer-arbitrator, in a system such as that of New York City, you can expect that the arbitrator will take a very active role in questioning the parties and witnesses.

Sooner or later, the defendant will get his or her chance. Defendants often get so angry at something the plaintiff has said ("Lies! Lies!") that when their turn comes, they immediately attack. This is silly and usually counterproductive. The defendant should present his or her side of the dispute calmly and clearly to the judge. If the plaintiff has made false or misleading statements, these should be answered—but at the end of the presentation, not the beginning. Tell your story first, then deal with the plaintiff's testimony if this seems necessary.

Here are a few tips that you may find helpful. These are merely suggestions, not rules written on golden tablets. You may wish to follow some and ignore others.

- Stand when you make your initial presentation to the judge. Standing gives most people a sense of presence and confidence at a time when they may be a little nervous. But this doesn't mean that you have to jump to your feet every time the judge asks you a question.
- Don't read your statement. Reading in court is almost always a bore. Some people find it helpful to make a few notes on a card to serve as a reminder if they get nervous or forget something. If you decide to do this, list the headings of the various points you want to make an outline form. Be sure your list is easy to read at a glance and that the topics are in the correct order.
- Be brief.
- Never interrupt your opponent or any of the witnesses, no matter how outrageous their "lies." You will get your chance to respond.
- Be prepared to present in another way any section of your case that is difficult to get across in words. This means bringing with you used car parts, damaged clothing, or other exhibits such as photographs or cancelled checks, and having them organized for easy presentation.

- There will be a blackboard in court. If drawings would be helpful, and they almost always are in cases involving car accidents, be sure that you have practiced at home. You will want to draw clearly and legibly the first time. If you wish to make a drawing and the judge doesn't ask you to, simply request permission to do so.

A Sample Contested Case

Now let's take a typical case and pretend that a court reporter is present making a transcript.

Clerk: The next case is John Andrews versus Robertson Realty. Will everyone please come forward? (Four people come forward and sit at the table facing the judge.)

Judge: Good morning. Which one of you is Mr. Andrews? OK, will you begin, Mr. Andrews?

John Andrews: (stands) This is a case about my failure to get a $200 cleaning deposit returned, your Honor. I rented a house from Robertson Realty at 1611 Spruce St. in Rockford in March of 1980, on a month-to-month tenancy. On January 10, 1981, I sent Mr. Robertson a written notice that I was planning to move on March 10. In fact, I moved out on March 8 and left the place extremely clean. All of my rent was properly paid. A few days after I moved out, I asked Mr. Robertson to return my $400 deposit. He refused, saying that the place was dirty and that he was keeping my deposit.

    I have with me a copy of a letter I wrote to Mr. Robertson on March 15, setting out my position in more detail. I also have some photographs that my friend Carol Spann, who is here as a witness, took on the day I moved out. I believe the pictures show pretty clearly that I did a thorough cleaning. (John Andrews hands the letter and pictures to the clerk who hands them to the judge.)

    Your Honor, I am asking not only for the $400 deposit but also for $200 in punitive damages that the law allows a tenant when a landlord improperly refuses to return a deposit.*

Judge: Mr. Andrews, will you introduce your witness.

Andrews: Yes, this is Carol Spann. She helped me clean up and move on March 7 and 8.

Judge: (looking at the pictures) Ms. Spann, were you in the apartment the day John Andrews moved out?

*Many states make some provision for "punitive damages" if a landlord retains a tenant's deposit in "bad faith." You should check to see if you are entitled to "punitive damages" before you file your suit. If you are entitled to them, the judge will not award them if you don't ask for them in your claim.

Carol Spann: (standing) Yes, I was, and the day before, too. I helped clean up and I can say that we did a good job. Not only did we do the normal washing and scrubbing but we waxed the kitchen floor and shampooed the rugs.

Judge: (turning to Mr. Robertson) OK, now it's your turn to tell me why the deposit wasn't returned.

Harry Robertson: (standing) I don't know how they could have cleaned the place up, your Honor, because it was filthy when I inspected it on March 9. Let me give you a few specifics. There was mildew and mold around the bathtub, the windows were filthy, the refrigerator hadn't been defrosted, and there was dog—how shall I say it?—dog manure in the basement. Your Honor, I have brought along Clem Houndstooth as a witness. Mr. Houndstooth is the tenant who moved in three days after Mr. Andrews moved out. Incidentally, your Honor, the place was so dirty that I charged Mr. Houndstooth only a $100 cleaning deposit, because he agreed to clean it up himself.

Judge: (looking at Clem Houndstooth) Do you wish to say something?

Clem Houndstooth: (standing) Yes, I do. Mr. Robertson asked me to come down and back him up, and I am glad to do it because I put in two full days cleaning that place up. I like a clean house, your Honor, not a half-way clean, halfway dirty house. I just don't think a house is clean if the oven is full of gunk, there is mold in the bathroom, and the insides of the cupboards are grimy. All these conditions existed at 1611 Spruce St. when I moved in. I just don't believe that anyone could think that that place was clean.

Judge: Mr. Andrews, do you have anything to add?

John Andrews: (standing up) Yes, I sure do. First, as to the mildew problem. The house is forty years old and there is some dampness in the wall of the bathroom. Maybe there is a leaky pipe someplace behind the tile. I cleaned it a number of times, but it always came back. I talked to Mr. Fisk in Mr. Robertson's office about the problem about a month after I moved in, and he told me that I would have to do the best I could because they couldn't afford to tear the wall apart. As to the cupboards and stove, they are both old. The cabinets haven't been painted in ten years, so, of course, they aren't perfect, and that old stove was a lot dirtier when I moved in than it is now.

Judge: What about the refrigerator, Mr. Andrews? Was that defrosted?

John Andrews: No, your Honor, it wasn't, but it had been defrosted about three weeks before I moved out and I thought that it was good enough the way it was.

Judge: OK, if no one else has anything to add, I want to return your pictures and letters. You will receive my decision by mail in a few days.

Now, I have a little surprise for you. This was a real case. As they used to say on *"Dragnet,"* "Only the names have been changed to protect the innocent." And I have another surprise for you. I spoke to the judge after the court session, and I know how the case came out. The judge explained his reasoning to me as follows.

"This is a typical case in which both sides have some right on their side. What is clean to one person may be dirty to another. Based on what I heard, I would have to guess that the old tenant made a fairly conscientious effort to clean up and probably left the place about as clean as it was when he moved in, but that the new tenant, Houndstooth, had much higher standards and convinced the landlord that it was filthy. The landlord may not have needed too much convincing since he probably would just as soon keep the deposit. But I did hear enough to convince me that Andrews, the old tenant, didn't do a perfect job cleaning up. My decision will be that Andrews gets a judgment for the return of $300 of the $400 deposit, with no punitive damages. I believe that $100 is more than enough to compensate the landlord for any damages he suffered."

I then asked the judge if he felt that the case was well presented. He replied substantially as follows:

"Better than average. I think I got a pretty good idea of what the problems were. The witnesses were helpful, and the pictures gave me an idea that the place wasn't a total mess. Both sides could have done better, however, Andrews could have had a witness to talk about the condition when he moved in if it was truly dirtier than when he left. Another witness to testify to the apartment's cleanliness when he moved out would have been good, too. His friend, Carol Spann, seemed to be a very close friend, and I wasn't sure that she was objective when it came to judging whether the place was clean. The landlord, Robertson, could also have done better. He could have presented a more disinterested witness, although I must say that Houndstooth's testimony was pretty convincing. Also, he could have had pictures documenting the dirty conditions and an estimate from a cleaning company for how much they would have charged to clean the mess up. Without going to too much trouble, I think that either side could have probably done somewhat better with more thorough preparation.''

Don't Forget to Ask for Your Costs

When you finish your presentation to the judge, you should be sure he realizes that you have incurred certain court costs. These can be added to the judgment amount. As we have mentioned, you can't recover for such things as time off from work, paying a babysitter or Xerox charges. In California and most other states you can recover for:

- Your filing fee
- Service of process
- Subpoenaed witness fees
- Cost of necessary documents, such as verification of car ownership by the motor vehicles bureau.

If you forget to have your costs added to the judgment in court and want to go to the trouble, you can file a "Memorandum of Costs" with the Small Claims Court clerk within five days after judgment. Forms are available at the clerk's office. For information on recovering costs incurred after judgment when your opponent won't voluntarily pay the judgment, see Chapter 23, "Recovering Collection Costs and Interests."

Motor Vehicle Repair Cases 16

Most Small Claims Court cases fall into a dozen or so broad categories, with perhaps another dozen subcategories. In the next six chapters, we look at the most common types of cases and discuss strategies to handle each. Even if your factual situation doesn't fit neatly in one of these categories, read them all. By taking a few hints here and a little information there, you should be able to piece together a good plan of action. For example, suggestions I make to handle motor vehicle repair disputes can be applied easily to cases involving major appliances such as television sets, washers, expensive stereos, etc.

Let's start by imagining that you go to the auto repair shop to pick up your trusty, but slightly graying, steed. The bill is $925 for a complete engine overhaul. This seems a little steep, but after the mechanic tells you all about the great job he did, and you remember that inflation is a fact of life, you drive out of the garage in something approaching a cheerful mood. One of life's little hassles has been taken care of, at least temporarily.

You're right—temporarily can sometimes be a very short time. In this case, it lasts only until you head up the first hill. What's that funny noise, you think? Why don't I have more power? Oh shit, you say (you never swear, but there are some extreme provocations where nothing else will do). You turn around and drive back to the garage. Not only are you out $925, but your car works worse than it did when you brought it in.

Funny, no one seems as pleasant as they did before. Funny, no one seems to have time to listen to you. Finally, after several explanations and a bit of foot stomping, you get someone to say that they will

look the car over again. You take a bus home, trying not to be paranoid. Two days later, you call. Nothing has been done. You yell at the garage owner and then call your bank to stop payment on the check. You are told that they cashed it yesterday. Another few days pass and the garage tells you that the problem is in a part of the engine that they didn't work on. You only paid for a ''short block job'' they keep telling you. ''Give us another $300 and we can surely solve this new problem,'' they add.

In disgust, you go down and pick up your crippled friend and drive it home—very, very slowly. You are furious and decide to pursue every legal remedy, no matter what the trouble. How do you start?

First, park your car, take a shower, and have a glass of wine. Nothing gets decided well when you're mad. Now, going back to the reasoning we used at the beginning of this book, ask yourself some basic questions.

Have I Suffered a Loss?

That's easy. Your car doesn't work, you paid out a lot of money, and the garage wants another bundle to fix it. Clearly, you have suffered a loss.

Did the Negligence of the Garage Cause My Loss?

Aha, now we get to the nitty gritty. In this type of case you can almost always expect the garage to claim that they did their work properly and that the car simply needs more work. Maybe they are right—it's your job to prove that they aren't. Doing so will make your case; failing to do so will break it. You'd better get to work.

STEP 1: Collect Available Evidence

First, get all evidence together; time is of the essence. In this particular situation, this means getting your used parts (it's a good idea to do this anytime you have major work done).* If the garage will not give them to you, make your request again by letter, keeping a copy for your file. If you get the parts, fine—if you don't, you have evidence that the garage is badly run or has something to hide.

STEP 2: Have the Car Checked

Before you drive many miles, have your car checked by one or more established local mechanics. Often it is possible to get free estimates from repair shops. But be sure that at least one of the people who looks the car over is willing to come with you to Small Claims Court if the need arises. A few states require that you present three written estimates in Small Claims Court. Whether this is required or not, it's a good idea to have them.

---

*In California and many other states you are entitled by law to get your parts back, just as you are entitled to a written estimate before repairs are made.

STEP 3: Try to Settle Your Case

By now you should have a pretty good idea as to what the first garage did wrong. Call them and ask either that the job be redone or that they give you a refund of part or all of your money. Often the repair shop will agree to do over some, or all, of the work in order to avoid further hassle. If they do agree to take the car back, try to get a written agreement detailing what they will do and how long it will take. Also, talk to the mechanic who will actually work on the car to be sure he understands what needs to be done.

STEP 4: Write a Demand Letter

If the garage isn't cooperative, it's time to write them a formal demand letter. Reread the discussion in Chapter 6. Your letter should be short, polite, and written with an eye to a judge reading it. In this situation you could write something like the letter in Exhibit 16.1.

Note: Most small independent garages don't make any written warranty or guaranty of their work. However, if you were given any promises in writing, mention them here in your letter.

STEP 5: File Your Court Papers

If you still get no satisfactory response from the garage, file your papers at the clerk's office of your local Small Claims Court. Reread Chapters 7–10.

STEP 6: Prepare for Court

If you want a third person (a judge) to understand your case, you must understand it yourself. Sounds simple, doesn't it? It does to me, too, until I get involved with machinery. My opinion of cars (and most other machinery) is low—they are supposed to work without trouble, but most of us know better.

For me to argue in Small Claims Court a case such as the one we are talking about here could be a disaster unless I did some homework. This sort of disaster is repeated often in Small Claims Court. I have seen many, many people argue cases about their cars knowing no more than "The car was supposed to be fixed, your Honor, and it's worse than ever." On some mornings when the roses are in bloom, the peaches are sweet, and the angels are in heaven, this is enough to win—usually it isn't. Why? Because the people from the garage are likely to have a terrific sounding story about the wonderful job they

```
                                    Jorge Sotomayor
                                    15 Orange St.
                                    Phoenix, AZ


Happy Days Motors
100 Speedway
Tempe, AZ

Dear People:

        On August 13, 19--, I brought my 1974 Datsun to your garage.  You
    agreed to do a complete engine rebuild job for $925.  You told me, "Your
    car will be running like a watch when we're through with it."  The car
    worked well when I brought it in, but was a little short on power.  Two
    days later when I picked up my car, it barely moved at all.  The engine
    made such a clanging noise that I have been afraid to drive it.

        I have repeatedly asked you to fix the car or to refund my money.
    You have refused.  Shortly after the work was done, I also asked for my
    used parts to be returned.  You refused to give them to me even though
    this is a violation of state law.

        I have had several mechanics look my car over since you worked on
    it.  They all agree that you did your job improperly and even installed
    some used parts that came from a 1975 Datsun.  The work you did on the
    piston rings was particularly badly done.

        After receiving no response from you, I had the work redone at a
    cost of $810.*  My car now works well.  Please refund my $925.  Should
    you fail to do so, I will exhaust all my legal remedies including com-
    plaining to interested state and local agencies and taking this dispute
    to Small Claims Court.

        May I hear from you promptly.



                                    Jorge Sotomayor
```

Exhibit 16.1

did. They will talk about pistons, rings, bearings, pulling the head, and turning the cam shaft. It's all likely to sound so impressive that you can easily find yourself on the defensive.

This sort of thing needn't happen if you are willing to learn a little about your car (or whatever machinery is involved). Fifteen minutes' conversation with a knowledgeable mechanic may be all you need to understand what's going on. Also, your local library will have manuals about every type of car, complete with diagrams, etc.

Most Small Claims Courts do not require that you actually have the work redone before going to court, but a few, such as New York City, require a repair bill marked "Paid."

Remember the Judge: Chapter 13 mentioned that it's important to pay attention to the person to whom you are presenting your case. Most Small Claims Court judges don't understand the insides of cars any better than you do. People often become lawyers because they don't like to get their hands dirty. So be prepared to deal with a person who nods his or her head but doesn't really understand the difference between the drive shaft and the axle.

STEP 7: Appearing in Court

When you appear in court, be sure than you are well organized. Bring all the letters you have written, or received, about your car problem, as well as written warranties (if any), photographs if they are helpful, and your used parts if they aid in making your case. Several times in cases involving machinery, I have seen people give effective testimony by representing a large drawing illustrating the screw-up. Also, be sure that you get your witnesses to the courtroom on time. The best way to do this is to pick them up at home or work and escort them personally.

If you are well prepared, you should win the sort of case outlined here without difficulty. Judges drive cars and have to get them fixed; they tend to be sympathetic with this type of consumer complaint. Simply present your story (see Chapter 15), your documentation, and your witnesses. If you feel that your opponent is snowing the judge with a lot of technical lingo, get his or her Honor back on the track by asking that the technical terms be explained in ordinary English. This will be a relief to everyone in the courtroom except your opponent. You will likely find that, once your opponent's case is shorn of all the magic words, it will shrink from tiger to pussycat.

STEP 8: Asking for a Continuance in the Middle of Your Presentation

The best-laid plans can occasionally go haywire. Perhaps a key witness doesn't show up, or maybe, despite careful preparation, you overlook some aspect of the case that the judge feels is crucial. If this occurs, you may want to ask the judge to reschedule the case on another day so that you can prepare better. It is proper to make this sort of request. Whether or not it will be granted is up to the judge. If he or she feels that more evidence isn't likely to change the result or that you are making the request to stall, it will not be granted. If there is a good reason for a delay, however, it will usually be allowed. But if you want a delay, you have to ask for it—the judge isn't going to be able to read your mind.

Motor Vehicle Purchase Cases 17

All too often, someone buys a motor vehicle, drives it a short way, and watches it fall apart. All too often, the seller won't stand behind the product sold or work out some sort of fair adjustment. There are major differences in approach, depending on whether you bought a new vehicle from a dealer, a used vehicle from a dealer, or a used vehicle from a private party. Let's look at each situation.

New Vehicles

Here the most common problem is the lemon with major manufacturing defects that the dealer won't fix under the new vehicle warranty. These sorts of cases are often won by irate consumers, but winning is no sure thing. The dealers have all been sued before; they know what to say and how to say it. Defending lawsuits is part of their business. Success will depend on your preparing your case carefully. Your goal is to prove that the vehicle was defective or latently defective when purchased, and that the defect should have been fixed under the warranty. You also must prove the amount of money you have lost as a result of the problem. You may also have to deal with a dealer's claim that the defect was caused by your improper use of the vehicle.

State Law Note: Many states have warranty laws that require that a product be reasonably fit for normal use. These laws have been interpreted to give the consumer more rights than the limited warranty that comes with the car. Contact a local consumer organization for advice about the law in your state.

Problems commonly develop with new vehicles just at the time the written warranty runs out. Sometimes it seems as though there is a little destruct switch set to flip 15 minutes after you hit "one year or ten thousand miles, whichever comes first." Often too, a problem starts to surface while the car is still under warranty and a dealer makes inadequate repairs that last scarcely longer than the remainder of the warranty term. When the same problem develops again after the warranty has run out, the dealer refuses to fix it.

Recently, I saw a case involving this sort of problem. A man with a new, expensive, European car sued the local dealer and the parent car company's West Coast representative. He claimed that he had brought the car repeatedly to the car dealer's repair shop with transmission problems while it was still under warranty. Each time, adjustments were made which seemed to eliminate the problem. But each time, after a month or so, the same problem would reappear. A few months after the warranty ran out, the transmission died. Even though the car was only a little over a year old, and had gone fewer than 10,000 miles, both the dealer and the parent car company refused to repair it. Their refusals continued, even though the owner wrote them repeatedly, demanding action.

How did the car owner go about dealing with his problem? First, because he needed his car, he went ahead and had the repairs made. This involved a cost in excess of the Small Claims Court limit. Then, he filed his Small Claims action. In doing this, he waived the amount of the claim over the Small Claims Court maximum. (See Chapter 4.) Because the dealer was located in the same city as he was, the man could sue locally.* In this situation it would have been adequate to sue only the local dealer and not the West Coast representative of the car company, but it didn't hurt to sue both, following the general rule, "when in doubt, sue all possible defendents."

In court, the car owner was well prepared and had a reasonably easy time. Both he and his wife testified to their trials and tribulations with the car. They gave the judge copies of the several letters they had written the dealer, one of which listed by date the fifteen times they had taken the car to the dealer's shop. They also produced a letter from the owner of the independent garage that finally fixed the transmission, stating that, when he took the transmission apart,

---

*In most states, only one defendant need be local to sue in a particular judicial district. (See Appendix.) The fact that the car company's West Coast headquarters was in a different part of the state didn't cause a problem with bringing the suit where the dealer was located. (See Chapter 9.)

he discovered a defect in its original assembly. The new car dealer simply testified that his mechanics had done their best to fix the car under the warranty. He then pointed out that, once the warranty had run out, he was no longer responsible. The dealer made no effort to challenge the car owner's story, nor did he bring his own mechanics to testify to what they had done while the car was still under warranty. The car owner won. He presented a convincing case to the point that the defect had never been fixed when it should have been under the warranty. The dealer did nothing to rebut it. As the judge noted to me after the hearing, a $9,000 car should come with a transmission that will last longer than 10,000 miles. The car owner would have had an even stronger case if he had brought the independent garage man to court, but the letters, along with his own testimony and that of his wife, were adequate in a situation where the dealer didn't put up much of a defense.

Note: In this sort of case it is very convincing to have documentation of all the trips you have made to the dealer's repair shop. You may be able to find copies of work orders you signed, or cancelled checks if you were charged. If you don't have this sort of record, sit down with a calendar and do your best to make an accurate list. Give the list to the judge in court. He will accept it as true unless the car dealer disputes it.

As noted above, even if your car is no longer covered by a written warranty when trouble develops, you may have a case. There are state law and general common law concepts of warranty that give you protection over and above the actual written paper that comes with the vehicle. Thus if the engine on your properly maintained car burns out after 25,000 miles, you will stand a good change of recovering some money even though the written warranty has expired. Engines are simply supposed to last longer than 25,000 miles. You may also wish to consider other remedies in addition to Small Claims Court, such as trying to enlist the help of state regulatory agencies. One strategy of last resort if you don't have much equity in the car is simply to drive it to the dealer and leave it there, refusing to make any more payments until it is fixed. This is an extreme remedy and should be considered only in an extreme situation. It does have the beauty of shifting the responsibility to take action, legal or otherwise, to the other side. If you do this, be sure to set forth in writing all the circumstances surrounding the mechanical deficiencies and your efforts to remedy the situation, and send a copy to both the car dealer and the bank or other financial institution that made the loan.

Used Vehicle Dealers

Recovering from used vehicle dealers can be tricky for several reasons. Unlike new vehicle dealers, who are usually somewhat dependent upon their reputation for honesty in the community, used vehicle dealers commonly have no positive reputation to start with and survive by becoming experts at self-protection. Also (and don't underestimate this one), judges almost never buy used vehicles, and therefore aren't normally as sympathetic to the problems used vehicle owners encounter. Chances are a judge has had a problem getting his (her) new car fixed under a warranty, but has never bought a ten year old Plymouth in "tip-top shape," only to have it die two blocks after leaving Honest Al's.

The principal self-protection device employed by used vehicle dealers is the "as is" designation in the written sales contract.* The salesperson may promise the moon, but when you read the fine print of the contract, you will see it clearly stated that the seller takes absolutely no responsibility for the condition of the vehicle.

Time and again I have sat in court and heard hard luck stories like this:

> I bought the car for $1,200 two months ago. The man at 'Lucky Larry's' told me that it had a completely reconditioned engine and transmission. I drove the car less than 400 miles and it died. I mean really died—it didn't roll over and dig itself a hole, but it may as well have. I had it towed to an independent garage and they told me that, as far as they could see, no engine or transmission work had ever been done. They estimated that to put the car right would cost $800. I got one more estimate, which was even higher, so I borrowed the $800 and had the work done. I feel I really got took by Lucky Larry. I have with me the canceled check for the $800 in repairs, plus the mechanic who did the work, who can testify to the condition of the car when he saw it.

Unfortunately, this plaintiff will probably lose. Why? Because, going back to the sort of issues that we discussed in Chapter 2, he has proven only half of his case. He has shown his loss (he bought a $1,200 car that wasn't worth $1,200), but he has not dealt with the

---

*A couple of states now require that used car dealers give customers a history of the car, as well as a statement as to what's wrong with it, and stand behind whatever they claim. The Federal Trade Commission is considering applying similar rules on a national basis.

issue of the defendant's responsibility to make the loss good ("liability"). Almost surely, the used car dealer will testify that he "had no way of knowing how long a ten-year-old Plymouth would last and that, for this very reason, sold the car 'as is'." He will then show the judge a written contract that not only has the "as is" designation, but which will say someplace in the fine print that "this written contract is the entire agreement between the parties and that no oral statements or representations made by the dealer or any salesperson are part of the contract."

How can you fight this sort of cynical semifraud? It's difficult to do so after the fact. The time for self-protection is before you buy a vehicle when you can have it checked by an expert and can insist that any promises made by the salesperson as to the condition of the car or the availability of repairs be put in writing. Of course, good advice such as this, after the damage has been done, "isn't worth more than a pitcher of warm spit," as former Vice-President John Nance Garner so graphically put it. If you have just been cheated on a used car deal, you want to know what, if anything, you can do now. Here are some suggestions.

- If the car broke down almost immediately after you drove it out of the used car lot, you can file in Small Claims Court and argue that you were defrauded. Your theory is that, no matter what the written contract said, there was also an implied warranty that you purchased a car, not a junk heap. When the dealer produces his "as is" contract, argue that it is no defense to fraud.
- You may want to consider having the car towed back to the lot and refusing to make future payments. This puts the burden on the bank or finance company to sue you, at which point you can defend on the basis of fraud. If you take this approach, be sure you have excellent documentation that the car was truly a lemon. Of course, you will probably have made some down payment, so even in this situation you may wish to initiate action in Small Claims Court.
- Have your car checked over by someone who knows cars and would be willing to testify if need be. If this person can find evidence confirming that you were cheated, it will greatly improve your Small Claims Court case. They might, for example, find that the speedometer had been tampered with, in violation of state law, or that a heavy grade of truck oil had been put in the crank case so that the car wouldn't belch smoke. Also, this is the sort of case in which a Subpoena Duces Tecum (subpoena for

documents) might be of help. (See Chapter 13.) You might wish to subpoena records the car dealer has pertaining to purchase price he or she paid for the car, or its condition when purchased. It might also be helpful to learn the name of the car's former owner with the idea of contacting him (her). With a little digging you may be able to develop information that will enable you to convince a judge that you have been defrauded.

• Consider other remedies besides Small Claims Courts. These can include checking with your state's consumer affairs division or the local motor vehicles department to see if used car lots are regulated. In most states, the motor vehicles department licenses used-car dealers and can be very helpful in getting disputes resolved, particularly if your complaint is one of many against the same dealer for similar practices. Also, contact your local district attorney's office. Most now have a consumer fraud division which can be of great help. If you can convince them that what happened to you smells rotten, or your complaint happens to be against someone they have already identified as a borderline criminal, they will likely call the used car dealer in for a chat. In theory, the DA's job is to bring legal actions against law violators. This will normally be of no direct aid in getting your money back, but in practice, negotiations often go on which can result in restitution. In plain words, this means that the car dealer will be told, "Look, buddy, you're right on the edge of the law here (or maybe over the edge). If you clean up your act, which means taking care of all complaints against you and seeing that there are no more, we will close your file. If you don't, I suggest you hire a good lawyer because you're going to need one."

Used Vehicles from Private Parties

Normally, it is easier to win a case against a private party than against a used-vehicle dealer. This runs counter to both common sense and fairness, as a private party is likely to be more honest than a dealer. But fair or not, the fact is that a nondealer is usually less sophisticated in self-protection than a pro is. Indeed, in most private party sales the seller does no more than sign over the title slip in exchange for the agreed upon price. No formal contract is signed that says the buyer takes the car "as is."

If trouble develops soon after you purchase the vehicle and you are out money for unexpected repairs, you may be able to recover. Again, the problem usually lies not in proving your loss, but in convincing the judge that the seller of the vehicle is responsible ("liable") to make your loss good. To do this, you normally must prove that the seller represented the vehicle to be in better shape than it was in fact, and that you relied on these promises when you made the deal.

Recently, I watched Barbara, a twenty-year-old college student, succeed in proving just such a case. She sued John for $325, claiming that the BMW motorcycle she purchased from him was in far worse shape than he had advertised. In court, she ably and convincingly outlined her conversations with John about the purchase of the motorcycle, testifying that he told her repeatedly that the cycle was "hardly used." She hadn't gotten any of his promises in writing, but she did a creative job of developing and presenting what evidence she had. This included:

- A copy (Exhibit 17.1) of her letter to John, which clearly outlined her position

14 Harrison St.
Moline, IL

January 27, 19--

John Malinosky
321 Adams St.
Moline, IL

Dear Mr. Malinosky:

This letter is a follow-up to our recent phone conversation in which you refused to discuss the fact that the 1975 B.M.W. motorcycle I purchased from you on January 15 is not in the "excellent condition" that you claimed.

To review: on January 12 I saw your ad for a motorcycle that was "almost new - hardly used - excellent condition" in the local flea market newspaper. I called you and you told me that the cycle was a terrific bargain and that you would never sell it except that you needed money for school. I told you that I didn't know much about machinery.

The next day you took me for a ride on the cycle. You told me specifically that:

1. The cycle had just been tuned up.
2. The cycle had been driven less than 10,000 miles.
3. The cycle had never been raced or used roughly.
4. That if anything went wrong with the cycle in the next month or two, you would see that it was fixed.

I didn't have the cycle more than a week when the brakes went out. When I had them checked, the mechanic told me that the carburetor also needed work (I confirmed this with another mechanic - see attached estimate). The mechanics also told me that the cycle had been driven at least 50,000 miles (perhaps a lot more) and that it needed a tune-up. In addition they showed me caked mud and scratches under the cycle which indicated to them that it had been driven extensively off the road in rough terrain and had probably been raced on dirt tracks.

The mechanic's low estimate to do the repairs was $325. Before having the work done, I called you to explain the situation and to give you a chance to arrange for the repairs to be made, or to make them yourself. You laughed at me and said, "Sister, do what you need to do - you're not getting dime one from me."

Again I respectfully request that you make good on the promises you made to me on January 15. I enclose a copy of the mechanic's bill for $325 along with several higher estimates that I received from other repair shops.

Sincerely,

Barbara Parker

Exhibit 17.1

- Copies of three estimates for repairing the motorcycle, all dated within a week of the purchase, the lowest of which was $325
- A copy of the repair bill for $325 dated within two weeks of her purchase of the cycle and marked "Paid"
- A copy of John's newspaper ad, which she had answered. It read: "BMW 500 cc 1975 model, almost new—hardly used—excellent condition—$900

Finally, Barbara presented the judge with the note in Exhibit 17.2 from the mechanic who fixed the cycle.

To Whom It May Concern:

    It's hard for me to get off work but if you need me, please ask the judge to delay the case a few days or call me at the job at 411-3700. All I have to say is this: the B.M.W. that Barbara Parker brought to me was in <u>fair</u> shape. It's impossible to be exact, but I guess that it had been driven at least 50,000-75,000 miles and I can say for sure that it was driven a lot of miles on dirt. I can say for sure that the brakes and carburetor were completely shot and had to be replaced, for which I charged $325.

                    Respectfully submitted,

                    Al "Honker" Green
                    February 3, 19--

Exhibit 17.2

Barbara quickly outlined the whole story for the judge and emphasized that she had saved for six months to get the money to make the purchase.*

Next, John had his turn. He helped Barbara make her case by acting like a weasel. His testimony consisted mostly of a lot of vague philosophy about machinery. He kept asking "How could I know just when it would break down?" When the judge asked him specific

---

*This sort of testimony isn't relevant, but it never hurts. As an old appeals court judge who had seen at least 75 summers told me when I graduated from law school feeling proud of my technical mastery of the law, "Son, don't worry about the law—just convince the judge that truth and virtue are on your side and he will always find some technicality to support you." No one ever gave me better advice.

questions about the age, condition, and previous history of the cycle, he clammed up as if he were a gangster called to testify by a Senate antiracketeering committee. Finally, the judge, in frustration, asked John if he had anything concrete to say. John said yes and started explaining how when you sell things, you "puff them up a little" and that "women shouldn't be allowed to drive motorcycles anyway." Finally, the judge asked him to please sit down.

Important: In this type of case, it's often one person's word against another's. Any shred of tangible evidence for either side can be enough to shift the balance to that side. Of course, if you have a friend who witnessed or heard any part of the transaction, his or her testimony will be extremely valuable. Getting a mechanic to check over a vehicle and then testify for you is also a good strategy. Sometimes you can get some help from the small blue book that lists wholesale and retail prices for used cars. Several times I have seen people bring this book (libraries and car dealers have them) into court and show the judge that they paid above the bluebook price for a used car "because the car was represented to be in extra good shape." This doesn't constitute much in the way of real proof that you were ripped off, but it is helpful at least to show the judge that you paid a premium price for unsound goods.

Cases in Which 18 Money Is Owed

From the Creditor's Point of View*

The job of the plaintiff in a case in which he or she is suing for non-payment of a debt is to prove that a valid debt exists and that it has not been paid. Here are a few suggestions.

SUE PROMPTLY

When you are owed money, be sure you sue promptly. You will find a discussion of the Statutes of Limitations applicable to different sorts of debts in Chapter 5. But even when there is no danger that the limitation period will run out, it makes sense to proceed as soon as reasonably possible. Judges just aren't as sympathetic to old claims. Several times when I have sat as judge, I have wondered why some people waited three years to sue for $500. Was it because they weren't honestly convinced that their suit was valid?

Another reason to sue early, especially when you're dealing with a small business that is not paying its bills, has to do with that old wisdom which tells us that it's usually the early bird that gets the worm. Any debtor who is not paying you is very likely not paying

---

Most states allow the person to whom money was owed to sue to collect it, whether or not the debt was a business or a personal one. However, many states bar assignees (collection agencies) from suing in Small Claims Court. Rules around the country vary—New York bars all corporations and insurers, Chicago bars partnerships and corporations, and Texas bars money lenders from suing in Small Claims Court.

others as well. Why? Usually because there is not enough money to go around. If you sue and move to collect quickly, you stand a change of getting a bit of the worm. If you delay and let the debtor put you off with excuses, you are very likely to end up with an empty craw.

WRITTEN CONTRACTS

If the debt is based on a written contract, be sure that your paperwork is in order. Bring to court the original copy of any written note proving the indebtedness so that the court can cancel it when the judgment is entered. Also bring any ledger sheets or other documentation of any payments made, interest charged, etc. Often I have seen otherwise sensible looking business people show up with botched records and become flustered when questioned closely by the judge. The courtroom is not the place to straighten out a poor accounting system. Some courts require that a copy of an unpaid bill or other evidence of indebtedness be submitted at the same time your action is filed. Check your local rules.

ORAL CONTRACTS

A debt based on an oral contract is legal as long as the contract could have been carried out in one year. However, you may face a problem proving that the debt exists if the defendant denies that he or she borrowed the money or bought the goods. Your best bet is to come up with some written documentation that your version of the story is true. If you have no written evidence (cancelled checks, letters, or requests for more time to pay, etc.), your next step is to try to think of any person who knows about the debt and who would be willing to testify. For example, if you asked the defendant to pay you and he or she said in the presence of your friend, "I'll pay you next month," or "You will never get your money back," or anything to indicate that a loan existed, bring your friend as a witness.

PROVING YOUR CASE

All too often, a business will send the same bookkeeper-type to court for every case. He or she will be competent enough in establishing that the books say that the money is owed, but will be helpless if the defendant starts raising questions about anything else. For example, if you own a TV repair business and are suing on an unpaid repair bill in a situation where the defendant claims that you did lousy work, you will want someone in court who knows the details of the job. As mentioned earlier, most states allow businesses to authorize an employee to represent them in court. If you find yourself in court suing on a debt and you suddenly realize that you don't have the right witness in court, ask that the case be delayed a few days. Many judges will do this if they feel that you made a sincere effort to be ready, but something came up that you couldn't foresee.

Note: Many businesses, and especially professionals such as doctors, dentists and lawyers, don't use Small Claims Court to collect unpaid bills because they think it takes too much of their own time, or is "undignified." You will have to worry about your "dignity" yourself, but I can tell you that Small Claims Court actions in most states can be handled with very little time and expense once you get the hang of it. This is especially true when you consider that the alternative is to turn the bill over to a collection agency or not to collect it at all. Wait until you have several cases and schedule them on the same day. Talk to the clerk when you set the cases for hearing and make sure they are scheduled for a light court day. When you get to court, speak to the clerk and point out that your cases are all (or mostly) defaults and that you have a busy schedule. Don't be aggressive; just ask politely if your cases can be heard first. You will find that, once you understand the system, you can often be in and out in fifteen minutes to a half hour. Once you get your judgment, your secretary should be able to handle the collection activities described in Chapter 23.

From the Debtor's Point of View

While there is an increasing number of private individuals using Small Claims Court, most plaintiffs trying to collect money are businesses or government entities, such as a library, hospital, or city tax office. Debt case defendants are often individuals with little in their pockets but holes. Not many years ago, debt collection cases dominated Small Claims Court dockets numerically to the degree that the court was in danger of becoming a "bill collectors' court." For a variety of reasons, perhaps the most important being the hopelessness of getting disputes resolved in more formal courts, Small Claims Courts have recently been used by a much wider variety of people to settle a broader range of disputes. This has been a healthy development, and now the representatives of the department stores, tire companies, and credit jewelers are only part of the crowd.

When I first watched debt collection cases, I did so with scant attention. I assumed that individuals being pursued by large institutions were bound to lose, especially since they mostly did owe the money. I even wondered why a lot of folks bothered to show up

—knowing in advance that they had no defense and no money. I thought it unjust that our society divided its bounty so unfairly, and sad that the poor had no better defense than their inability to pay, but I didn't have any positive suggestions to offer as to how they might win their cases. But then a curious thing happened. Many of the "downtrodden" I had dismissed so easily refused to play their docile parts. Instead of shuffling in with heads down and nothing constructive to say, they argued back, stamped their feet, and acted like the proud and dignified people they were. I realized suddenly that I was the only person in the courtroom who had dismissed them. I learned that morning, and on dozens of later mornings, that there are lots of ways to constructively defend nonpayment of debt cases. Here are some examples:

A local hospital sued an unemployed man for failure to pay an emergency room bill for $278. It seemed an open and shut case—the person from the hospital had all the proper records, and the defendant hadn't paid. Then the defendant told his side of it. He was taken to the emergency room suffering from a gunshot wound. Because it was a busy night and he was not about to die, he was kept waiting four hours for treatment. When treatment was given, it was minimal, and he suffered later complications that might have been avoided if he had been treated promptly. He said he didn't mind paying a fair

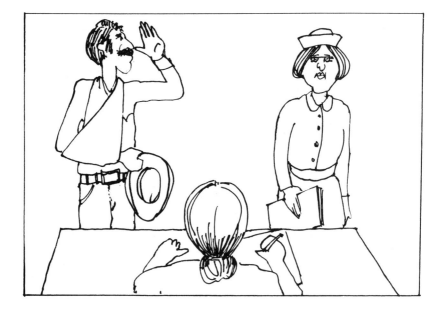

amount, but that he didn't feel he had received $278 worth of care during the half an hour he had spent with the doctor. The judge agreed and awarded the hospital $90, plus court and service of process costs of $4.00. After the defendant explained that he had only his unemployment check, the judge ordered that he be allowed to pay off the judgment at the rate of $10 per month.

A large tire company sued a woman for not paying the balance on a tire bill. She had purchased eight tires for two pickup trucks and still owed $512.50. The tire company properly presented the judge with the original copy of a written contract along with the woman's payment record, and then waited for judgment. They are still waiting. The woman, who ran a small neighborhood gardening and landscaping business, produced several advertising flyers from the tire company which strongly implied, but didn't quite state, that the tires would last at least 40,000 miles. She then testified and presented a witness to the fact that the tires had gone only 25,000 miles before wearing out. The defendant also had copies of four letters written over the past year to the headquarters of the tire company in the Midwest complaining about the tires. Both in the letters and in court, she stated repeatedly that the salesperson at the tire company told her several times that the tires were guaranteed for 40,000 miles. Putting this all together, the judge decided the tires should be prorated on the basis of 40,000 miles and gave the tire company a judgment for only $302, instead of the $512.50 requested. The woman wrote them out a check on the spot and departed feeling vindicated.

A rug company sued a customer for $686 and produced all the necessary documentation showing that the carpet had been installed and that no payment had been received. The defendant testified that the rug had been poorly installed with an uneven seam running down the center of the room. He had pictures that left no doubt that the rug layer was either drunk or blind. The defendant also presented drawings that illustrated that there were obviously several better ways to cut the carpet to fit the room. The rug company received nothing.

The point of these examples is not the facts of the individual situations—yours will surely differ. The point is that there are all sorts of defenses and partial defenses, and that it makes sense to defend yourself creatively if you feel that goods or services you received were worth less than the amount for which you are being sued. It is usually not enough to tell the judge that you were dissatisfied with what you received. A little more imagination is required. If shoddy goods are involved, show them to the judge. If you received bad service, bring a witness or other supporting evidence. If, for example, you had roof repairs done that resulted in more holes than you had before, take pictures of the rain leaking in and get an estimate from another roofer.

There is often a tactical advantage for the debtor in the fact that the person who appears in court on behalf of the creditor is not the same person with whom the debtor dealt. If, for example, you state that a salesperson told you X, Y, and Z, that person probably won't be present to state otherwise. This may tilt a closely balanced case to you. It is not inappropriate for you to point out to the judge that your opponent has only books and ledgers, not firsthand knowledge of the situation. The judge may sometimes continue the case until another day to allow the creditor to have whatever employee(s) you dealt with present, but often this is impossible because the employee in question will have left the job, or be otherwise unavailable.

A Little More Time to Pay: In California, the District of Columbia, New York, and many other areas, the judge has considerable discretion to order that a judgment be paid in installments. Thus a judge could find that you owe the phone company $200, but allow you to pay it off at $20 per month instead of all at once. Time payments can be particularly helpful if you don't have the money to pay all at once, but fear a wage attachment or other collection activity by the creditor. Don't be afraid to ask the judge for time payments—he or she won't know that you want them if you don't ask for them. Several recent studies bear out this point—time payments are almost never ordered unless they are requested.

Vehicle Accident Cases 19

It is a rare Small Claims Court session that does not include at least one fender bender. Usually these cases are badly prepared and presented. The judge commonly makes a decision at least partially by guess. I know from personal experience that it sometimes wouldn't take much additional evidence for me to completely reverse a decision. In Chapter 2, I discuss the concept of negligence and what's involved in proving it. It might be profitable to reread Chapter 2 before proceeding.

The average vehicle accident that ends up in Small Claims Court doesn't involve personal injury, but is concerned with damage to one, or both, parties' car, cycle, r.v., moped, or whatever.* Because of some quirk of character that seems to be deeply embedded in our overgrown monkey brains, it is almost impossible for most of us to admit that we are bad drivers or are at fault in a car accident. We will

---

*Cases involving all but the most minor personal injuries don't belong in Small Claims Court, as they will result in settlements of more than the Small Claims maximum. And in states that have no-fault insurance, even simple property damage cases may not be allowed unless you've complied with certain requirements of your state's no-fault insurance law. In Massachusetts (one of the first states to enact no-fault), Small Claims Court is actually considered to be a sort of court of appeal from an earlier administrative determination of who gets paid what. New Jersey allows auto accident claims for property damage only, not for personal injury; Montana and Rhode Island don't allow suits arising out of any accidents to be brought in Small Claims Courts.

cheerfuly acknowledge that we aren't terrific looking or geniuses, but we all believe that we drive like angels. Out of such fantasies are these lawsuits made.

Who Can Sue Whom?

The owner of a vehicle must sue for damage to the vehicle, even if he or she wasn't driving when the damage occurred. Any person injured, whether driver, passenger or pedestrian, must sue for his or her own personal injuries. Suit should be brought against the negligent driver and, if the driver is not the registered owner of the car, against the registered owner, too. Both the driver and the registered owner are liable. To find out who owns a car, contact the department of motor vehicles. As long as you can tell them the license number, they can tell you the registered owner.

Be particularly wary when you are opposing a driver of a bus or truck. Many of these people suffer problems on their jobs if they are found to be at fault in too many accidents. As a result they deny fault almost automatically. Judges usually know this and are often unsympathetic when a busdriver says that there has never been a time when he "didnt look both ways twice, count to ten, and say the Lord's Prayer" before pulling out from a bus stop. Still, it never hurts to question the driver in court as to whether his company has any demerit system or other penalty for being at fault in an accident.

Was There a Witness to the Accident?

Because the judge has no way of knowing what happened unless one or more people tell him or her, a good witness can make or break your case. It is better to have a disinterested witness than a close friend or family member, but any witness is better than no witness. If the other guy is likely to have a witness and you have none, you will have to work extra hard to develop other evidence to overcome his advantage. Reread Chapter 14 for more information on witnesses.

Police Accident Reports

It is always wise to have a police accident report prepared after any accident if possible. They are admissible as evidence in Small Claims Court in most states. The theory is that an officer investigating the circumstances of the accident at the scene is in a better position to establish the truth about what happened than is any other third party. So, if there is an accident report, spend a few dollars to buy a copy from the police station. If it supports you, bring it to court. If it doesn't, be prepared to refute what it says. This can best be done with the testimony of an eyewitness. If both an eyewitness and a police report are against you, try prayer.

Diagrams

After witnesses and police accident reports, the most effective evidence is a good diagram. It is almost impossible for a judge to understand based on words alone how an accident happened. Several times I have seen a good case lost because the judge was unable to visualize properly what had happened. All courtrooms have chalkboards, and it is proper to draw out what happened as part of your presentation. If you are nervous about your ability to do this, you may want to prepare your diagram in advance and bring it to court. Use crayons or magic markers and draw on a large piece of paper about three feet square. Do a good job and pay attention to detail. Exhibit 19.1 shows a sample drawing that you might prepare to aid your testimony if you were eastbound on Rose St. and making a right-hand

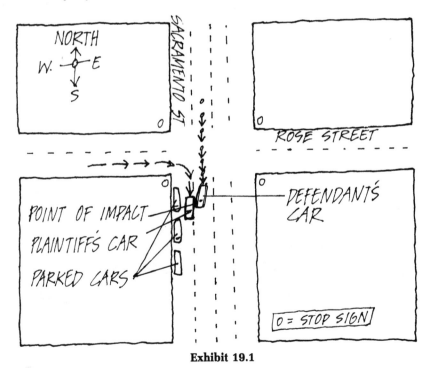

Exhibit 19.1

turn on Sacramento St. when you were hit by a car that ran a stop sign on Sacramento. Of course, the diagram doesn't tell the whole story—you have to do that.

Photos

Photographs can sometimes be of aid in fender bender cases. They can serve to back up your story about how an accident occurred. For example, if you claimed that you were sideswiped while you were parked, a photo showing a long series of scratches down the side of your car would be helpful. It is also a good idea to have pictures of the defendant's car if you can manage to get them, and photos of the scene of the accident.

Estimates

In a vehicle accident case you are entitled to recover for damage to your vehicle, personal injuries, uncompensated time off from work as a result of personal injuries, damages to things inside your car, and money for transportation while your car was out of commission.* Of course, disputes involving major accidents will not be heard in Small Claims Court, and most Small Claims cases involve only damage to a vehicle. Get three written estimates for the cost of repairing the vehicle. If you have already gotten the work done, bring your canceled check or receipt from the repair shop.† Be sure to get your estimates from reputable shops. If, for some reason, you get an estimate from someone you later think isn't competent, simply ignore it and get another. You have no responsibility to get your car fixed by anyone suggested to you by the person who caused the damage. Common sense normally dictates that you don't. Unfortunately, you can't recover money from the other party to cover the time you put in to get estimates, take your car to the repair shop, or appear in court.

Defendant's Note: Sometimes dishonest plaintiffs try to get already existing damage to their car fixed as part of getting the legitimate accident work done. If you think the repair bill is high, try developing your own evidence that this is so, such as letters from repair shops saying that they would have done the work in question for less. If you have a picture showing the damage to the plaintiff's car, this can be a big help. Also, remember that the plaintiff is entitled only to an amount for repairs that does not exceed the total value of the car before the accident. If the car was worth only $800 and the reapirs cost $1,000, the plaintiff is entitled only to $800. (See Chapter 5.)

See Chapter 5 for a more thorough discussion of damages. As far as getting money for transportation while your car is out of commission, you can only recover for the minimum time it would normally take to get your car fixed. Thus if you could arrange to get a fender put right in one day, you are entitled to a rented car for only one day, even if the mechanic takes four.
†*In a few courts, such as in New York City, you must have the repairs completed and paid for before you can collect. See your local rules.*

Your Demand Letter

Here again, as in almost every other type of Small Claims Court case, you should write a letter to your opponent with an eye to the judge reading it. See the exhibits in Chapter 6. Exhibit 19.2 shows another.

---

18 Channing Way
Eugene, OR

August 27, 19--

R. Rigsby Rugg
27 Miramar Crescent
Eugene, OR

Dear Mr. Rugg:

   On August 15, 19-- I was eastbound on Rose Street in Eugene, Oregon at about 3:30 on a sunny afternoon. I stopped at the stop sign at the corner of Rose and Sacramento and then proceeded to turn right (south) on Sacramento. As I was making my turn, I saw your car coming southbound on Sacramento. You were about 20 feet north of the corner of Rose. Instead of stopping at the stop sign, you proceeded across the intersection and struck my car on the front left fender. By the time I realized that you were coming through the stop sign, there was nothing I could do to get out of your way.

   As you remember, after the accident the Fullerton police were called and cited you for failure to stop at a stop sign. I have gotten a copy of the police report from the police and it confirms the facts as I have stated them here.

   I have gotten three estimates for the work needed on my car. The lowest is $412. I am proceeding to get this work done as I need my car fixed as soon as possible.

   I will appreciate receiving a check from you as soon as possible. If you wish to talk about any aspect of this situation, please don't hesitate to call me, evenings at 486-1482.

Sincerely,

Carmina Rocique

Exhibit 19.2

Presenting Your Case in Court

Assuming the demand letter failed to settle the case, Carmina would present her case in the following way:

Clerk: Next case, Rocique versus Rugg. Please come forward.
Judge: Please tell me what happened, Ms. Rocique.

Carmina Rocique: Good morning. This dispute involves an auto accident that occurred at Rose and Sacramento Streets on the afternoon of August 15, 19—. I was coming uphill on Rose (that's east) and stopped at the corner. There is a four-way stop sign at the corner. I turned right, or south, on Sacramento Street, and as I was doing so, Mr. Rugg ran the stop sign on Sacramento and crashed into my rear left fender. Your Honor, may I use the chalkboard to make a quick diagram?"

Judge: Please do. I was about to ask you if you would.

Carmina Rocique: (Makes drawing like the one in Exhibit 19.1, points out the movement of the cars in detail, and answers several questions from the judge.) Your Honor, before I sit down, I would like to give you several items of evidence. First, I have a copy of the police accident report from the Fullerton police that states that Mr. Rugg got a citation for failing to stop at a stop sign. Second, I have some photos which show the damage to the fender of my car. Third, I have my letter to Mr. Rugg, trying to settle this case, and finally I have several estimates for the cost of repairing the damage to my car. As you can see from my canceled check, I took the lowest one.

Judge: Thank you, Ms. Rocique. Now, Mr. Rugg, it's your turn.

R. Rigsby Rugg: Your Honor, my case rests on one basic fact. Ms. Rocique was negligent because she made a wide turn into Sacramento Street. Instead of going from the right hand lane of Rose to the right hand, or inside lane, on Sacramento Street, she turned into the center lane on Sacramento Street. (Mr. Rugg moves to the blackboard and points out what he says happened.) Now it might be true that I made a rolling stop at the corner. You know, I really stopped, but maybe not quite all the way—but I never would have hit anybody if she had kept to her own side of the road. Also, your Honor, I would like to say this—she darted out; she has one of those little foreign cars, and instead of easing out slow like I do with my Lincoln, she jumped out like a rabbit being chased by a red fox.

Judge: Do you have anything else to say, Ms. Rocique?

Carmina Rocique: I am not even going to try to argue about whether Mr. Rugg can be rolling and stopped at the same time. I think the policeman who cited him answered that question. I want to answer his point about my turning into the center lane on Sacramento St., instead of the inside lane. It is true that, after stopping, I had to make a slightly wider turn than usual. If you will look again at the diagram I drew, you will see that a car was parked almost to the corner of Sacramento and Rose on Sacramento. To get around this car, I had to drive a little farther into Sacramento before starting my turn than would have been necessary otherwise, I didn't turn into the center lane, but as I made the turn, my outside fender crossed into the center lane slightly. This is when Mr. Rugg hit me. I feel that since I had the right of way and I had to do what I did to make the turn, I wasn't negligent.

Judge: Thank you both—you will get my decision in the mail.

The judge decided in favor of Carmina Rocique and awarded her $412 plus service of process and filing costs.

Note: As discussed in Chapter 5, you can win, or partially win, a case involving negligence in most states even if you were not completely in the right. If the other person was more at fault than you were, you have a case. This concept of "comparative" negligence is a new one in many states. It used to be that if you were even a little at fault, you couldn't recover because of a legal doctrine known as "contributory negligence."

Landlord– Tenant Cases 20

Small Claims Court can be used by a tenant to sue for money damages for such things as the failure of a landlord to return a cleaning or damage deposit. A landlord may use it to sue a tenant or former tenant for damage done to the rental property. In some situations, it is also possible in some states for a landlord to turn to Small Claims Court to evict a tenant for nonpayment of rent or some other reason. (See Appendix for state-by-state information.) This is an exception to the general rule that only money damage cases can be handled by Small Claims Court. It almost always makes great sense to use Small Claims Court for landlord–tenant cases involving money damages. However, it sometimes makes much less sense to use it for evictions, even in states where this is allowed. Why? Because, unfortunately, the appeal laws of a few states (e.g., California) are drafted in such a way that the defendant can remain in the living unit while appealing a judgment ordering an eviction, without either paying rent or posting a bond. So before you bring an eviction action in Small Claims Court, check out the following questions in your state rules:

- If you win an eviction order, can you get the sheriff or marshal to enforce it immediately?
- If the defendant appeals, can he or she stay in the dwelling while the appeal is pending?
- If the defendant can stay in the dwelling during an appeal, is there a requirement that he or she must post some money in the form of a bond that will go to you to cover lost rent if the appeal fails?

165

If you find that a tenant can stay in the dwelling unit pending an appeal and is not required to post a bond, you should not use Small Claims Court for your eviction action but rather should sue in formal court. You might also consider getting involved in the political processes necessary to change this rule, so that all landlord–tenant cases (including evictions) can automatically be heard in a special division of Small Claims Court. Both landlord and tenant should have quick access to an inexpensive dispute resolution forum where hassles can be settled quickly, cheaply, and fairly.

Deposit Cases

The most common landlord–tenant disputes concern the failure of a landlord to return a tenant's cleaning and damage deposits after the tenant moves out. These days, deposits can add up to many hundreds of dollars, and tenants understandably want them returned.

Getting deposits back can be easy or difficult, both depending on the facts of the situation and on how much homework a tenant has done in advance of filing suit. Many landlords are experienced with Small Claims Court proceedings and come to court prepared with a long list of damaged and dirty conditions that they claim the tenant left behind. All too often, the landlord's presentation leaves the tenant sputtering with righteous indignation. Unfortunately evidence, not indignation, wins cases. Think about it—if the tenant testifies that the apartment was clean, and the landlord that it was dirty, the judge (unless he or she is psychic) is stuck making a decision that is little more than a guess. Faced with this sort of situation, most judges will split the difference.

How should a tenant prepare a case involving failure to return deposits? Ideally, preparation should start when he or she moves in. Any damage or dirty conditions already existing should be noted as part of the lease or rental agreement. The tenant should also take photographs of substandard conditions and have neighbors or friends look the place over. When the tenant moves out and cleans up, he or she should do much the same thing—take photos, have friends check the place over, keep receipts for cleaning materials, and try to reach an understanding with the landlord.*

*All of this is discussed in more detail in Moskovitz, Warner, and Sherman, 1980, The California Tenants' Handbook, Nolo Press. The California Tenants' Handbook contains a tear-out, room-by-room inventory sheet valid in all states on which landlord and tenant can record jointly the results of their inspection of the premises on the dates when the tenant moves in and leaves.

In most states, the burden of proof that conditions exist that justify the landlord keeping all or part of a deposit falls on the landlord. Usually state law also provides that if a deposit is not returned within a short time after the tenant moves out (usually somewhere between 14–30 days, depending on the state), and if the landlord acted in bad faith in retaining the deposits, the tenant may be entitled to "punitive" damages over and above the actual amount of the deposits.* Whether or not the tenant actually gets punitive damages is a matter of judicial discretion, but it never hurts to bring your suit for an amount that includes them. Remember the general rule that you have to request damages when you file your suit if you wish to receive them.

Now let's assume that you are a tenant and have not had $300 in cleaning and damage deposits returned even though you moved out of an apartment three weeks ago, having paid all your rent and having given proper notice. Start by writing the landlord a letter like the one shown in Exhibit 20.1.

If you get no satisfactory response, file your case. Sometimes it is hard to know whom to sue, as rent isn't always paid to the owner, but to a manager or other agent. In most states, multiple occupancy buildings must have ownership information posted on the premises, or specify on the rental agreement the name of the owner or the agent for suit. If this is required but the manager hasn't complied, you can sue the owner and serve your Small Claims Court papers on the manager as the owner's "agent for service of process." If you are in doubt as to who owns your unit, you are probably safe if you sue both the person to whom you pay your rent and the person who signed the rental agreement, unless you have received notice that the building has been transferred to a new owner, in which case you would sue that person.

On court day a well-prepared tenant would show up in court with as many of the following pieces of evidence as possible:

- Photos of the apartment taken on the date the tenant moved in which show any dirt or damage that already existed.

*California allows $200 as punitive damages. A large number of states provide for recovery of double (Illinois, New Jersey, Michigan, Ohio, Pennsylvania, and others) or even triple (Georgia, Maryland, Texas) the amount wrongfully withheld. Some of these states also provide that the tenant may be awarded attorney's fees if applicable. Texas seems toughest on landlords; there the landlord can be assessed a maximum of $100 plus three times the amount wrongfully withheld plus attorney's fees. To check the law in your state, look under the heading "Landlord–Tenant" and the subheading "Deposits" in your state's legal code.

```
                                          1700 Walnut Street
                                          Costa Mesa, CA

                                          October 15, 19--


    Anderson Realty Co.
    10 Rose St.
    Costa Mesa, CA

    Dear People:

        As you know, until September 30, 19--, I resided in apartment #4 at
    1700 Walnut Street and regularly paid my rent to your office.  When I
    moved out, I left the unit cleaner than when I moved in.

        As of today, I have received neither my $150 cleaning deposit nor my
    $150 damage deposit.  Indeed I have never received any accounting from
    you for any of my money.  Please be aware that I know my rights under
    California Civil Code 1950.5 and that, if I do not receive my money
    within the next week, I will regard the retention of these deposits as
    showing "bad faith" on your part and shall sue you, not only for the
    $300 in deposits, but also for the $200 punitive damages allowed by Sec-
    tion 1950.5 of the California Civil Code.

        May I hear from you soon.

                                          Sincerely,



                                          Farah Shields
```

Exhibit 20.1

- Photos of the apartment taken when the tenant moved out which show clean conditions.
- Receipts for cleaning supplies used in the final clean-up.
- The tenant's copy of any written lease or rental agreement.
- A copy of a demand letter to the landlord such as the one shown in Exhibit 20.1.
- At least two witnesses who were familiar with the property and saw it after you cleaned up, and who will testify that it was immaculate. People who helped in the clean-up are always particularly effective witnesses. If you also have a witness who saw the place when you moved in and who will say that it wasn't so clean (or that damage already existed), so much the better.
- A copy of an inventory of conditions on the dates when the tenant moved in and moved out, signed by the landlord and tenant, if one was prepared.

Proceedings in court should go something like this:

Clerk: Shields versus Anderson Realty. Please step forward.

Judge: Good morning. Please tell me your version of the facts, Ms. Shields.

Farah Shields: I moved into the cottage at 1900 Chestnut St. in Costa Mesa in the spring of 19__ . I paid Mr. Anderson here my first and last months' rent which totaled $500. I also paid him $300 in deposits. The deposits were divided $150 for cleaning and $150 for damage. Here is a copy of the rental agreement (hands it to the clerk) which specifically states that these deposits are to be returned to me if the apartment is left clean and undamaged.

When I moved into 1900 Chestnut, it was a mess. It's a nice little cottage, but the people who lived there before me were sloppy. The stove was filthy, as was the bathroom, the refrigerator, the floors, and just about everything else. In addition, the walls hadn't been painted in years. But I needed a place and this was the best available, so I moved in despite the mess. I painted the whole place—everything. Mr. Anderson's office gave me the paint, but I did all of the work. And I cleaned the place thoroughly, too. It took me three days. I like to live in a clean house.

Here are some pictures of what the place looked like when I moved in. (Hands photos to clerk who gives them to the judge.) Here is a second set of photos which were taken after I moved out and cleaned up. (Again hands pictures to clerk.) Your Honor, I think these pictures tell the story—the place was clean when I moved out. I also have receipts (hands to clerk) for cleaning supplies and a rug shampooer that I used during the clean-up. They total $28.25. I have also brought two people who saw the place the day I left and can tell you what it looked like.

Judge: (looking at one of the witnesses) Do you have some personal knowledge of what this cottage looked like?

John DeBono: Yes, I helped Farah move in and move out. I simply don't understand what the landlord is fussing about. The place was a smelly mess when she moved in, and it was spotless when Farah moved out.

Judge: (addressing the second witness) Do you have something to add?

Puna Polaski: I never saw 1900 Chestnut when Farah moved in because I didn't know her then. But I did help her pack and clean up when she moved out. I can tell you that the windows were washed, the floor waxed, and the oven cleaned because I did it. And I can tell you that the rest of the cottage was clean too, because I saw it.

Judge: Mr. Anderson, do you want to present your case?

Adam Anderson: Your Honor, I am not here to argue about whether the place was clean or not. Maybe it was cleaner when Miss Shields moved out than when she moved in. The reason I withheld the deposits is that the walls were all painted odd, bright colors and I have had to paint them all over. Here are some color pictures of the walls taken just after Miss Shields moved out. They show several pink, light blue, and purple rainbows, a dancing hedgehog, six birds apparently laughing, a purple dog, and several unicorns of various sizes. I ask you, your Honor, how was I going to rent that place with a purple bulldog painted on the living room wall, especially with an orange butterfly on his nose. It cost me more than $300 to have the place painted over white.

Judge: (looks at the pictures and gives up trying to keep a straight face, which is OK, as everyone in the courtroom is laughing except Mr. Anderson) Let me ask a few questions. Was it true that the place needed a new coat of paint when you moved in, Ms. Shields?

Farah Shields: Yes.

Judge: Do you agree, Mr. Anderson?

Adam Anderson: Yes, that's why my office paid her paint bills, although we never would have if we had known about that bulldog, not to mention the rainbows.

Judge: How much did the paint cost?

Adam Anderson: Ninety-five dollars.

Judge: I normally send decisions by mail, but today I am going to explain what I have decided. First the apartment needed repainting anyway, Mr. Anderson, so I am not going to give you any credit for paying to have the work done. However, Ms. Shields, even though the place looks quite—shall I say, cheerful—decorated with its assorted wildlife, Mr. Anderson does have a point in that you went a little beyond what is reasonable. Therefore, I feel that it's unfair to make Anderson Realty pay for paint twice. My judgment is this: The $95 for the paint that was given to Ms. Shields is subtracted from the $300 deposits. This means that Anderson Realty owes Farah Shields $205 plus $4.00 for costs.

Note: We have focused here on deposit cases from the tenant's point of view. The reason for this is that tenants are the ones who initiate this sort of case. However, landlords, too, should benefit from a careful reading with a special focus on the list of evidence that is helpful in court. Often, the best witness for a landlord is the new tenant who has just moved in. This person is more likely to feel that the place isn't clean than is the person who just moved out.

Money Damage Cases—Unpaid Rent

Landlords most commonly initiate Small Claims Court actions to sue for unpaid rent. Often the tenant has already moved out and doesn't bother to show up in court. If this happens, the landlord wins by default. Sometimes the tenant does show up, but presents no real defense and is there only to request the judge to allow him or her to make payments over time (see Chapter 22, "Time Payments").

The landlord should bring the lease or rental agreement to court and simply state the time periods for which rent is due but unpaid. Nothing else is required unless the tenant claims that he or she did pay the rent. Sometimes a landlord will sue for three times the amount of rent owed (triple damages) under a lease or rental agreement that states that he or she is entitled to do so if the tenant fails to pay rent but stays in the rental unit. Doing this will almost guarantee that the tenant will put up a fight. In my experience landlords are rarely awarded more than their actual out-of-pocket loss, and it makes little sense to request more.

There are several valid defenses to a suit based on a tenant's failure to pay rent. The principal one is where the tenant claims that rent was withheld because the condition of the premises was "uninhabitable." This amounts to the tenant saying to the landlord: "I won't pay my rent until you make necessary repairs."* It is legal to

*Under California law it is also legal for a tenant to have repairs done under some circumstances, and to deduct the cost from one month's rent. See California Civil Code Section 1941–42. This "repair and deduct" remedy is also discussed in detail in The California Tenants' Handbook. Often a tenant who fails to pay rent is brought to court by the landlord as part of an eviction action. If the tenant can prove that rent was withheld for a valid reason, he or she can't be evicted for exercising this right in California and the majority of other states.

do this in California under the decision in *Green v. Superior Court*, 10 CAL 3d 616.* The important thing for a tenant to understand in all states, however, is that rent withholding is not legal where the landlord refuses to fix some minor defect. For rent to be withheld legally, the condition needing repair must be sufficiently serious as to make the home "uninhabitable." In addition, the landlord must have been given reasonable notice of the problem. Thus a broken furnace that a landlord refused to fix would qualify as a condition making a home uninhabitable in the winter, but lack of heat in the summer would not.

If you are involved as a tenant in a rent-withholding case, your job is to prove (through pictures, witnesses, etc.) that the condition that caused you to withhold rent is indeed serious. Thus you might call the building inspector or an electrician to testify that the wiring was in a dangerous state of decay. The landlord, of course, has to prove the opposite—that the rental unit is in fundamentally sound shape, even though there may be some minor problems. A landlord has the right to inspect his or her properties at reasonable hours of the day as long as he or she gives the tenant reasonable notice. In many states 24-hours' notice is presumed by the law to be reasonable in the absence of an emergency. The landlord cannot use his or her right to inspect to harass the tenant, but the law has set down no absolute guidelines as to what harassment is.

Note: The present cumbersome procedure does not allow a tenant to sue in Small Claims Court to get needed repairs made, but instead requires the tenant first to withhold rent and then to defend himself in an eviction action. We need to reform our landlord–tenant law to provide for an effective procedure that tenants can institute when a landlord abdicates his responsibility to maintain rental property properly.

*If you live outside of California, check with a tenants' rights project or consumer group before withholding rent. Many states allow rent withholding by statute or court decision when conditions are awful, but others do not. Some states, particularly in the South and Midwest, require that tenants living in uninhabitable housing continue to pay rent while bringing legal action to get repairs made. If you live in California, see Moskovitz, Warner, and Sherman, 1980, The California Tenants' Handbook, Nolo Press, which goes into rent withholding and retaliation eviction in detail.

Evictions

(Known technically as "unlawful detainer," "summary dispossess," and "forcible entry and detainer," depending on the state.) Without question, landlords should have a simple and cheap way to free themselves of tenants who don't pay their rent. As noted at the beginning of this chapter, in some states, if a landlord wants to be sure to get a tenant out without ridiculous delays, an "unlawful detainer" action must be filed in formal court. Traditionally this has required the expense of a lawyer, but more and more landlords are learning to handle their own eviction actions.

A large number of states do not permit eviction actions to be brought in Small Claims Court at all. (See Appendix.) A few, including Illinois, New York, and Massachusetts, have in their larger cities separate "landlord–tenant" courts that amount to Small Claims Courts for this one specific purpose. But in many other states it is legal to bring eviction actions in Small Claims Court, provided the amount of rent involved in the suit is under the Small Claims Court dollar limit. Check your local rules with the Small Claims Court clerk. For example, in California only certain types of evictions are allowed in Small Claims Court. These include the situation in which a tenant of residential property has a written or oral, month-to-month (or week-to-week) rental agreement and is behind in the rent.* In California, if a lease is involved that gives the tenant a set term of occupancy longer than 30 days, or if the eviction is for some reason other than nonpayment of rent, the eviction action cannot be brought in Small Claims Court. Again, see your local rules.

Important: Let me repeat—before bringing an eviction action in Small Claims Court, a landlord should check the rules governing the tenant's right to appeal. This can be a trap for the unwary. In some

---

Before the landlord files an unlawful or forcible detainer action (eviction), he or she must first serve the defendant (tenant) a notice to pay rent or leave the premises. A carbon of this notice should be retained to be shown in Small Claims Court. Only after the notice period (three days in many states) has run out can an unlawful or forcible detainer lawsuit be filed. The notice may normally be served on the tenant personally by the landlord or by anyone else. Alternatively, a copy may be left at the defendant's address with a responsible person, and another copy mailed to him or her. A proof of service should be filled out. (See Chapter 11.)

states, including California, the defendant has an automatic right to appeal, and there is no requirement that an adequate bond be posted. In this situation a tenant's appeal can mean a long and costly delay for the landlord who is trying to get the tenant out. In California, for example, a tenant who knows the rules can often delay eviction three or four months simply by appealing the Small Claims Court eviction decision, even though he or she pays no rent and has no chance of winning the case in Superior Court.

Of course, the worst doesn't always happen. Many times a tenant who is served with Small Claims eviction papers moves out without a fight. If this occurs, you are ahead of the game and have saved time over the formal court procedure. It's a bit of a gamble, although you may be able to shorten the odds a little by giving some thought to the personality and sophistication of your tenant. If you think he or she is going to try to hold on to the apartment like a tick to a tasty dog, in many states you are better off going to a formal court.

A landlord who gets to court need prove only that the rent was not paid and that a correct notice was properly served. Bring a copy of the notice to court and a "proof of service" form filled out by the person who performed the service. The fact that a tenant is suffering from some hardship such as illness, poverty, birth of a child, etc., is not a defense to failure to pay rent. Possible tenant defenses are discussed briefly under "Money Damage Cases—Unpaid Rent" in this chapter. In many states, including those that have passed the Uniform Residential Landlord and Tenant Act (URLTA), these include rent withholding and deducting from the rent the cost to a tenant of repairing an item personally. A tenant cannot legally claim for the first time on the day of the court hearing that he or she withheld rent because of some defect. The landlord must be given reasonable notice that a defect exists before rent is withheld or the tenant makes repairs.*

---

*The length of such "reasonable" notice varies with the situation. For minor problems (dripping faucets, cracked windows, etc.) that don't present an immediate threat to health or safety, one month is usually presumed to be reasonable. For no heat in the winter, totally clogged drains or toilets, no hot water, etc., a day or two may be reasonable.

Miscellaneous Cases 21

By now you should have a clear idea of how a Small Claims Court case can be presented sensibly. The facts of each situation will vary, but the general approach will not. Here I will discuss a few of the more common types of cases. If I haven't covered yours in detail, simply make your own outline of steps to be taken, adapting the general approaches I have suggested to your own case.

Clothing (Alteration and Cleaning)

Several years ago, before I started attending Small Claims Court regularly, I stopped by one morning when I had a few free moments to kill before a criminal hearing. The case being argued involved an elderly German-American gentleman with a strong accent, suing an equally aged Armenian tailor, who was also seriously uncomfortable with the English language. The dispute centered around whether a suitcoat that the tailor had made for the plaintiff should have had two or three buttons. After ten minutes of almost incomprehensible testimony, I understood little more than that the plaintiff had never owned a suit with two buttons and the tailor had never made one with three. The two men ended by standing facing one another— each pulling a sleeve of the suitcoat and each yelling as loud as he could in his own language, apparently about how many buttons a suit ought to have. Much to their credit, the judge and bailiff just sat and smiled. What happened? I don't know. I was still actively practicing law then and had to bustle off to argue before another judge that my client thought that the two pounds of marijuana he was carrying in a money belt was really oregano. You can probably guess how *that* argument ended.

While I have never seen another clothing case quite as colorful as that of the two button suit, I have been consistently surprised at how often I have encountered people in Small Claims Court clutching an injured garment. We must indeed come to view our clothing as an extension of ourselves, because so many of us react with an indignation out of proportion to our monetary loss when some favorite item is damaged. I will never forget the morning I saw a particularly sour-looking fellow with neither word nor smile for anyone, including his obviously long-suffering wife, draw himself up to full height and wax poetic for five minutes about a four-year-old leather vest that a cleaner had mutilated.

Winning a significant victory in a case involving clothing is often difficult. Why? Because, while the liability is often easy to prove (i.e., the seamstress cut off the collar instead of the cuff), a reasonable amount of compensation for damages is difficult or impossible to establish, for the obvious reason that used clothing has little actual market value, even though it may have cost a lot to start with or have enormous sentimental value to its owner. In theory a court can award a plaintiff only the fair market value of the damaged clothing, not its replacement cost. But because this rule of law commonly works a severe injustice in clothing cases (a $400 suit bought last week may be worth only $100 this week), many judges tend to bend it a little in favor of the person who has suffered the loss.

They do this by allowing an amount pretty close to the original purchase price when the clothing involved was almost new, even though its fair market value for resale would be much less. Thus, the owner of a $300 dress that had been ruined by a seamstress after only one wearing might recover $250. Judges are not required to take this approach, but many do. With older clothing, I have also seen some judges take a flexible approach. They do this by making a rough estimate of the percentage of total use that remains in a garment and then awarding the plaintiff this percentage of the original purchase price. Thus, if a cleaner ruined a $300 suit that had been worn for about 50 percent of its useful life, the plaintiff might recover $150.

Here are some hints:

- Bring the damaged clothing to court. It's hard for a tailor to say much when confronted with a coat that is two sizes too big or has three sleeves.

- Be ready to prove the original purchase price with a canceled check, newspaper ad, credit card statement, etc.
- Be sure that the person you are suing (tailor, cleaner, seamstress, etc.) caused the problem. As noted in the example of the suede coat in Chapter 2, some problems that develop during cleaning or alterations may be the responsibility of the manufacturer.

Note: Cleaners are particularly apt to offer "proof" from "independent testing laboratories" that damage caused during cleaning wasn't their fault. You will want to ask: How much did the cleaner pay the testing lab for the report? How many times had the same cleaner used the same testing lab before? How did the cleaner know about the testing lab (does it solicit business from cleaners)? etc.*

Dog-Bite Cases

Reread Chapter 2, where I used several dog-bite cases as examples. To review: be ready to prove the extent of the injury, the location where it occurred, time off from work without compensation, doctor's bills, etc. If the dog is mean-looking, a picture will be a great help.† If the dog bite occurred someplace other than the dog owner's property, you have an excellent chance of recovery. If the attack occurred on a part of the owner's property on which you had a clear right to be (the front walk, or even the backyard if you were there by invitation), you also stand to win. However, if you were on a part of the dog owner's property that people normally would not go without invitation and you had no such invitation, chances are that you will lose.

In cases where one dog attacks another, there is normally no recovery unless the attacking dog entered the other's property, or

---

*In a creative deviation from the normal, unimaginative way of running Small Claims Court, Minneapolis, Minnesota periodically sets a special day aside in its Small Claims Court for "cleaning" cases. The court has its own independent expert come in and advise it as to who should recover what. Commonly, but not always, the expert finds that the cleaners have been negligent.

†Getting the picture without being bitten again is a serious problem, of course. I have heard that a ham bone can be quite helpful, but I don't guarantee it.

the attacking dog was loose and the victim was on a leash. When two loose dogs get into a mix-up on neutral ground, there is usually no award of damages to the loser.

Damage to Real Property (Land, Buildings, etc.)

There is no typical case of this nature, as facts vary greatly. So instead of trying to set down general rules, let's look at a situation that happened recently to a friend of mine. (Let's call her Babette.)

Babette owns a cinder-block building that houses two stores. One morning when she came to work, she noticed water pouring in through the back of her building. Because the building was set into a hill, it abutted about eight feet of her uphill neighbor's land. (Let's call her neighbor Boris). After three days of investigation involving the use of green dye in Boris's plumbing system, it was discovered that the water came from an underground leak in Boris's sewer pipe.

At this point, Babette had spent considerable effort and some money to pay helpers to get the water mopped up before it damaged anything in the stores.

Instead of fixing the leak promptly, Boris delayed for four days. All of this time, Babette and her helpers were mopping frantically. Finally, when Boris did get to work, he insisted on digging the pipe out himself, which took another four days. (A plumber with the right equipment could have done it in one.) In the middle of Boris's digging, when his yard looked as though it was being attacked by a herd of giant gophers, it rained. The water filled the holes and trenches instead of running off as it normally would have. Much of it ran through the ground into Babette's building.

When the flood was finally over, Babette figured out her costs as follows:

First three days (before the source of the water was discovered)	$148 (for help with mopping)
Next four days (while Boris refused to cooperate)	$188 (for help with mopping)
Final four days (including day it rained)	$262 (for help with mopping)
One secondhand water vacuum purchased during rain storm	$150
Her own time, valued at $5.00 per hour	$400

Assuming that Boris is unwilling to pay Babette's costs, for what amount should she sue and how much is she likely to recover? If you remember the lessons taught in Chapter 2, you will remember that before Babette can recover for her very real loss, she must show that Boris was negligent or caused her loss intentionally. Probably, she can't do this for the first three days, when no one knew where the water was coming from. However, once the problem was discovered and Boris didn't take immediate steps to fix it, he was clearly negligent, and she can recover at least her out-of-pocket loss ($450 for labor and $150 for the water vacuum). Can Babette also recover for the value of her own time? The answer to this question is *maybe*. It would depend on the state and the judge. If Babette could show that she had to close her store or take time off from a job to stem the flood, she probably could recover. Were I she, I would sue for about $1000, and count on getting a judgment for most of it.

Police Brutality—False Arrest Cases

Now and then actions against the police end up in Small Claims Court. Usually, the plaintiff is an irate citizen who has tried and failed to get an attorney to represent him in a larger suit and, as a last resort, has filed for the maximum amount.* Put simply, most of the people I have seen bringing this sort of case have been run out of court in a hurry. Why? Because the police and jailors have excellent legal advice and aren't afraid to lie to back each other up. The unwritten rule in any law enforcement agency is to protect your own derriere first, and to protect your buddies' derrieres right after that. Police officers are not going to sit still politely and collect black marks on their service records without fighting back. Most law enforcement people have testified many times before and know how to handle themselves in court.

The reason that many plaintiffs must use Small Claims Court to sue law enforcement people pretty much tells the story. Lawyers normally won't invest their time and money in this sort of case because they find them almost impossible to win. Does this mean that I believe that people bringing false arrest, police brutality, and similar types of cases are wasting their time? Balancing the trouble involved against the unlikely chance of success, I would have to say yes. That said, let me also say that I believe that lots of things that make little sense at a practical level are worthwhile at many other levels. I can't help but admire people who will fight for principle even though they have small chance of winning.

If you do sue a police officer, jailor, or anyone else with a badge, be sure that you have several witnesses who will back you up and won't be intimidated into keeping their mouths shut. Never, never rely on one officer to testify against another. They simply won't do it. It may be cynical but it is also realistic to assume that all law enforcement personnel will tell whatever lies necessary to protect themselves and each other. This isn't always true, but it happens often enough so that you may as well be prepared for the worst. You would also be wise to spend a few dollars and talk to a lawyer who specializes in criminal cases. For a $25–$50 fee, you can probably pick up some valuable pointers on how to convince the judge that you were treated in an illegal and unreasonable way.

*In most cases of this sort, you will want to sue the city, county, or state government that employs the officer, as well as the individual involved. In California, before you can sue a government entity, you must file an administrative claim. (See Chapter 8.)

Libel, Slander, etc.

In California, libel and slander cases may be brought in Small Claims Court. However, many states, among them Colorado, Connecticut, Massachusetts, Michigan, New Hampshire, Ohio, and Oklahoma, bar libel and slander cases from Small Claims Court. Actions for false arrest, malicious prosecution, and other "personal torts" that are hard to win and for which damages are difficult to ascertain are also commonly barred. Check your state's Small Claims Court laws.

Suits against Airlines or Hotels

Because of overbooking, it is not uncommon for an airline or a hotel to refuse to honor your reservation. In some situations this can cause considerable financial loss, especially if, in the case of an airline bumping, you miss work or an important meeting. Airlines are required by the CAB to pay some amount of compensation, which will vary in accordance with the length of the delay.* But the amount that they are required to pay may not cover your loss.

You can use Small Claims Court to get an additional recovery.† To prepare your case for Small Claims Court, do as much of the following as possible:

- At the airline gate when you are being bumped, tell the airline that you will suffer financial loss if you don't get to your destination promptly and ask that they request other passengers to take a later flight.
- Find out the name of the local airline manager and put him or her on notice that you will sue if you are bumped.
- Note down all out-of-pocket expenses that the delay causes you.
- Compute any loss of wages, commissions, or paid vacation time that the delay causes.

*If the airline provides an alternative flight that arrives within two hours of the original flight, compensation is limited to the amount of the one-way fare (not to exceed $200). If the delay is more than two hours, the airline must pay double the one-way fare, not to exceed $400.

†The information contained in this section was suggested to me by an excellent article by syndicated columnist and financial writer Peter Weaver, entitled "When Airlines Bump, Bump Back." The article appeared in the April 21, 1978, issue of Medical Economics.

- Write to the airline requesting payment of your loss, and inform them that you will file in Small Claims Court if they don't pay up.
- File your case in Small Claims Court for the amount of your out-of-pocket expenses and lost business. If your claim appears reasonable, the airline may pay voluntarily or allow you to win on a default judgment.

Judgment and Appeal 22

The Judgment

In most states, including California, the decision in your case will be mailed to the address on record with the clerk any time from a few days to a few weeks after your case is heard. The exception to this rule occurs when one side doesn't show up (or doesn't file an answer within the proper time, in states that require it), and the other wins by default. Default judgments are normally announced right in the courtroom.* The truth is that in the vast majority of contested cases the judge has already made up his or her mind at the time your case is heard and notes down his or her decision before you leave the courtroom. Decisions are sent by mail because the court doesn't want to have to deal with angry, unhappy losers, especially those few who might get violent. As one bailiff recently put it, "The county simply can't afford to clean the blood off the floor every time the loser goes after the winner or the judge." But is this fear realistic? Several studies have found that it is not and that there have been no serious disruptions where decisions are announced in court by the judge. As

---

*Chapters 10, 12, and 15 discuss default judgments and the fact that people who have had defaults entered against them can often get them set aside if (1) they had a reasonable excuse for not being present, and (2) they notified the court clerk immediately of their desire to have the judgment set aside. In most states a motion to vacate a default judgment must be filed immediately if the defaulting party was properly notified of the case to start with. If the defaulting defendant was never properly served, he or she must move to set aside the default as soon as the default is discovered.

185

a result, more and more states are now following a policy of announcing the decision in court. My experience has been that this is a better approach, especially when the judge takes a moment to explain his or her reasoning in making the decision.

Often when a judgment is entered against a person, he or she feels that the judge would surely have made a different decision if he or she hadn't gotten mixed up, or overlooked some crucial fact, or had properly understood an argument. On the basis of my experience on the bench, I can tell you that in the vast majority of Small Claims Court cases there is little likelihood that the judge would change his or her decision even if you had a chance to argue the whole case over. In any event, you don't. You have had your chance and the decision has gone against you. Don't call the judge, or go to see him, or send him documents through the mail. You had your chance in court; you don't get another chance in the judge's office. (See "The Appeal" later in this chapter.)

Note: Now that a judgment has been entered, we need to expand our vocabulary slightly. The person who wins the case (gets the judgment) now becomes "the judgment creditor" and the loser is known as "the judgment debtor."

Time Payments

We have mentioned the fact that in a great many states, including California, Connecticut, Michigan, New York, and Minnesota, a judge may order that the loser be allowed to pay the winner over a period of time, rather than all at once.* The judge won't normally give this sort of order unless you request it. If you are in a state in which the judge announces his or her decision in court, this is not a problem, as you are present to ask for time payments if you lose. However, if you are in a state in which decisions are sent by mail, you will have to make your request in advance. You will want to do this if you have no real defense to a claim, or if you have a fairly good case but aren't sure which way the judge will decide.

*Many other states also allow time payments. Be sure to ask about this possibility in your Small Claims Court.

"In closing my presentation, I would like to say that I believe I have a convincing case and should be awarded the judgment, but in the event that you rule for my opponent, I would like you to allow me time payments of no more than (whatever amount is convenient) per month."

Or, if you have no real defense:

"Your Honor, I request that you enter the judgment against me for no more than (an amount convenient to you) per month."

If you neglect to ask for time payments in court and wish to make this request after you receive the judgment, first contact the other party to see if he or she will voluntarily agree to accept the money on a schedule you can afford to pay. If he or she agrees, it would be wise to write your agreement down and have your opponent sign it. If your opponent is an all-or-nothing sort of person and refuses time payments, promptly contact the court clerk and ask that the case again be brought before the judge—not to rehash the facts, but only to set up a payment schedule that you can live with. The clerk should arrange things for you, but if there is a problem, write a letter (similar to the one in Exhibit 22.1) to the judge.

Honorable Felix Hamburg   47 West Adams St.
Judge of the Small Claims Court   Brooklyn, NY
111 Centre St.   October 17, 19--
New York, NY 10013

Dear Judge Hamburg: Re: Elliot v. Toller
                                                      Index No. _____

    I recently appeared before you in the case of Elliot v. Toller
(Index No. _____). Mr. Elliot was awarded a judgment in the amount
of $526.00. Paying this amount all at once would be nearly impossible
because of (lack of employment, or illness, or whatever). I can pay
$25 per month.

    Please change the order in this case to allow for a $25 per month
payment. If it is necessary for me to make this request in court,
please inform me of the time I should be present.

                                Sincerely,

                                John Toller

Exhibit 22.1

Satisfaction of Judgment*

Exhibit 22.2 shows a sample "Satisfaction of Judgment" form that is available from the Small Claims Court clerk. It must be signed by the judgment creditor. It is a good idea to get the satisfaction form filled out and signed when you pay the judgment. This saves the trouble of having to track down the other party later. Besides, people are much more willing to be cooperative when you are waving money under their nose than when they have already spent it. Once signed, the Satisfaction of Judgment must be filed with the Small Claims Court clerk. This clerk can give you a certified copy of the satisfaction if you ever need one. This may be necessary to clear up your credit history at a credit bureau or with someone else with whom you want to establish your good credit.

THE RIGHT TO A "SATISFACTION OF JUDGMENT"

The law of all states says that a "judgment debtor" is entitled to get a "Satisfaction of Judgment" from the "judgment creditor" when the judgment is paid. All the debtor need do is ask for it. Commonly, state law requires that the "Satisfaction of Judgment" must be provided within 15 to 30 days of request, but it is an excellent idea to insist that one be filled out at the time the money is paid. Ask your Small Claims Court clerk for local rules. You may also be entitled to a partial "Satisfaction of Judgment" if you pay off part, but not all, of the judgment. However, as a practical matter, a partial Satisfaction of Judgment doesn't help you much, and you will probably want to wait to get a full "Satisfaction of Judgment" when the debt is paid. In the meantime, save your canceled checks or money order receipts.

GETTING A "SATISFACTION OF JUDGMENT" FROM A PERSON WHO WON'T COOPERATE

There are penalties for refusing to give a judgment debtor a "Satisfaction of Judgment" after he or she has paid off the judgment. In California these can amount to $100 in addition to any actual damage the delay caused, unless the judge finds that the judgment creditor had just cause for his or her action. Rules in other states are similar. To get your complaint that the judgment creditor will not sign a

*The rules I discuss here, including time limits, fees, etc., are for California. Other states have similar regulations.

211-150

SMALL CLAIMS COURT, BERKELEY-ALBANY JUDICIAL DISTRICT,
COUNTY OF ALAMEDA, STATE OF CALIFORNIA

_____   NO. SC _____
                          Plaintiff(s)
                    vs   SATISFACTION OF JUDGMENT

_____
                          Defendant(s)

I hereby acknowledge full satisfaction of the judgment in the above entitled action.

Executed at _____ , California on _____

_____
                                        Judgment Creditor

Exhibit 22.2

"Satisfaction of Judgment" before the court, go to the clerk's office. The clerk will help you bring the matter before a judge. This is done by serving papers (often entitled "Notice of Motion to Satisfy Judgment") on the judgment creditor. This service may be done by mail. Once you get to court, show the judge your proof that the judgment has been paid in full and he or she will do the rest.

GETTING A "SATISFACTION OF JUDGMENT" FROM A PERSON YOU CAN'T FIND

Sometimes people forget to get a "Satisfaction of Judgment" when they pay a judgment, only to find later that they can't locate the judgment creditor. If this happens, consult the court clerk. You will have to prepare an affidavit concerning your unsuccessful attempt to find the judgment creditor and submit it to the court with your proof that the judgment was paid.

The Appeal

If, in the face of justice, common sense, and all of your fine arguments, the judge turns out to be a big dummy and rules for your opponent, you can appeal to a higher court, right? Not necessarily. Although most states allow either side the right to appeal, California, Massachusetts, Washington, and some other states do not allow the person who brought the suit (the plaintiff) to appeal; in these states, if you are the plaintiff and you lose, you are finished, done, through. Why? Because that's how the legislature made the rules. However, if you are the defendant and lose, you can appeal to a formal court if, and only if, you do it promptly.

Isn't it unfair, maybe even unconstitutional, for some states to allow appeal rights for defendants and none for plaintiffs? I will leave it to you to decide the fairness issue, but it's not unconstitutional for the simple reason that the plaintiff knows before filing that he or she doesn't have a right to an appeal. The plaintiff has a choice in most states of bringing suit in Small Claims Court in which there is no right for plaintiffs to appeal, or in a formal court in which both sides can appeal. The defendant doesn't have this opportunity to pick the court and, therefore, the legislature decided that his or her appeal rights should be preserved.

In the Appendix you will find a very brief summary of the appeal rules of all states. Appeal rules vary considerably. Some states, such as Connecticut, Maryland and Hawaii, allow no appeal. New York allows an appeal of a judge's decision, but not an attorney-arbitrator's decision. Determining whether you can appeal is important, but it is only *part* of the information you need. Just as important is determining what kind of appeal is permitted in your state. While it may be true, as Gertrude Stein suggested, that "a rose is a rose is a rose," appeals are not nearly so consistent. Some states allow an appeal only on questions of law, while others allow the whole case to be replayed from scratch (this is often called a hearing "de novo"). Let's pause for a moment and look at the difference.

TRIAL DE NOVO ON APPEAL

In 14 states, including Pennsylvania and Texas, either party can appeal and have the case heard over from scratch. In seven other states, including California and Massachusetts, only the defendant can appeal, but when he or she does, the case is also presented again as if the first trial hadn't occurred. When an appeal is "de novo," you simply argue the case over, presenting all of your witnesses, documents, and testimony, etc. This is necessary because no records are kept at Small Claims Court hearings. Of course, both sides should give some thought to how their presentation can be improved. This is particularly true of the person who has already lost once. It is probably true that many judges have a bias toward the person who won the first time because they believe that Small Claims Court appeals are not worth the time they take and should be discouraged.

APPEAL ON QUESTIONS OF LAW ONLY

In over 20 states, including Ohio, Wisconsin, and Vermont (see Appendix for a complete list), appeals can be based only on questions of law, not on the facts of the case. This is the sort of appeal that the United States Supreme Court and the other formal appellate courts normally hear. As most appeals are about the interpretation of fact ("The apartment was really clean, your Honor"), states that hear only questions of law on appeal have far fewer appeals. Thus in a landlord–tenant case, the appeal court would not review the Small Claims Court judge's determination that a tenant moved out and left his or her apartment dirty, but would review the judge's decision if he or she awarded $500 in damages when the law of the state called for $250. In most states appeals made on the basis of a mistake of law must be backed up by a written outline of what the mistakes were. This can put nonlawyers at a great disadvantage because they are unfamiliar with legal research and legal writing techniques. Thus all too often the theoretical right to appeal is frustrated by the reality of our convoluted legal system.*

Filing Your Appeal

Now let's look at the mechanics of the appeal. In California, the defendant must file a notice of appeal within 20 days of the entry of the judgment. As judgments are mailed, this means that there will be fewer than 20 days to file an appeal from the day that the defendant receives the judgment. In New York, appeals must be filed in 30 days. In many other states, including Massachusetts and Arizona, appeals must be filed within ten days, while Washington, D.C., requires that appeals be on file within three days. In all states, appeals must be filed promptly, so wherever you are, don't delay.

To file your notice of appeal, go to the Small Claims Court clerk's office and fill out a paper such as the one illustrated in Exhibit 22.3. The appeal fee is often higher than the original filing fee; $20–40 is

---

*If you wish to do some legal research on your own, start by reading Peter Jan Honigsberg, 1979, Cluing into Legal Research, Golden Rain Press. This book shows you how to really break the "secret" code of the law library.

```
COMMONWEALTH OF MASSACHUSETTS

MIDDLESEX, SS.                              THIRD DISTRICT COURT
                                            OF EASTERN MIDDLESEX
                                            SC NO._____

_____PLTF.

                    vs

_____DEFT.


       DEFENDANT'S APPEAL AND CLAIM OF TRIAL BY JURY

    Now comes the defendant in the above entitled action and
claims a TRIAL BY JURY in the Superior Court and further upon
affidavit makes oath that said trial is entered in good faith
and that there are questions of law and fact requiring trial
by jury with specification as follows;

_____

_____

_____

_____

_____

_____

    Signed under the pains and penalties of perjury


                    _____Name

                    _____Address

                    _____City

                    _____Phone

Date_____
```

Exhibit 22.3

average. You are now going into formal court and you must pay according to the formal court's fee schedule. If you ultimately win your appeal (that is, get the original decision turned around in your favor), you can add these court costs to the judgment. In many states, the party filing an appeal must post a bond (or written guarantee by financially solvent adults) to cover the amount of the judgment if he or she loses. This is not required in California and some other states.

When you file your appeal, the court will notify the other side that you have done so. You need not do this yourself. Once your appeal is on file at the next higher court, your next step is to wait. When you are done waiting, you will probably have to wait some more. You are in the formal court system now, where traditionally very little happens and happens very slowly. Those who have been in the armed services will understand. All the deadlines apply to you—never to the bureaucracy. Eventually (normally two to six months, depending on your area) you will get a notice giving you a court date in the formal court.

Exhibit 22.3 illustrates an appeal notice in use in Massachusetts. The one in use in your state may look different, but the information requested will be similar.

Note: Appeal rights are almost always restricted to those who showed up in Small Claims Court, argued their case, and lost. If you defaulted (didn't show up), you normally can't appeal until you get the default set aside. You must act to do this almost immediately. (See Chapter 10, "If One Party Doesn't Show Up.")

Arguing Your Appeal

You are entitled to have an attorney in formal court. But as your case is not worth a lot, you will probably decide that it is not wise to hire one. Indeed there should be little practical reason for an attorney, as you probably have an excellent grasp of the issues by this time. However, it's often true that judges pay more attention to the same argument made by an attorney than made by an ordinary citizen. I find this to be yet another manifestation of the sickness of our judicial system, but you are stuck dealing with the system as it is, not as it should be.

As noted above, the procedure for appealing a Small Claims Court judgment varies considerably from state to state, depending on whether the appeal is for an entirely new ("de novo") trial or is based only on a question of law. In the former situation, you must be prepared to argue your entire case from scratch, while in states that limit appeals to questions of law you will have to be prepared to explain to the judge hearing the appeal exactly what mistake the other judge made. Because state procedures vary so much in this area, the best I can do is to suggest that you go down to your courthouse and watch a few Small Claims Court appeals. The clerk will be able to tell you when they are scheduled.

Collecting Your Money 23

OK, you won. What does that mean? Simply that you are entitled to the dollar amount of the judgment from the opposing party or parties. How are you going to get it? Try asking politely. This works in the majority of cases, especially if you have sued a respectable business. If you don't have personal contact with the person who owes you the money, try a note like the one shown in Exhibit 23.1. If appeals are allowed in your state, it is wise to wait until after the last possible day to appeal has passed before asking for your money. (See Appendix.) Why? Because if you make your request for money too soon, you may remind the defendant to take advantage of his or her right to appeal. In a number of states, you can't begin formal collection activity (garnishments, attachments, etc.) until after the time to appeal has elapsed. Check with the clerk for rules in your state.

If you receive no response to your polite note, you will have to get serious about collecting your money or forget it. The emphasis in the previous sentence is on the word "you." Much to many people's surprise, the court does not enforce its judgments and collect money for you—you have to do it yourself.

There are only a few relatively easy ways to collect money from a debtor. We mentioned these briefly in Chapter 3. I hope you gave some thought to collection before you brought your case. If you only now realize that your opponent doesn't have the money to buy a toothbrush and never will, you are better off not wasting more time and money trying to get him to pay up. Also, remember that a judgment is valid for many years (ten in most states) and can be renewed

---

SAMPLE COLLECTION NOTE

P.O. Box 66
Springfield, IL

February 15, 19--

Mildred Edwards
11 Milvia Street
Springfield, IL

Dear Mrs. Edwards:

As you know, a judgment was entered against you in Small Claims Court on January 15 in the amount of $457.86. As the judgment creditor I will appreciate your paying this amount at your earliest convenience.

Thank you for your consideration.

Very truly yours,

John Toller

Exhibit 23.1

for an additional period of years if you can show that you have tried to collect it but failed. In some situations you may simply want to sit on it, with the hope that your "judgment debtor" will show a few signs of solvency in the future.

Important: A few states, such as New York, are putting some teeth in their collection rules. In New York, if a business that has the ability to do so doesn't pay three or more Small Claims Court judgments, a judgment creditor can get triple the judgment as damages, plus attorney fees. If you are in New York, contact the Small Claims Court clerk for details.

Levying on Wages, Bank Accounts, Business Assets, Real Property, etc.

If a polite letter doesn't work (two weeks is plenty of time to wait), and you know that the person who owes you the money (the "judgment debtor") has it, you will have to start acting like a collecting agency.*

If you know where the judgment debtor works, you are in good shape. Federal and state laws normally allow you to take approximately 25 percent of a person's net wages to satisfy a debt.† Knowing where a judgment debtor banks can also be extremely valuable, as you can order a sheriff or marshal to levy on a bank account and get whatever it contains at the time of the levy. Of course, a bank account levy will work only once, as the debtor is pretty sure to move the account when he or she realizes that you have emptied it. Other types of property are normally much more difficult to grab. Why? Because all states have a number of "exemption" laws that say even though a person owes money, certain types of his or her property can't be taken to satisfy the debt. Items protected typically include equity in a family house up to a certain dollar amount, furniture, clothes, and much more.‡ Practically speaking, the only assets other than wages and bank accounts that are normally worth thinking about to satisfy a Small Claims Court judgment are motor vehicles in which the judgment debtor has an equity of more than $500, real property other than the place in which the debtor lives, and the receipts of an operating business. Theoretically, there are many other assets that you could reach, but in most cases they are not worth the time and expense involved considering that your judgment is for the Small Claims Court maximum or less.

*It is possible to turn your debt over to a real collection agency, but this probably doesn't make too much sense as the agency will take 50 percent of what they can collect. Unless you are a regular customer, the agency probably won't treat your debt with much priority unless they believe that it is easy to collect. If it is easy for them to collect, it probably won't be hard for you to do it yourself and save the fee.

†If a person has a very low income, the amount you can recover can be considerably less than 25 percent. Wage garnishments are not allowed in Nevada, New Mexico, North Dakota, South Carolina, and Texas. Some other states make it difficult to garnishee the wages of a head of family in a situation where the family has a low income and needs all of its income to survive. A few states, such as New York, limit garnishments to 10 percent of a person's wages. The sheriff or marshal's office in your area can supply you with rules in your state.

‡All states exempt some property from attachment, but the details vary considerably. For more information, look in the index to your state laws under the heading "Attachments" or "Garnishments" and the subheading "Exempt Assets." State exemption regulations are also set out in Kosel, 1980, A Legal Guide to Bankruptcy, Addison-Wesley. For a thorough discussion of debtors' rights in California, see Warner and Honigsberg, 1979, The California Debtors' Handbook—Billpayers' Rights, Nolo Press.

THE WRIT OF EXECUTION

Before you can levy on a person's wages or other property, you need to get a court order. This is called a "Writ of Execution." A sample is shown in Exhibit 23.2. If you have a Small Claims Court judgment, you are entitled to this writ. You get your Writ of Execution in most states from the Small Claims Court clerk by filing a form entitled "Application and Order for Issuance of Writ of Execution." The clerk will help you fill it out. There is often a small charge for filing this form, which is a recoverable cost. (See "Recovering Collection Costs and Interest" later in this chapter.)

Civil Court of The City of New York
COUNTY OF NEW YORK
SMALL CLAIMS PART

Claimant
Judgment Creditor,

vs.

Index No. S.C. _____ 197 .

Defendant
Judgment Debtor.

THE PEOPLE OF THE STATE OF NEW YORK

TO ANY SHERIFF OR TO ANY MARSHAL OF THE CITY OF NEW YORK

WHEREAS, judgment was entered on   , 197 , in the Civil Court of the City of New York, County of
NEW YORK . Small Claims Part, in favor of
Judgment Creditor and against
Judgment Debtor whose last known address is
for the sum of $, and the sum of $
is now actually due thereon together with interest.

YOU ARE HEREBY DIRECTED to levy upon and sell only the property in which the above named Judgment Debtor, who is not deceased, has an interest, or upon debts owed to the Judgment Debtor; and

WHEREAS, the Judgment Debtor is receiving or will receive income of more than $85.00 per week from
address
, you are further directed to collect in installments 10% from each payment, in accordance with Section 5231 of the Civil Practice Law and Rules.

WITNESS, Hon. **Stanley S. Danzig**   , one of the Judges of said Civil Court of the City of New York, the   day of   . 197 .

PHOENIX INGRAHAM
Chief Clerk of the Court

TO THE JUDGMENT DEBTOR: Please take notice that you shall commence payment of the installments above mentioned to the said Sheriff or Marshal forthwith, and that upon your default, this execution will be served upon the aforesaid employer.

TO THE EMPLOYER: Please take notice that you are to withhold and pay over the installments above mentioned to the said Sheriff or Marshal forthwith.

TO THE GARNISHEE (other than employer) name
address
: You are required by law to pay over or deliver to the said Sheriff or Marshal forthwith all money or other property in your possession in which the above-named judgment debtor has an interest.

Delivered to Marshal   on   , 197 . Delivered to the Sheriff of the City of New York in the County of   on   , 197 .

Exhibit 23.2

THE SHERIFF (OR MARSHAL)

Once your "Writ of Execution" form is filled out, take or send it to the sheriff or marshal in the county in which the assets are located. The Small Claims Court clerk will direct you. Do it right away because the Writ of Execution expires within a certain period (often 60-90 days) if it is not served by the sheriff or marshal. If this time runs out, you will have to go back to the Small Claims Court clerk and get another "Writ of Execution" issued. Give the sheriff (marshal):

- The "Writ of Execution" (original) and one to three or more copies, depending on the asset to be collected.*
- His fees for collecting (this will vary as to the type of asset, so you should inquire).
- Instructions on what and where to collect: The sheriff or marshal may have a form they wish you to use when giving them instructions. Ask about the fee for this when you call. Normally, a letter is sufficient.

HOW TO LEVY ON WAGES AND BANK ACCOUNTS

To seize a person's wages or bank account you need the original and one copy of a "Writ of Execution," the sheriff's (marshal's) fee ($10-20 in most states), and a letter of instruction like that shown in Exhibit 23.3

LEVYING ON MOTOR VEHICLES (INCLUDING PLANES, BOATS, AND RVS)

Getting money from wages or bank accounts is fairly easy. Selling a person's motor vehicle is more difficult for several reasons, including the following:

- A portion of the equity in a car is exempt from your levy in many states. (California exempts $500.)†

Example: A judgment debtor in California has a car worth $1,500 on which he owes $1,000. This means that his equity is $500—the bank owns the rest. As an equity of $500 is exempt under California law, you would end up with nothing.

Don't forget to keep a copy of the "Writ of Execution" for your files.
†*Some states have no exemption for motor vehicles and some exempt a higher amount of equity. Check your state legal codes, or call your local sheriff or marshal's office.*

```
                                    P.O. Box 66
                                    Berkeley, CA

                                    March 1, 19--


Sheriff (Civil Division), Alameda County
Alameda County Courthouse
Oakland, CA

                         Re:  John Ehrman v. Mildred Edwards
                              Albany-Berkeley Judicial Dis-
                              trict
                              Small Claims Court No. 81-52

Dear Sir:

     Enclosed you will find the original and one copy of a Writ of Execu-
tion issued by the Small Claims Court for the Oakland Judicial District
in the amount of $   (fill in total due)   .  I also enclose a check
for your fee in the amount of $_____.

     I hereby instruct you to levy on the wages of Mildred Edwards, who
works at the Graphite Oil Co., 1341 Chester St., Oakland, CA.  Please
serve the Writ on or before March 15, 19--.*


                                    Very truly yours,


                                    John Ehrman
```

Exhibit 23.3

- In many states a motor vehicle is exempt from attachment up to a higher limit if it is a "tool of a person's trade." (A limit of $2,500 in California, $600 in Ohio, etc.)

Example: A California judgment debtor has a pickup truck worth $2,000 which she uses every day in her gardening business. The truck would be exempt under C.C.P. 690.4

- The judgment debtor may not own the car he or she drives. It may be in someone else's name, or the driver may owe a bank or finance company as much or more than the car is worth.

  To find out if a judgment debtor owns the car he or she drives, go to the Department of Motor Vehicles and give them

For a bank account, you would simply substitute "all monies in the checking account of Mildred Edwards, located at the Bank of Trade, 11 City St., Oakland, Calif." You do not need to know the account number. If a bank account is in the name of defendant and someone else, you may have to post a bond, depending on your state's laws. Ask the sheriff or marshal for details.

the license number. In most states, for a small fee, they will tell you who owns the car and whether or not a bank or finance company is involved. Once you have this information, you can determine whether it is worthwhile to have the sheriff pick up the car and sell it. Levying on motor vehicles can be expensive. The storage fees and the sheriff's cost of sale average about $175 and must be paid in advance. This money is recoverable when the vehicle is sold. Call the sheriff or marshal (Civil Division) of the county in which the car is located to find out how much money the sheriff or marshal requires as a deposit with your Writ of Execution and how many copies of the Writ you need. Then write a letter similar to the one in Exhibit 23.4.

```
                              P.O. Box 66
                              Berkeley, CA

                              March 1, 19--


Sheriff (Civil Division)
Alameda County
Alameda County Courthouse
Oakland, CA

                         Re:  John Ehrman v. Mildred Edwards
                              Small Claims Court
                              Albany-Berkeley Judicial Dis-
                              trict
                              No. SC 81-52

Dear Sir:

     You are hereby instructed, under the authority of the enclosed Writ
of Execution, to levy upon and sell all of the right, title and interest
of Mildred Edwards, judgment debtor, in the following motor vehicle:

     (Type here all information regarding the description of the
     car from your D.M.V. report, including the license number.)

     The vehicle is registered in the name(s) of Mildred Edwards and is
regularly found at the following address(es:

     (List home and work address of owner)

     Enclosed is my check for $_____ to cover your costs of levy
and sale.


                              Very truly yours,



                              John Ehrman
```

Exhibit 23.4

REAL PROPERTY

It normally makes little sense to go through the complicated procedures involved in selling, or trying to sell, a person's real property to satisfy a Small Claims Court judgment—especially when the simple act of recording an "Abstract of Judgment" against the property at the County Recorder's office gives you a lien against that property.* When the judgment debtor wishes to sell his or her real property, the title will be clouded by your lien and the judgment debtor will have to pay you off to be able to transfer clear title to a third party. Thus, sooner or later, you will get your money.†

To record your judgment against real property, first get an "Abstract of Judgment" from the Small Claims Court clerk's office. The clerk will prepare this paper for you for a small fee. Then take the "Abstract of Judgment" to the County Recorder's office in the county in which the property is located and pay a small recording fee. They will do the rest.

Note: In some states you have to identify the property you're putting the lien on.

OTHER PERSONAL PROPERTY

Normally, it isn't worth the trouble to try to levy on small items of personal property, such as furniture or appliances, because they are commonly covered by one or another of the state exemption laws that declare certain possessions exempt from being taken to satisfy debts.

BUSINESS ASSETS

In most states it is possible to have someone from the sheriff or marshal's office sent to the business of a person who owes you money to collect it from the cash on hand. You will want to ask your court clerk about your local rules. In California and many other states there are several ways to proceed.

*In most states you must record your "Abstract of Judgment" against the record of each piece of property, but in a few states, recording a judgment at the County Recorder's office gives you an automatic lien against all property in that county. Check with your county clerk for local details.
†The only exception to this rule is that, under the law of many states, the owner of a home on which the judgment debtor has filed a homestead prior to your filing your "Abstract of Judgment" can sell it and use the money (up to the amount of equity protected by the "homestead" law in your state) to buy another homesteaded home without paying off your lien.

- **Till Tap**   A deputy goes to the business one time and picks up all the money in the till. The fee for this service normally varies from $10–$35.

- **Eight-Hour Keeper**   A deputy stays all day at the place of business and collects all the money that comes in. Average fee—$35–$70.

- **48-Hour Keeper** The deputy stays at the business for a much longer period of time and collects what comes in. Average fee—$200–$350, depending on the state and county.

Talk to the sheriff or marshal in your area to get more details. They will want an original and three copies of your Writ of Execution together with instructions telling them where and when to go. The creditor must pay the fees in advance, but they will be taken from the debtor in addition to the amount of the judgment, assuming, of course, that there is money in the till.

PENSIONS AND RETIREMENT BENEFITS

You can get at money in individual or self-employment retirement plans held in any bank or savings institution. You go after this money just as you do any other money kept in a bank. Of course, you need to know where the money is.

Private company retirement plans and state or local government retirement plans can't be touched until the money is paid over to the employee.

Federal government payroll checks and pension and retirement benefits may not be garnisheed to satisfy any debts, except those for alimony and child support.

Finding Phantom Assets— The Order Of Examination

As you now understand from reading the section above, collecting money isn't difficult if the judgment creditor has some and you know where it is. But what do you do when you know only that the money exists, but have no idea how to find it? For example, you may know that a person works, but not where, or that he or she has money in the bank, but not which bank. Wouldn't it be nice to be able simply to ask the judgment debtor a few questions he or she had to answer?

Well, you can, if you go through a procedure known as an "Order of Examination." Again, I refer here to California rules, but similar procedures exist in other states and you will wish to ask the Small Claims Court clerk for information. An "Order of Examination" allows you to require the presence of the judgment debtor in court* on a certain day so that you can ask questions.

*Ohio has a very helpful procedure for allowing the "judgment creditor" to ask questions by mail on a standard form available from the clerk. The "judgment debtor" will be held in contempt of court if he or she fails to answer the questions fully within a week.

To get the judgment debtor to show up in court, you must get a copy of a "Declaration and Order of Examination" form from the Small Claims Court clerk. Exhibit 23.5 shows a sample.

The clerk of the Small Claims Court will help you fill it out and get the judge to sign it. Then the form must be served personally on the judgment debtor and a "Proof of Service" returned to the court. (See Chapter 11, "Notifying the Court That Service Has Been Accomplished" ("Proof of Service")).

211-33

| Name, Address and Telephone No. of Attorney(s) | Space Below for Use of Court Clerk Only |

Peter Plaintiff
123 Broadway
Albany, CA.

848-7938

Attorney(s) for ...IN PRO PER...................

MUNICIPAL COURT OF CALIFORNIA, COUNTY OF ALAMEDA
BERKELEY-ALBANY JUDICIAL DISTRICT
2000 Center St., Berkeley, Calif. 94704

Peter Plaintiff

Plaintiff(s) vs.

Doris Defendant

Defendant(s)
(Abbreviated Title)

CASE NUMBER

(Fill in number)

DECLARATION AND
ORDER OF EXAMINATION

ORDER

To___Doris Defendant_____:
(Name and Capacity (judgment debtor/debtor of judgment debtor/garnishee))

You are ordered to appear personally in this court before a judge, or a referee appointed by him, on _____ at _____ .m., _____ , to answer
(Date)   (Time)   (Department No., if any)

concerning the property or indebtedness, credits or other personal property belonging to the defendant(s) as set forth in the declaration below.
Failure to appear may subject you to arrest and punishment for contempt of court.

Dated _____   _____
                                                Judge

DECLARATION

For the purpose of securing an order requiring _____
(Name and Capacity—judgment debtor/
_____ to appear and answer concerning his property
debtor of judgment debtor garnishee)

or indebtedness, credits or other personal property belonging to defendant(s), I declare that:
Check applicable boxes

☐ Judgment was entered in this action on _____ against the debtor and has not
(Date)

been satisfied. Debtor's residence or place of business is _____ County, or within 150 miles of the place of trial.

☐ Execution may properly be issued at this time upon the judgment.

☐ Debtor has been previously examined on _____ .
(Dates of examinations in chronological order)

☐ Affidavit in support of application for order under Section 717, Code of Civil Procedure, is filed herewith.

☐ Affidavit in support of application for order under Section 545, Code of Civil Procedure, is filed herewith. Garnishee's residence or place of business is in _____ County, or within 150 miles of the place of trial.

I declare under penalty of perjury that the foregoing is true and correct.

Executed on _____ , at _____ , California.
(Date)   (Place)

_____
(Signature of Declarant)

_____
(Type or print name of declarant)

DECLARATION AND ORDER OF EXAMINATION

C.C.P. Secs. 545, 545.1,
714, 715, 717, 717.1,
2015.5

Exhibit 23.5

THE ORDER OF EXAMINATION

At the "Order of Examination" hearing, you are entitled to have a court reporter present if you wish. This is expensive and probably is not necessary to collect a Small Claims Court judgment. If you wish a court reporter, you must arrange for the reporter yourself (see Yellow Pages) and pay for it. You may be able to recover this cost from the judgment debtor if the judge thinks that a court reporter's presence was necessary. (See "Recovering Collection Costs and Interest" beginning on page 210.)

On the day in question you (and the court reporter if you have arranged for one) will show up in court to meet the "judgment debtor." It the "judgment debtor" doesn't show up, the judge, on your request, will issue a bench warrant which can lead to the debtor's arrest. Assuming that the debtor does show up, what happens? You will go to the corner of the courtroom or to some free room in the courthouse and ask your questions. In theory, the judge can ask the questions for you, but since there are normally a number of examinations going on at the same time, the judge will leave it to you. You are entitled to straight answers, and if you don't think that you are getting them, tell the judge.

Important: There is one question that you don't want to overlook: "Do you have any money in your pocket?" If the debtor has money (it might be a few hundred dollars), you can ask the judge to order that it be turned over to you on the spot.

Exhibit 23.6 gives some sample questions that were originally prepared by Eileen Luboff and Constance Posner for their wonderfully thorough book, *How to Collect Your Child Support and Alimony,* 1977, Nolo Press. Not all will apply to you, so go through them carefully in advance of the hearing and ask only those that are relevant.

Note: After you have finished asking your questions, you may feel that not all your questions were answered candidly or you may wish to request the judge to order a turnover of the money the judgment debtor has with him or her, as suggested above. If so, return to the courtroom with the judgment debtor and make your request.

QUESTIONNAIRE FOR EXAMINATION OF JUDGMENT DEBTOR

Date of the Examination _____ 19__ Town _____

ESTABLISHING IDENTITY OF THE DEBTOR

Your full name and address
Your telephone numbers Home _____ Work _____
Date of Birth _____ 19__ Place Born _____ Town _____ State
Are you presently married? _____ If so, your wife's full name _____
What was her maiden name? _____

Do you have any children? _____
What are their names and ages? _____

Do they live with you? _____ If not, what is their address(es)? _____

Does your wife have any children from previous marriages? _____
How many? _____ What are their names and ages? _____
Do they live with you? _____

Who supports them? _____ How? _____
Which do you live in: apartment, condominium, townhouse or house? _____
Is your dwelling owned by you or your wife? _____

QUESTIONS TO BE ASKED IF DWELLING IS OWNED BY DEBTOR OR WIFE
Who is shown as the owner of the property on the title? _____
Is the title to the property in more than one name? _____
If so, who are all of the owners? _____
Give date the property was purchased _____ For how much money? _____
How much was the down payment? _____ How much are the payments? _____
How much is presently owed on the property? _____ Who is the
Mortgage Company? _____ What is the present market value
of the property? _____ Is there a second trust deed? _____
Against the property? _____ For how much? _____ What are the
payments? _____ Who do you pay them to? _____
How about any other kinds of liens? _____ What are they? _____
_____ How much are they for? _____
Who are the lien holders? _____

Who pays the actual mortgage payments on your house? _____
Are they paid by cash, check or money order? _____
How many rooms do you occupy? _____ Do you rent any out? _____
How much income from rents? _____

QUESTIONS TO BE ASKED IF DEBTOR RENTS
Do you have a lease agreement? _____ How much rent do you pay? _____
Who pays the rent? _____ Is it by check, cash or money order? _____
Is your rent paid up to date? _____
What is the landlord's name and address? _____

How long have you rented at this address? _____
What is your previous address? _____
Did you rent or own there? _____

QUESTIONS TO BE ASKED WHETHER DEBTOR OWNS OR RENTS HIS HOME
Do you or your wife own any property anywhere other than what we've already discussed? _____ If so, please state precisely where _____

On what date was the property purchased? _____
Who purchased it? _____ In whose name(s) is the property held? _____ What kind of property is it: recreation land? apartments? vacant land? farm land? commercial property? _____ Is there any sort of building on the land? _____ If so, what kind? _____
What was the purchase price? _____ Was it bought for cash or financed? _____ If financed, by whom? _____
Address _____
How much was paid as down payment? _____ What are the terms on the balance owing? _____ How much is the property worth today? _____

QUESTIONS REGARDING EMPLOYMENT
Are you presently employed? _____ By whom? _____
What is their address? _____
What is your social security number? _____
What is your job classification? _____

Exhibit 23.6

What is your gross monthly pay? _____ How long have you been in their employ? _____

What is the union and local? _____ Are you a union member? _____

Do they have a credit union? _____ What is their name and address? _____

_____ Are you a member? _____

Do you have a savings account with them? _____ How much is in your account? _____ Do you have an outstanding loan with them? _____ For how much and on what kind of a loan? _____

Do you receive commission or incentives or bonuses from your employer? _____ What are they for and how much and when do you get them? _____

_____

Are you in any type of full or part-time self employment? _____

If so, what kind and where? _____

What is the name of your business? _____

How long have you been in it? _____ Did you start the business or purchase an existing business from someone? _____

If purchased, for how much? _____ How long ago was it started or acquired? _____ Will you agree to give me as the examiner a letter to the Bureau of Old Age and Survivors Insurance requesting that they send a transcript of your account over the last five years, so that I can verify the statements you have made today? _____

If the debtor is in business for himself, make the additional request as outlined.

Question: Will you agree to provide a financial statement, prepared by a Certified Public Accountant, of your business to me as the Judgment Creditor within 30 days of this examination? _____

What is your accountant's name? _____

Who prepares your business and personal income tax returns? _____

Do you have a contract for employment? _____ Who is your contract with? _____ What is your salary, commissions or other compensation under that contract? _____ Is your employer presently in arrears on payments? _____ For how much? _____

Do you have any part-time employment, either for yourself or someone else? _____ How much are you paid for your services? _____ What do you do? _____ How many hours do you work per week, month, year in your full-time or part-time employment? _____

When did you write your last check on a bank account? _____

Do you have access to any business account for which you are an authorized signature? _____ Where and in what name? _____

Where is each account kept? Bank name and branch? _____

What is the account number? _____

Do you have your checkbook with you right now? _____ What is your account #? _____ How much cash do you have on your person right now? _____

Do you or your wife have any savings bonds? _____ What kind and for how much? _____

When were they purchased? _____

PROPERTY QUESTIONS

VEHICLES

Have you an automobile driver's license? _____ A chauffeur's license? _____

Does your wife have a license? _____

If either of you is licensed, state what vehicles you drive _____

Do you own any recreational vehicles, boats or airplanes? _____

If so, how much did they cost, when did you buy them _____

Do you owe any money on them? _____ How much? _____

To whom do you owe the money? _____

Their address _____

REAL PROPERTY

Do you or your wife separately or in joint tenancy own any real estate in California? _____ If so, please give all the details as to location, what kind of property, price and value, unless we have already covered this area fully when we discussed your dwelling _____

Do you or your wife own any stocks, bonds or other securities of any description, either in your possession or held by someone else for you? _____ If so, what are they, how much and who holds them? _____

Do you or your wife own any mortgages on real or personal property? _____ If so, how much and where? _____

MISCELLANEOUS QUESTIONS

Are your wife (husband) or your children employed or in business for themselves? _____ What is the name and nature of the business?

Where is it located? _____ What income do they receive from their employment?

If you are not the sole support of your family, state the amount of money contributed by each family member toward the family income _____

Do you, your wife or any other members of your family own stock or serve as directors or officers of any business which employs you or your wife? _____ If so, please explain in detail _____

Please state your employment or businesses you have conducted in the last five years. Give your position in the firm, how long, their name and address and the amount earned on each job or from each business (if you were self-employed) _____

Are you now an officer, director or stockholder of any corporation? _____ If so, give the details _____

Please answer yes or no to the following questions and then we will go back for additional information:

Do you or your wife have a checking account? _____ Is it joint? _____

Do you or your wife have a savings account? _____ Is it joint? _____

Do you or your wife have a commercial savings account? _____

A Christmas Club Savings Plan? _____ A safe deposit box? _____

Now go back to any question that he (she) answered "yes" to and continue with the following questions relating to that type of account.

When did you make your last deposit? _____ How much was it for? _____ How often do you make deposits? _____

How often does your wife make deposits? _____ When is the last time you made a withdrawal from that account? _____ What are the present balances in any type of bank account which you or your wife now maintain? When and where did you last open, have or close a bank account?

Do you or your wife own any judgments?

Do you or your wife own a watch, diamonds or other jewelry or antiques of any character which are valued over $50?

Do you or your wife own a stamp collection? _____ A coin collection? _____ What is the value of either?

Do you or your wife own any other property (personal) not discussed before that has a value over $50?

Do you or your wife have any property in pawn right now? _____ How much did you borrow against it? _____ When are you supposed to redeem it?

Have you or your wife any interest in the estate of any deceased person? _____ Whose estate? _____ Where is the estate located?

Have you or your wife ever inherited any money or property? _____ If so, give the full details.

Are you the beneficiary in any will?

In the past year have you received any payments of money other than as already described? _____ If so, state when, the amounts and all details, including what was done with the money _____

Have you ever been injured in an accident? _____ Did you sue the person or persons responsible? _____ When did this occur? _____

Did you receive a settlement? _____ Is there a suit pending? _____ Name of suit _____ Where?

Have you sold or transferred any property out of your name in the last five years? _____ What and when?

Did you get an income tax refund from the federal or state government last year? _____ How much? _____ Do you anticipate one this year?

Have you filed a copyright, trade name certificate or partnership certificate in the last five years? _____ If so, please detail the transaction

Has any license, permit or appointment been issued or granted to you by either the county, city, state or federal government or an agency or department thereof? _____ If so, give the details

Are you acting as the guardian, trustee or in any capacity under any will, agreement or court appointment? _____ If so, explain _____

Exhibit 23.6 (cont.)

Recovering Collection Costs and Interest

Costs incurred prior to recovering a judgment should be included in the judgment total. This is discussed in Chapter 15, "Don't Forget to Ask for Your Costs."

Here I am concerned with costs incurred after judgment. These are the costs that result when the judgment debtor doesn't pay voluntarily and you have had to levy on his or her assets. This can be expensive and you will want to make the judgment debtor pay, if possible. Many costs of collecting a judgment are recoverable; some are not. Generally speaking, you can recover your direct costs of collecting which include such things as sheriff fees, fees to get papers (e.g., "Writ of Execution", "Abstract of Judgment") issued, and recording fees. In most states you can also recover interest on the judgment. Indirect costs such as babysitting costs, time off from work, postage, gasoline, etc., can't be recovered. There are two principal ways to collect your costs.

WRIT OF EXECUTION

In most areas the costs for having the sheriff or marshal levy on wages, bank accounts, automobiles, business assets, etc. can simply be added to the total to be collected. Normally, this includes the fee for issuing the "Writ of Execution." These fees can really add up, especially when a law-enforcement officer has to spend time at a business or sell an automobile. Be sure you get a copy of your local rules—they vary so much from state to state that I can give you only a general outline here. But be warned! If you don't ask for your costs, it is extremely likely that you won't recover them.

MEMORANDUM OF CREDITS, ACCRUED INTEREST, AND COSTS AFTER JUDGMENT

Other costs such as money expended for an "Abstract of Judgment," County Recorder fees, and costs for unsuccessful levies on wages, bank accounts, businesses, or motor vehicles can be recovered only after court approval in most states. To get this, you must file some additional papers to inform the court of the amounts you have expended. The name of this form will vary in the different states, but it is often called something like "Memorandum of Costs, Accrued Interest, and Costs after Judgment" (Exhibit 23.7). The Small Claims

9-15

211 21

Name, Address and Telephone No. of Attorney(s)

Peter Plaintiff
123 Broadway
Albany, CA

848-7938

Attorney(s) for IN PRO PER

Space Below for Use of Court Clerk Only

MUNICIPAL COURT OF CALIFORNIA, COUNTY OF ALAMEDA

BERKELEY-ALBANY JUDICIAL DISTRICT

Peter Plaintiff

Plaintiff(s) vs

Doris Defendant

Defendant(s)

(Abbreviated Title)

CASE NUMBER
(Fill in number)

MEMORANDUM OF CREDITS, ACCRUED INTEREST AND COSTS AFTER JUDGMENT

MEMORANDUM OF CREDITS

CREDIT for payments and partial satisfaction of judgment, including direct payments and executions partially satisfied: $ ___ (if none, state none)

INTEREST ACCRUED AFTER JUDGMENT

INTEREST ACCRUED AFTER JUDGMENT at 7% from date of entry of judgment on balance due after dates of payments or credits acknowledged above: $ ___

MEMORANDUM OF COSTS AFTER JUDGMENT

1 Costs after judgment claimed on memorandum filed heretofore . . . . $ ___
2 Clerk's fees: . . . . $ ___
3 ___ $ ___
4 Sheriff's, marshal's or constable's fees: . . . . $ ___
5 ___ $ ___
6 Serving supplementary proceedings: . . . . $ ___
7 ___ $ ___
8 Notary fees: . . . . $ ___
9 ___ $ ___
10 ___ $ ___
TOTAL $ ___

I am the ___ of the party(s) who claim(s) these costs.
To the best of my knowledge and belief the foregoing items of cost are correct and have been necessarily incurred in this action.
I declare under penalty of perjury that the foregoing is true and correct.

Executed on ___ at ___, California.
(Place)

(Signature of Declarant)

(Type or Print Name of Declarant)

NOTE: A notice of motion to tax costs shall specify the items of the cost bill to which objection is made.
(See reverse side for Declaration of Service and Acknowledgment of Service)

MEMORANDUM OF CREDITS, ACCRUED INTEREST AND COSTS AFTER JUDGMENT   C.C.P. Secs. 682.2, 1033.7, 2015.5

Exhibit 23.7

Court clerk will help you prepare this form. File one copy with the clerk and have a friend mail another copy to the judgment debtor. Then have your friend fill out a "Proof of Service" (see Chapter 11, "Notifying the Court That Service Has Been Accomplished ("Proof of Service")") to be filed with the clerk.

Where Do We Go from 24 Here?

It's easy to criticize the existing legal system—almost everyone knows that it's on the rocks. The $350-a-day experts with their degrees, titles, and well-funded consulting companies have studied the problem to death with no positive results. And this is hardly surprising, since most of the experts involved in the studies and in the resulting decisions are lawyers who, at bottom, are unable to understand a problem of which they are so thoroughly a part.*

But instead of my lecturing you about all the things that are wrong at the local courthouse, let's sit down at the kitchen table with a pot of tea and a bowl of raspberries and see if we can't design a better system. After all, this republic was founded by ordinary people taking things into their own hands—they had to because most of the governor, judge and lawyer-types were quite comfortable in England, thank you. And don't forget that we have already agreed that the present legal structure doesn't work, so we obviously have nothing to lose by making our own suggestions. Hey, leave a few raspberries for me, and why don't you jot down a few of your own ideas as we go along, so that this becomes a two-way communication.

---

*Not everyone believes that a rotten court system is a bad thing. David Hapgood, in his interesting book, The Average Man Fights Back, Doubleday 1977, reports the following statement by the Chinese Emperor K'and Hsi: ". . . lawsuits would tend to increase to a frightening extent if people were not afraid of the tribunals and if they felt confident of always finding in them ready and perfect justice. . . . I desire therefore that those who have recourse to the tribunals should be treated without pity and in such a manner that they shall be disgusted with law and tremble to appear before a magistrate."

Before we get to specific suggestions for change, let's take a brief look around to see where we are starting from. As a society, we obviously have a fixation with trying to solve problems by suing one another. Nowhere in the world do people come close to being as litigious as we do. The result of this love of lawsuits, or perhaps its cause—it's one of those chicken and egg problems—is the fact that, whenever we get into any sort of spat with anyone, or even think that we might get into one in the future, we run to a lawyer.* It's become so bad that people who suffer an injury have been known to call their lawyer before their doctor. But there is a paradox here. At the same time that we tolerate vast numbers of lawyers eating at the top end of our societal trough and are more and more likely to use them, public opinion polls tell us that our respect for lawyers has fallen so that we rate their trustworthiness below that of used-car salespeople, undertakers, and loan sharks. It's as if the less we respect lawyers, the more we use them. Perhaps we're afraid that if we don't sue first, someone will get the jump on us. If you eat one more of those raspberries, I'll see you in court.

Have you ever thought about how people solved their disputes in other ages? Let's pretend for a moment that we are members of a society of deer hunters in an age when such things were still possible.† One fine fall morning we each set out, bow in hand, you to the east and I to the west. Before long, you hit a high cliff and turn north. My way is blocked by a swift river, and I too turn north. Without our realizing it, our paths converge. Suddenly, a great stag jumps from the underbrush and we both pull back our bows and let fly. Our arrows pierce the deer's heart from opposite sides, seemingly at the same instant.

For a moment we stand frozen, each surprised by the presence of the other. Then we realize what has happened and that we have a problem. To whom does the deer belong? We carry the deer back to the village, each unwilling to surrender it to the other. After the deer is gutted and hung, we go to speak to the chief of our group, who convenes a council of elders to meet late in the afternoon. We both have our say as to what happened. The deer carcass is examined. Anyone

---

*There are over half a million lawyers in the United States. New York City alone has more than 40,000. The New York Times reported that by 1977 many hot-shot lawyers were charging $25 for each six minutes of their time. Today that amount is probably a bargain for the real crème de la crème. In San Francisco, one out of every three hundred people is a lawyer.
†Anthropologists will, I hope, accept this little fable as just that.

else who has knowledge of our dispute is invited to speak. Tribal customs (laws) are consulted, our credibility is weighed, and a decision is made—in time for dinner.

Now, let's ask ourselves what would happen today if you and I simultaneously shot a deer (instead of each other) on the first day of hunting season and were unable to agree to whom it belonged. Assuming we didn't fight it out on the spot but wanted the dispute resolved by "proper" legal procedures, lawyers would have to be consulted, court papers filed and responded to, a court appearance scheduled, words spoken in legalese, and a formal court decision written and issued. All of this for a deer that would have long since rotted away unless it had been put in cold storage. If the deer had been frozen, the storage costs would have to be added to court costs and attorney fees, which all together would surely add up to a lot more than the value of the deer. Oh well, next time we had better go hunting at McDonald's where everything is delivered safely wrapped in plastic.

Seriously, what were the differences between the ways that the two societies resolved the problem of who owned the deer? The so-called primitive one did a better job, but why? Obviously because its solution was in proportion to the problem, while today we make the solution process so cumbersome and expensive that it dwarfs most disputes. The hunting society handled the disagreement quickly, cheaply, and most importantly, through a process that allowed the disputing parties to participate in and understand what was going on.* Simple, you say. Why then can't our dispute resolution procedure achieve even one of these goals? In large measure, because lawyers have vested financial and psychic interests in the present cumbersome way of doing things and have neither the motivation nor the perspective to make changes.

But isn't my view a bit radical? Isn't there something uniquely valuable about the great sweep of the common law down through the ages? Doesn't the majestic black-robed judge sitting on his throne mumbling esoteric nonsense somehow guarantee that God is in heaven, the republic safe, and that "justice will be done"? Not necessarily. History is arbitrary—our dispute resolution mechanisms could have developed in a number of ways. If our present system worked well, imposing it on the future would make sense. As, in fact, it hardly

---

In a criminal case (if one hunter had attacked and injured the other) you would also want to think about restitution (making whole) to the injured person, and perhaps to his or her dependents.

works at all, continuing it is silly. Those who get quite misty-eyed re-
counting the history, traditions and time-tested forms behind our
present ways of doing things are almost always people that benefit
by their continuance. Consider, too, that in North America we have
no pure legal tradition, having borrowed large hunks of our jurispru-
dence from England, Spain, France, Holland, and Germany, as well
as various native American cultures.

OK, granted that there have been legal systems that worked better than ours, and granted that at least some change is overdue, what
should we do? One significant reform would be to expand Small
Claims Court. Like the system followed by the deer hunters, but unlike the vast majority of our legal system, Small Claims Court is simple, fast, cheap, and allows for the direct participation of the disputing parties. Never mind that up to now Small Claims Court has been
tolerated as a way to keep lawyers' offices clear of penny-ante people with penny-ante disputes. It's there, it works, and we can expand
it to play a meaningful role in our lives.

As you know by now, Small Claims Court as it is presently set up
has several disadvantages. First, the amount for which suit can be
brought is ridiculously low. Second, the court only has the power to
make judgments that can be satisfied by the payment of money damages.* Third, many kinds of cases, such as divorces, adoptions, etc.,
aren't permitted. Fourth, many states still allow lawyers to represent
people in Small Claims Court, even though a recent study by the National Center for State Courts indicates that people win just as often
without lawyers. Why not start our effort to improve things by doing
away with these disadvantages? Let's raise the maximum amount for
which suit can be brought to $10,000.† I would like to suggest
$20,000, but perhaps we should take one step at a time to limit at-
torney opposition. An increase to $10,000 would be a significant re-
form that would allow tens of thousands of disputes to be removed
from our formal legal system. One logical reason to pick $10,000 is
that people can't afford lawyers to handle disputes for amounts

---

*A few states are beginning to allow judges to make some decisions that
don't involve the payment of money. This is a step in the right direction.
†While most states limit Small Claims jurisdiction to $750 (California) or
$1,000 (New York), there are exceptions. For example, the United States Tax
Court has a very successful Small Claims procedure which allows claims up
to $5,000 and a few states are beginning to increase limits substantially.

below this.* To illustrate, let's take a situation in which Randy the carpenter agrees to do $20,000 worth of rehabilitation to Al's home. When the work is completed, an argument develops about whether the work was done properly according to the agreement. Al pays Randy $15,000, leaving $5,000 in dispute. Randy goes to his lawyer, and Al to his. Each has several preliminary conferences after which the lawyers exchange several letters and telephone calls. Eventually, a lawsuit is filed and answered, a court date is obtained many months in the future and then changed several times, and finally, a two-hour trial is held. Randy's lawyer bills him $1,250 (25 hours + $50 per hour) and Al's charges $960 (24 hours + $40 per hour), for a total fee of $2,210. The dispute takes eleven months to be decided. In the end, Randy is awarded $3,500 of the $5,000.

This is a typical case with a typical solution. Between them, the lawyers collected almost half of the amount in dispute and took most of a year to arrive at a solution that very likely left both Randy and Al frustrated. Don't you think that Randy and Al would have preferred presenting their case in Small Claims Court in which it would have been heard and decided in a month? Of course, either of them could have done worse arguing the case himself, but remember, when the legal fees are taken into consideration, the loser would have had to do a lot worse before he was out of pocket any money. Randy recovered $3,500 with a lawyer, but after subtracting the $1,250 lawyer fee, his net gain was only $2,250. Al ended up paying $4,460 ($3,500 for the judgment and $960 for his attorney). Thus if a Small Claims Court judge had awarded Randy any amount from $2,251 to $4,459, both men would have done better than they did with lawyers. Of course, if this sort of case were permitted in Small Claims Court, there would be two big losers. Can it be a coincidence that these losers (through their control of every state legislature) make sure that Small Claims Court maximums are kept as low as possible and that lawyers must be hired to handle most disputes?

*I believe that there are persuasive reasons for limiting the role of lawyers in addition to the fact that they cost too much. Such a limitation would require fundamental changes in our adversary system and is the subject for a broader book. For a good history of how our adversary system evolved from barbaric practices such as trial by battle, how it all too often serves to obscure rather than expose the truth, and how it protects the interests of the already strong and powerful (those who can afford a good mouthpiece) at the expense of everyone else, see Strick, 1977, Injustice for All, Putnam, $8.95.

The second great barrier to bringing cases in Small Claims Court is the fact that, with minor exceptions, the court is limited to making money judgments.* Think back for a moment to our problems with the twice-shot deer. How does the award of money make sense in this situation? In Small Claims Courts, the hunter who didn't end up with the carcass would have had to sue the other for the fair market value of the deer. What nonsense—if we are going to have a dispute resolution procedure, why not permit a broad range of solutions, such as the deer being cut in half, or the deer going to one hunter and six ducks going to the other in compensation, or maybe even the deer going to the person who needed it most. Using an example more common at the end of the 20th century, why not allow a Small Claims Court judge to order that an apartment be cleaned, a garage repainted, or a car properly fixed, instead of simply telling one person to pay X dollars to the other. One advantage of this sort of flexibility is that more judgments would be meaningful. Under our present system, tens of thousands of judgments can't be collected because the loser has no obvious source of income. We need to get away from the notion that people who are broke have neither rights nor responsibilities. All people need both.

Lawyers and judges often contend that it would be impossible to enforce judgments granted under a more flexible approach. Perhaps some would be hard to keep track of. Certainly it might require some experimentation to find out what types of judgments will work and which will not; however, since it is often impossible to collect a judgment under the present system, it can't hurt to try some alternatives.

The third big change that I propose, and the one that would truly make over our court system, involves expanding the types of cases that can be heard in Small Claims Court. Why not be brave and take the 20 most common legal problems and adopt simplified procedures enabling all of them to be handled by the people themselves without lawyers? Why not open up our courthouses to the average person who, after all, pays the bills?

To accomplish this democratization of our dispute resolution procedures, I suggest dividing Small Claims Court into several separate divisions, each one responsible for a broad area of common concern. For example, there would be a landlord–tenant and a do-

*Some states allow judgments to include several types of equitable relief, such as recission, restitution, and specific performance, but this sort of relief is limited in scope and rarely used.

mestic relations division.* Each division would have the authority to consider a broad range of problems and solutions falling within its area of concern. Today, if you have a claim against your landlord (or your landlord has one against you) for money damages, you can use Small Claims Court only if the claim is under the dollar limit. If you want to have a roof fixed, to have a tenant evicted, or to protect your privacy, etc., most Small Claims Courts can't help you. The Canadian province of British Columbia and a few West Coast cities have already put all landlord–tenant disputes in what amounts to a Small Claims Court format, easily and cheaply available to both landlord and tenant. Why can't this be done everywhere?

A domestic relations Small Claims Court could include simplified procedures to help people handle their own uncontested divorces, adoptions, name changes, guardianships, etc., safely and cheaply. And why not? Even with considerable hostility from lawyers and court personnel, over 30 percent of the divorces in California are already handled without a lawyer. When I suggest that people should be encouraged to handle their own domestic problems in a forum of the Small Claims type, I'm not advocating that sensible safeguards be dropped. For example, if a divorce involves children, we want to have someone trained in the field to examine carefully the parents' plans for custody, visitation, and support to see that they are reasonable.

Without going into detail, I suggest that if we took lawyers out of our domestic relations courts we would not only save millions of dollars and hours, but more importantly, we would lighten the heavy burden of hostility and anxiety that the parties must now bear. Our present system, in which parents and children become clients to a "hired gun" (the lawyer), is a bad one. By definition, the client role is weak and the gun fighter role strong. This imbalance commonly results in lawyers making critical decisions affecting the clients' lives, sometimes obviously, sometimes subtly. All too often these decisions benefit the lawyer and his or her bank balance to the detriment of both the client's psyche and pocketbook. The lawyer, after all, is paid more to fight, or at least to pretend to fight, than to compromise. I have seen dozens of situations in which lawyers have played on people's worst instincts (paranoia, greed, ego, one-upmanship) to fan

---

There is nothing new about the idea of dividing a court by subject matter. This is already done in our formal trial courts and works well.

nasty, little disagreements into flaming battles. Perhaps mercifully, the battles normally last only as long as the lawyers' bills are paid.*

I could list a number of other areas of law that could be converted to a Small Claims approach (auto accidents, simple probates, perhaps even some criminal cases), but I am sure you get the point. We must take control of the decision-making processes that affect our lives. We must make ourselves welcome in our own courts and legislatures. We must stop looking at ourselves as clients and start taking responsibility for our own legal decisions.

Let's assume now that no matter what the obstacles, we are going to expand drastically the role of Small Claims Court. In the process of doing so, we will need to make a number of changes in the way the court now operates. It will be a good opportunity to throw out a number of existing procedures that owe more to history than to common sense. Here are a few ideas:

- Before people present their dispute for resolution as part of a court proceeding, they should be encouraged to talk it over among themselves. This seems to be basic common sense, but a face-to-face meeting to find out if a compromise is possible isn't part of the present system. A meeting with someone who has training as a mediator could occur at the courthouse, or perhaps at a less intimidating location in the community, as a regular part of every case.
- Let's make our court one of truly easy access. This means holding weekend and evening sessions. This is being done now experimentally in a few areas, but such sessions should be as routinely available everywhere else as they are in New York City. When court is held at 9 A.M. on weekdays, it often costs more than the case is worth in lost job time for all the principals and witnesses to show up. And who wants to wait around half a day for a case to be heard? Scheduling should be done so that people are asked to come at 9:00, 10:00, 11:00, and so on—not all at once, as is now common.
- Let's get the judge out of the black robe and off of the throne. There is a part of all of us that loves the drama involved in seeing our magistrate sitting on high like the king of England, but I am convinced by my own brief experience as a "pro tem" judge that

---

*In an interesting article entitled "Valuable Deficiencies, A Service Economy Needs People in Need," in the Fall 1977 Co-Evolution Quarterly, John McKnight points out that "The Latin root of the word 'client' is a verb which translates 'to hear,' 'to obey.' "

this is counterproductive. We would have a lot less confrontation and a lot more willingness to compromise if we got rid of some of the drama.

• While we're making changes let's make a big one—let's throw out the adversary system.* It contributes a great deal to posturing and obfuscation and little to arriving at a dispute resolution process that everyone can live with. We must move toward systems of mediation and arbitration in which, instead of a traditional judge, we have someone whose role is to facilitate the parties arriving at their own solution—deciding it for them only if they arrive at a hopeless impasse. Big business, big labor, and increasingly even lawyers are coming to realize that arbitration and mediation are good ways to solve problems.† What I have in mind is something like this: All the parties to the dispute sit down at a table with the Small Claims Court mediator. (Let's drop the word "judge.") This person would be trained for the job, but would not normally be a lawyer. The mediator helps the parties search for areas of agreement and possible compromise and then helps them define any areas still in dispute. If no agreement is possible, the dispute is referred to another person for decision.‡

I don't mean to suggest that the changes I propose in this short chapter are the only ones necessary. If we are going to put the ma-

*Roscoe Pound, distinguished legal scholar, said it better than I can, "The doctrine of contentious procedure . . . is peculiar to Anglo-American law . . . (it) disfigures our judicial administration at every point . . . (it) gives to the whole community a false notion of the purpose and end of law . . . Thus, the courts . . . are made agents or abettors of lawlessness." This quote is reported by Anne Strick in Injustice For All.

†California has adopted a procedure that even allows cases that have been filed in court to be diverted to an arbitration procedure.

‡As noted in Chapter 13, reform plans not too dissimilar to some suggested here are being tried in several areas. Unfortunately, the people who are doing the mediation and arbitration are all lawyers, raising the dangerous possibility that legislatures will pretend to expand the Small Claims concept while, in fact, turning it into another court controlled by and for lawyers. State Bar Associations and other lawyer groups have supported so-called reforms to add lawyer-advisors to Small Claims Court under a theory of "consumer protection," even though studies tend to show that Small Claims Court is a great equalizer and that people who have not finished eleventh grade do just as well as those who have years of higher education. (Small Claims Courts, A National Examination) Ruhnka et al., 1979 National Center for State Courts.)

jority of our routine legal work in Small Claims, it will require turning our dispute resolution process on its head. Legal information must be stored and decoded so that it is available to the average person. Clerk's offices and the other support systems surrounding our courts must be expanded and geared to serve the nonlawyer. Legal forms must be translated from "legalese" into English.

Let's illustrate how things might change by looking at a case I recently saw argued in a Small Claims Court. One party to the dispute (let's call her Sally) arranged fishing charters for business and club groups. The other (let's call him Ben) owned several fishing boats. Sally often hired Ben's boats for her charters. Their relationship was of long standing and had been profitable to both. However, as the fishing charter business grew, both Sally and Ben began to enlarge their operations. Sally got a boat or two of her own and Ben began getting into the charter booking business. Eventually they stepped on one another's toes and their friendly relationship was replaced by tension and arguments. One day a blowup occurred over some inconsequential detail, phones were slammed down, and Sally and Ben each swore never to do business with the other again.

Before the day of the final fight, Sally had organized two charters on Ben's boat. These were to have taken place a week after the phones were slammed down. For reasons unconnected with the argument, the charters were canceled by the clubs that had organized them. Ben had about a week's notice of cancellation. He also had $600 in deposits that Sally had paid him. He refused to refund the deposits. Sally sued him in Small Claims Court for $700 ($600 for the charter fee and $100 for general inconvenience).*

Testimony in court made it clear that charters were commonly canceled and were often replaced by others booked at the last minute. Ben and Sally had signed a "Standard Marine Charter Agreement" because it was required by the Coast Guard, although they had never in the past paid attention to its terms. They had always worked out sensible adjustments on a situation-by-situation basis, depending on whether substitute charters were available and whether the club or business canceling had paid money up front, etc.

When Ben and Sally first presented their arguments about the $700, it seemed that they were not too far apart as to what would be a fair compromise. Unfortunately, the adversary nature of the court system encouraged both to overstate their cases and to dredge up all

---

*As we learned earlier, Sally can't recover for inconvenience, so her maximum recovery would be $600.

sorts of irrelevant side issues. "What about the times you overloaded my boat?" Ben demanded. "How about those holidays when you price gouged me?" Sally replied. As the arguments went back and forth, each person got angrier and angrier and was less and less able to listen to the other.

The result was that after an hour of testimony the judge was left with a confused mishmash of custom, habit, maritime charter contracts, promises made or not made, past performance, etc. No decision at which the judge arrived was likely to be accepted as fair by both Ben and Sally. Indeed, unless the judge gave one or the other everything he or she requested, both of them would surely feel cheated. That is not to say that the hearing was all bad—some good things did occur. The dispute was presented quickly and cheaply, and each person got to have his or her say and blow off some steam. All of these things would have been impossible in our formal court system. However, if Small Claims Court could be changed along the lines suggested above, a better result might have been reached.

Suppose that instead of a formal courtroom approach Ben and Sally are first encouraged to sit down and talk the dispute out. If this fails, then the next step is to sit down somewhere outside the courtroom with a court employee who is trained as a mediator and whose purpose is to help Ben and Sally arrive at a fair compromise—a compromise that might provide a foundation for Ben and Sally to continue to work together in the future. Only if compromise is impossible would there be recourse to more formal proceedings.* I am convinced that Ben and Sally would have worked out a compromise at the first or second stage.

One final point. Today lawyers are still trying to plug the holes in the rotten dike of our present legal system. Tomorrow the dike will burst and many of our present ways of doing things will be washed into the history books. Small Claims Court will survive the deluge and will expand. The danger is that lawyers will try to control Small Claims Court so that their attitudes and prejudices dominate it as they have dominated every other mechanism our society has to resolve disputes. To allow this to happen is to destroy much of the value of expanding Small Claims Courts. And don't minimize the danger. As I have noted, under a so-called consumer-reform approach, lawyers

---

*If we put domestic cases into Small Claims Court (and even if we don't), it is essential that we work out a nonadversary way of handling them so that bitterness and bad feelings are kept to a minimum instead of being inflated as is now the case.

are already serving in the role of mediator and arbitrator in several California judicial districts. This is now being done on a voluntary basis, but you can expect an effort to have it institutionalized soon. It is all too likely that under the guise of trying to protect us from ourselves, an effort will also be made to have everyone see a lawyer as part of the Small Claims procedure. Remember, it is our lawyer-dominated state legislature that makes Small Claims Court rules and our lawyer-dominated judicial councils that carry them out.

Have I rambled for a long time? I guess I have. But now it's your turn. If you have any ideas and comments on how you would like to see Small Claims Court changed or expanded, let me know—care of Nolo Press, 950 Parker Street, Berkeley, California 94710.

Appendix: Small Claims Court Rules for the Fifty States, the District of Columbia, and Puerto Rico

ALABAMA Small Claims (District Court)

STATUTES: Code of Alabama (1978): Sec. 12-21-31 (amount), and Alabama Small Claims Rules, Rules A through N.

DOLLAR LIMIT: $500.

WHERE TO SUE: County or district where any defendant resides, or injury or property damage occurred. A corporation "resides" wherever it is doing business.

SERVICE OF PROCESS: Sheriff, constable, disinterested adult (with court's permission), or certified mail.

TRANSFER: No provision.

ATTORNEYS: Allowed.

APPEALS: Allowed by either party within 14 days to Circuit Court for new trial.

EVICTIONS: Yes.

NOTES: (1) The defendant must file a written answer within 14 days of service (7 days for eviction suits) or he or she will lose by default; a form for this purpose accompanies the summons. All that is needed is "a short and plain reply showing what defendant admits, what he denies, and why he denies it." It need not be served on the plaintiff.

(2) Equitable relief is available.

ALASKA Small Claims (District Court)

STATUTES: Alaska Statutes (1979): 22.15.040 (amount), and District Court Rules of Civil Procedure, Rules 8 through 22.

DOLLAR LIMIT: $2,000.

WHERE TO SUE: Court nearest to the defendant's residence, place of employment, or business, or court in district in which injury or property damage occurred.

SERVICE OF PROCESS: Peace officer or registered or certified mail. Certified or registered mail service is binding on defendant who refused to accept and sign for the letter. After such refusal, the clerk remails it regular first class, and service is assumed.

TRANSFER: Defendant (or plaintiff against whom a counterclaim has been filed) or judge may transfer to regular District Court procedure.

ATTORNEYS: Allowed; required for assignees (collection agencies).

APPEALS: Allowed by either party within 30 days (on claims over $50) to Superior Court based on law—not facts.

EVICTIONS: Yes.

NOTE: The defendant must file a written answer within 20 days of service, or he/she will lose by default; a form for this purpose accompanies the summons, as should a copy of the Alaska Small Claims Handbook.

ARIZONA Justice Court (No Small Claims system)

STATUTES: Arizona Revised Statutes (1979): Sec. 22-201 (amount) through 22-283.

DOLLAR LIMIT: $1,000.

WHERE TO SUE: Precinct where any defendant resides, act or omission occurred, or obligation was to be performed. Corporations "reside" in any precinct where they have an agent or representative, or conduct any business.

SERVICE OF PROCESS: Sheriff, constable, or disinterested adult (with court's permission).

TRANSFER: Allowed to Superior Court only if defendant counterclaims over dollar limit.

ATTORNEYS: Allowed; required for corporations.

APPEALS: Allowed by either party within ten days (on claims over $25) to Superior Court on law—not facts.

EVICTIONS: Yes.

NOTES: (1) The defendant must give an oral or written answer within 5 to 15 days (depending on where defendant served) to the justice after service or he or she will lose by default.

(2) A jury trial may be demanded by either party.

ARKANSAS Urban: Small Claims (Municipal Court or Boone County Circuit Court).

Rural: Justice of the Peace.

STATUTES: Arkansas Statutes Annotated (1979): Constitution Article 7, Sec. 40, 43 (amount). Regular Statutes, Secs. 22-758.1 through 22-758.16 (Small Claims), Sec. 26-301 through 26-1302 (Justice of the Peace).

DOLLAR LIMIT: $300; $500 in Boone County Circuit Court Small Claims division.

WHERE TO SUE: Small Claims—County in which any defendant resides, act or omission occurred, or obligation was to be performed. Justice of the Peace—Township in which any defendant resides; a nonresident of the county in which the JP is located cannot be a defendant in a county other than his or her own county of residence.

SERVICE OF PROCESS: Sheriff, constable (JP Court only), disinterested adult, or certified mail (Small Claims only); certified mail service in Small Claims is binding on a defendant who refuses to accept and sign for the letter. After such refusal, the clerk remails it first class, and service is assumed.

TRANSFER: In Small Claims, if the judge learns that any party is represented by an attorney, he or she must transfer it to regular Municipal Court procedure; no transfer provision in Justice of the Peace Courts.

ATTORNEYS: Small Claims: Not allowed; see above.
Justice of the Peace: Allowed.

APPEALS: Allowed by either party within 30 days to Circuit Court (except Boone County) for new trial.

NOTE: For purposes of where to sue, a corporation "resides" only where its principal place of business is located or where its chief officer (president) resides. Exceptions to this are banks and insurance companies, which may be sued wherever a bank branch or insurance agency is located.

CALIFORNIA Small Claims (Municipal or Justice Court)

STATUTES: West's Annotated California Codes (197): Code of Civil Procedure Sec. 116 through 118.7, Sec. 116.2 (amount).

DOLLAR LIMIT: $750 ($1500 in the Oakland-Piedmont, Compton, Fresno, West Orange County, East Los Angeles, and San Bernardino (Chino Division) jurisdictions).

WHERE TO SUE: Judicial district where any defendant resides (or resided when promise or obligation was made), act or omission occurred, or obligation was to be performed. A corporation "resides" where its principal place of business is located.

SERVICE OF PROCESS: Sheriff, disinterested adult, or certified or registered mail.

ATTORNEYS: Not allowed.

APPEALS: Allowed by defendant (or plaintiff who lost on a counterclaim) within 20 days to Superior Court for new trial.

EVICTIONS: Yes, if month-to-month tenancy and rent is less than $600/month.

NOTES: (1) Assignees (collection agencies) cannot sue in Small Claims Court.
(2) Equitable relief is available.

COLORADO Small Claims (County Court).

STATUTES: Colorado Revised Statutes (1977): Sec. 13-6-401 through 13-6-413, 13-6-403 (amount), and Colorado Rules of Civil Procedure, Rules 501 through 521.

DOLLAR LIMIT: $500.

WHERE TO SUE: County in which any defendant resides or plaintiff resides if the defendant served there, or where act or omission occurred. Actions on "consumer contracts" can only be brought in a county where any defendant resides (or resided when the obligation was entered into), or the obligation was entered into (where goods were purchased). Other actions on "goods sold and delivered" may be brought in county where the plaintiff resides.

SERVICE OF PROCESS: Sheriff, disinterested adult, or certified mail. Certified mail service is binding on a defendant who refuses to accept and sign for the letter, and no further notice is given.

TRANSFER: Allowed by defendant who wishes to be represented by an attorney or who has a counterclaim over the dollar limit (if he/she actually files it in Small Claims, any excess over the dollar limit is waived).

ATTORNEYS: Allowed only if attorney is plaintiff or defendant, or full-time employee or one of the following with respect to these types of plaintiffs or defendants: general partner (partnership), officer (corporation), active member (corporation or association). If an attorney does appear as permitted above, the other party may have one also.

APPEALS: Allowed by either party within 10 days to District Court on law—not fact.

NOTES: (1) Assignees (collection agencies) cannot sue in Small Claims Court. Actions to "disaffirm, avoid, or rescind a contract" are allowed.

(2) Equitable relief is available.

CONNECTICUT Small Claims (Superior Court)

STATUTES: Connecticut General Statutes Annotated (1979): Sec. 51-15.

DOLLAR LIMIT: $750.

WHERE TO SUE: County or judicial district where the defendant resides or does business, or where act or omission occurred.

SERVICE OF PROCESS: Peace officer or disinterested adult.

TRANSFER: Allowed by defendant to regular Superior Court procedure, upon showing that he/she has a valid defense or by counterclaiming over dollar limit.

ATTORNEYS: Allowed; required for corporations.

APPEALS: Not allowed.

EVICTIONS: No.

NOTE: A jury trial may be demanded by either party.

DELAWARE Justice of the Peace (No Small Claims system)

STATUTES: Delaware Code Annotated (1978): 10 Sec. 9301 (amount) through 10 Sec. 9570.

DOLLAR LIMIT: $1,500.

WHERE TO SUE: Anywhere in the state.

SERVICE OF PROCESS: Sheriff, constable, or certified mail.

TRANSFER: Defendant can transfer to Superior Court by demanding jury trial.

ATTORNEYS: Allowed.

APPEALS: Allowed by either party within 15 days (on claims over $5) to Superior Court for new trial.

EVICTIONS: Yes.

DISTRICT OF COLUMBIA Small Claims and Conciliation Branch (Superior Court)

STATUTES: District of Columbia Code (1979): Sec. 11-1301 through 11-1343, 11-1321 (amount), 16-3901 through 16-3910, and D.C. Code Encyclopedia Court. Rules—Rules for the Small Claims and Conciliation Branch.

DOLLAR LIMIT: $750.

WHERE TO SUE: This should be easy—there's only one such court in Washington, D.C. It's at 613 G St. N.W., telephone (202) 727-1760. You sue there, provided the defendant can be served within Washington, D.C.

SERVICE OF PROCESS: U.S. Marshal, disinterested adult (with court's permission), or certified or registered mail.

TRANSFER: Transferable to regular Superior Court procedure only if defendant counterclaims and the counterclaim mentions something about real property (land or housing).

ATTORNEYS: Allowed; required for corporations.

APPEALS: Allowed by either party within three days to D.C. (not U.S.) Court of Appeals on law—not fact.

EVICTIONS: No.

NOTES: (1) Certified or registered mail service is binding on defendant who refused to accept and sign for the letter. After such refusal, the clerk remails it regular first class, and service is assumed. A jury trial may be demanded by either party.

(2) Evening sessions every Wednesday at 6:30 P.M.

(3) Arbitration is available.

FLORIDA Summary Procedure (County Court)

STATUTES: Florida Rules of Court (1979): Rules of Summary Procedure, Rules 7.010 (amount) through 7.341.

DOLLAR LIMIT: $1,500.

WHERE TO SUE: County where the defendant resides, or act or omission occurred. A corporation "resides" wherever it "has or usually keeps an office for transaction of its customary business."

SERVICE OF PROCESS: Peace officer, disinterested adult (with court's permission), or registered mail.

TRANSFER: Allowed to regular County Court procedure only if defendant counterclaims over dollar limit.

ATTORNEYS: Allowed; court may require corporate collection agencies to have an attorney.

APPEALS: Allowed by either party within 30 days to Circuit Court on law—not fact.

EVICTIONS: Yes.
NOTES: (1) A jury trial may be demanded by either party.
         (2) The summons is designed to notify a defendant of his or her right to insist that the plaintiff sue in the right place, and informs how to object if the plaintiff has not done so.

GEORGIA

NOTE: Georgia has a strange patchwork quilt of county-run Small Claims Courts in some counties, with procedure varying from county to county, and Justice of the Peace courts in other counties. Since the Small Claims rules are different for each county, only Fulton County (Atlanta) Small Claims Court is represented here. Justice of the Peace rules are uniform statewide.

STATUTES: Code of Georgia (1978): Title 24, Part IV, Editorial Note (Small Claims), and 24-1001 (amount) through 24-1305 (Justice of the Peace).

JUSTICE OF THE PEACE COURTS

DOLLAR LIMIT: $200.
WHERE TO SUE: On bills and notes—militia district in which any defendant resides, but a nonresident of the county cannot be sued except in his/her own county.
SERVICE OF PROCESS: Constable.
TRANSFER: Allowed upon defendant's counterclaim over the dollar limit.
ATTORNEYS: Allowed.
APPEALS: Allowed by either party within 30 days (on claims over $50) to Superior Court for a new trial. Also, a new trial may be had in a JP case originally heard without a jury by appealing to the JP and demanding a jury trial.
EVICTIONS: Yes.

SMALL CLAIMS COURT (State Court—Fulton County)

DOLLAR LIMIT: $300.
WHERE TO SUE: County (Fulton County) in which the defendant resides.
SERVICE OF PROCESS: Marshal or disinterested adult (with court's permission).
TRANSFER: Allowed to regular State Court procedure upon defendant's counterclaim over the dollar limit or demand for a jury trial.
ATTORNEYS: Not allowed.
APPEALS: Allowed by either party within 30 days to Court of Appeals on law—not facts.
EVICTIONS: Yes.
NOTES: (1) A defendant in Fulton County Small Claims Court must file a written answer or "appearance card" within the time noted on the summons or he/she will lose by default.
         (2) A corporation "resides" wherever it "has an office and transacts business in that county."
         (3) Justices of the peace cannot try personal injury cases.

HAWAII Small Claims (District Court)

STATUTES: Hawaii Revised Statutes (1978): 633-27 (amount) through 633-26.
DOLLAR LIMIT: $300; no limit in landlord–tenant residential deposit cases.
WHERE TO SUE: Judicial district in which the defendant or a majority of defendants reside, or act or omission occurred.
SERVICE OF PROCESS: Sheriff, County Chief of Police, or certified or registered mail.
TRANSFER: Either party may transfer the case to Circuit Court by demanding a jury trial. Otherwise, a counterclaim over the dollar limit will not cause a transfer.
ATTORNEYS: Allowed (but in landlord–tenant residential deposit cases, attorneys are *not* allowed); also, with court permission, a nonattorney may represent another if he/she does not charge any fee.
APPEALS: Not allowed.
EVICTIONS: No.

IDAHO Small Claims (Magistrate Division of District Court)

STATUTES: Idaho Code (1979): Sec. 1-2301 (amount) through 1-2315.
DOLLAR LIMIT: $1,000.
WHERE TO SUE: County where the defendant resides. A corporation "resides" in the county where its principal place of business is located.
SERVICE OF PROCESS: Sheriff, disinterested adult, or certified or registered mail.
TRANSFER: No provision.
ATTORNEYS: Not allowed.
APPEALS: Allowed by either party within 30 days to District Court for new trial.
EVICTIONS: No.
NOTE: Assignees (collection agencies) cannot sue in Small Claims Court.

ILLINOIS Small Claims (Circuit Court), Cook County "Pro Se" branch

STATUTES: Smith-Hurd Illinois Annotated Statutes (1979): 110A Sec. 281 (amount) through 110A Sec. 288.
DOLLAR LIMIT: Small Claims $1,000, Cook County "Pro Se" $500.
WHERE TO SUE: County in which any defendant resides, corporation conducts business, partner of partnership resides or has office, or act or omission occurred.
SERVICE OF PROCESS: Sheriff, disinterested adult (with court's permission), or certified mail (for service within the county only).
TRANSFER: No provision.
ATTORNEYS: Small Claims: Allowed, required for corporations. Cook County "Pro Se": Not allowed.

APPEALS: Allowed by either party within 30 days to Appellate Court on law—not facts.

EVICTIONS: No.

NOTE: A jury trial may be demanded by defendant in Cook County "Pro-Se" branch, and by either party elsewhere.

INDIANA Small Claims (Circuit, County, or Superior Court)

STATUTES: Burns' Indiana Statutes Annotated (1979): Sec. 33-10.5-3-3 (amount), 33-10.5-7-1 (amount) through 33-10.5-7-10, 33-11.6-1-3, 33-11.6-4-1 through 33-11.6-4-15, 33-11.6-4-2 (amount), 33-11.6-4-3 (amount), and Indiana Rules for Small Claims, Rules 1 through 14.

DOLLAR LIMIT: $1,500.

WHERE TO SUE: County in which any defendant resides or is employed, act or omission occurred, or obligation was incurred or was to be performed by defendant.

SERVICE OF PROCESS: Certified or registered mail first; if that fails, then by sheriff or police officer.

TRANSFER: Defendant may transfer to regular civil court only by demanding a jury trial.

ATTORNEYS: Allowed.

APPEALS: Allowed by either party to Court of Appeals on law—not fact. In Marion County, appeal is by new trial in Circuit or Superior Court.

EVICTIONS: Yes, if rent is less than $500/month. (No such rent limitation in Marion County.)

IOWA Small Claims (District Court)

STATUTES: Iowa Code Annotated (1979): Sec. 631.1 (amount) through 631.16.

DOLLAR LIMIT: $1,000.

WHERE TO SUE: County in which any defendant resides, act or omission occurred, or obligation was to be performed.

SERVICE OF PROCESS: Peace officer, disinterested adult, or certified mail (not allowed in eviction suits).

TRANSFER: Even if the defendant counterclaims over the dollar limit, transfer is still at judge's discretion. But defendant can transfer to regular formal court by demanding jury trial.

ATTORNEYS: Allowed.

APPEALS: Allowed by either party to District Court within ten days on law—not facts.

EVICTIONS: Yes.

NOTE: The defendant must file a written answer within the time stated on the summons, or he or she will lose by default; a form for this purpose accompanies the summons.

KANSAS: Small Claims (District Court)

STATUTES: Kansas Statutes Annotated (1979): 61-2701 through 61-2713, 61-2703 (amount).

DOLLAR LIMIT: $300.

WHERE TO SUE: County in which the defendant resides. Also, a defendant may be sued in any county where he/she/it can be served if employed or conducting business there, or if the plaintiff resides there.

SERVICE OF PROCESS: Sheriff or disinterested adult (with court's permission).

TRANSFER: Even if the defendant counterclaims over the dollar limit, transfer is still at the judge's discretion.

ATTORNEYS: Not allowed.

APPEALS: Allowed by either party within ten days (5 days in eviction suits) to new District Court Judge.

NOTE: Assignees (collection agencies) cannot sue in Small Claims Court.

KENTUCKY Small Claims (District Court)

STATUTES: Kentucky Revised Statutes (1979): Sec. 24A.200 through 24A.360, 24A.230 (amount).

DOLLAR LIMIT: $500.

WHERE TO SUE: Judicial district in which the defendant resides or the "defendant or defendant's agent is doing business."

SERVICE OF PROCESS: Certified or registered mail first; if that fails, then by sheriff or constable.

TRANSFER: Allowed to regular District Court procedure upon defendant's demand for a jury trial or counterclaim over the dollar limit.

ATTORNEYS: Allowed.

APPEALS: Allowed by either party within 10 days to Circuit Court on law—not facts.

EVICTIONS: Yes.

NOTES: (1) Collection agents, or agencies or lenders of money at interest cannot sue in Small Claims Court.

(2) Jefferson County has a special "Consumer Court" docket, where only consumer plaintiffs may file on consumer disputes.

LOUISIANA Urban: Small Claims (City Court)
Rural: Justice of the Peace

STATUTES: Louisiana Statutes Annotated (1979): 13:5202(A) (amount), and Sec. 13:5200 through 13:5210, Code of Civil Procedure, Articles 4832 (amount) through 4840, 4892 through 4921, 4941, 4942.

DOLLAR LIMIT: $300.

WHERE TO SUE: Parish in which the defendant resides. A corporation or partnership may also be sued in a parish or district in which a business establishment or office is located if the lawsuit resulted from some connection with that particular office or establishment.

SERVICE OF PROCESS: Sheriff, constable, or certified mail (Small Claims only).

TRANSFER: Small Claims may transfer case to regular City Court procedure for any reason, including a counterclaim ("reconventional demand") over the dollar limit. No transfer provision in Justice of the Peace Court.

ATTORNEYS: Allowed.

APPEALS: Allowed by either party in JP courts within 10 days to District Court for new trial. No appeal from Small Claims Court.

EVICTIONS: Yes.

NOTE: Equitable relief is available in Small Claims Court.

MAINE Small Claims (District Court)

STATUTES: Maine Revised Statutes Annotated (1979): 14 Sec. 7451 (amount) through 14 Sec. 7456.

DOLLAR LIMIT: $800.

WHERE TO SUE: District Court "division" in which the defendant resides. A corporation may be sued where it has "an established place of business."

SERVICE OF PROCESS: Ordinary mail.

TRANSFER: No provision.

ATTORNEYS: Allowed.

APPEALS: Allowed by either party within ten days to Superior Court for new trial.

EVICTIONS: Yes.

MARYLAND Informal Procedure (District Court)

STATUTES: Annotated Code of Maryland (1977): Courts and Judicial Proceedings Sec. 6-403 (amount).

DOLLAR LIMIT: $500.

WHERE TO SUE: County in which any defendant resides, is employed, or does business, or where injury to person or property occurred.

SERVICE OF PROCESS: Sheriff or constable.

TRANSFER: No provision.

ATTORNEYS: Allowed.

APPEALS: Allowed by either party within 30 days to Baltimore City Court or Circuit Court (outside of Baltimore) for new trial.

EVICTIONS: Yes.

NOTE: Unincorporated associations may sue and be sued in their common business name.

MASSACHUSETTS Small Claims (Boston—Municipal Court; Elsewhere—District Court)

STATUTES: Massachusetts General Laws Annotated (1979: 93A (consumer complaints) 218 Sec. 21 (amount) through 218 Sec. 25.

DOLLAR LIMIT: $750. ($2,250 on consumer complaints against business.)
WHERE TO SUE: Judicial district in which the defendant resides, is employed, or does business. Actions against landlords can also be brought in the district in which the property is located.
SERVICE OF PROCESS: Sheriff, constable, or registered mail.
TRANSFER: Allowed only at court's discretion.
ATTORNEYS: Allowed.
APPEALS: Allowed by defendant within 10 days to Superior Court for jury trial ($100 bond) where the *defendant* will have the burden of proof (in District Court).
EVICTIONS: No.
NOTES: (1) The dollar limit does not apply to review in Small Claims Court of arbitration awards in auto accident property damage cases. Also, additional statutory penalties (like extra double damages to tenant in security deposit cases) are *not* included in the dollar limit.
   (2) Mediation is available.

MICHIGAN Small Claims (District Court)

STATUTES: Michigan Statutes Annotated (1979): Sec. 27A.8401 (amount) through 27A.8425.
DOLLAR LIMIT: $300.
WHERE TO SUE: District in which any defendant resides, conducts business, or has a place of business, or act or omission occurred.
SERVICE OF PROCESS: Sheriff, disinterested adult, or certified mail.
TRANSFER: Either party may transfer to regular District Court procedure. Defendant's counterclaim over dollar limit will also cause transfer.
ATTORNEYS: Not allowed.
APPEALS: Not allowed.
EVICTIONS: No.
NOTE: Assignees (collection agencies) cannot sue in Small Claims Court.

MINNESOTA Conciliation Court (Municipal or County Court)

STATUTES: Minnesota Statutes Annotated (1978): Municipal Court: Sec. 491.01 through 491.08, 491.04 (amount). County Court: Rules for the Conciliation Courts, Rules 1.01 through 1.26, 1.02 (amount).
DOLLAR LIMIT: Municipal Court—$1,000; County Court—$500.
WHERE TO SUE: County in which any defendant resides or automobile accident occurred. A corporation may be sued in any county in which it has "an office, resident agent, or business place."
SERVICE OF PROCESS: Sheriff, police officer, disinterested adult, registered or unregistered mail. Municipal Court judges or clerks can also effect service "orally, or by telephone."
TRANSFER: If defendant counterclaims over the dollar limit, judge must dismiss case if he/she determines the counterclaim not to be frivolous, and plaintiff must start over again using regular Municipal or County Court procedure.

ATTORNEYS: Allowed in Minneapolis/St. Paul only.
APPEALS: Allowed by either party within 10 days to regular Municipal or County Court for new trial.
EVICTIONS: No.

MISSISSIPPI Justice of the Peace

STATUTES: Mississippi Code Annotated (1978): Sec. 9-11-9 (amount), 11-9-101 through 11-9-143.
DOLLAR LIMIT: $500.
WHERE TO SUE: Justice of the Peace of the district in which any defendant resides, act or omission occurred, or obligation entered into. A corporation "resides" where its registered office is located.
SERVICE OF PROCESS: Sheriff, constable, or disinterested adult (only in "emergency" with court's permission).
TRANSFER: No provision.
ATTORNEYS: Allowed.
APPEALS: Allowed by either party within 10 days to Circuit Court for new trial.
EVICTIONS: Yes.
NOTE: Either party may demand a jury trial.

MISSOURI Small Claims (Circuit Court—Associate Judge)

STATUTES: Vernon's Annotated Missouri Statutes (1979): Sec. 482.300 through 482.365, 482.305 (amount). Missouri Rules of Court (1979): Rules of Practice and Procedure in Small Claims Courts, Rules 140.01 through 155, 140.06 (amount).
DOLLAR LIMIT: $500.
WHERE TO SUE: County in which any defendant resides (or can be found, if plaintiff lives there), or act or omission occurred. A corporation "resides" wherever an "office or agent for the transaction of its usual and customary business" is located.
SERVICE OF PROCESS: Sheriff or certified mail.
TRANSFER: Allowed to regular Magistrate Court procedure only if defendant counterclaims over dollar limit and the counterclaim arises out of the same incident.
ATTORNEYS: Allowed.
APPEALS: Allowed by either party within 10 days for new trial before regular Circuit Court judge.
EVICTIONS: No.

MONTANA Small Claims (Justice's Court)

STATUTES: Montana Code Annotated (1978): District Court: Secs. 3-12-101 through 3-12-203, 3-12-106 (amount), 25-34-101 through 25-34-404; Justice Court: Secs. 3-10-1001 through 3-10-1005, 3-10-1004 (amount), 25-35-101 through 25-35-406.
DOLLAR LIMIT: Small Claims Court—$750; Justice's Court—$750.

WHERE TO SUE: County or judicial district in which any defendant resides or obligation was to be performed. Service of summons limited to within county boundaries.

SERVICE OF PROCESS: Sheriff, constable (Justice's Court), or disinterested adult (Justice's Court only).

TRANSFER: Not allowed, even on defendant's counterclaim over dollar limit. (If defendant has such a counterclaim he/she must sue later in another court.)

ATTORNEYS: Not allowed, unless *all* parties present have attorneys.

APPEALS: Allowed by either party within 10 days to District Court. New trial if originally tried in District Small Claims Court; on law only—not facts—if originally tried in Justice's Small Claims Court.

EVICTIONS: No.

NOTES: (1) Montana does not allow Small Claims based on injury or property damage.

(2) Assignees (collection agencies) cannot sue in Small Claims Court.

(3) In District Court defendant who does not counterclaim may demand jury trial.

(4) Small Claims Court is allowed by local option. The result is that it exists only in parts of the state.

NEBRASKA Small Claims (County or Municipal Court)

STATUTES: Revised Statutes of Nebraska (1979): Sec. 24-521 through 24-527, 24-522 (amount).

DOLLAR LIMIT: $1000.

WHERE TO SUE: County in which any defendant resides (or can be found, if plaintiff lives there), or injury or property damage occurred. A corporation "resides" wherever it regularly does business through an office or agent.

SERVICE OF PROCESS: Sheriff, or certified or registered mail.

TRANSFER: Transferable to regular civil court procedure on defendant's request or counterclaim over the dollar limit.

ATTORNEYS: Not allowed.

APPEALS: Allowed by either party within 10 days to District Court for new trial.

EVICTIONS: Yes.

NOTE: Equitable relief is available.

NEVADA Small Claims (Justice's Court)

STATUTES: Nevada Revised Statutes (1977): Sec. 4.370 (amount), 73.010 (amount) through 73.060, and Justice's Courts Rules of Civil Procedure, Rules 80A (amount) through 80J.

DOLLAR LIMIT: $750.

WHERE TO SUE: City or township in which the defendant resides.

SERVICE OF PROCESS: Sheriff, constable, Justice of the Peace, disinterested adult, or certified or registered mail.

TRANSFER: No provision.
ATTORNEYS: Allowed.
APPEALS: Allowed by either party within five days to District Court on law or facts; the District Court may at its discretion grant a new trial there.
EVICTIONS: No.

NEW HAMPSHIRE Small Claims (District or Municipal Court)

STATUTES: New Hampshire Revised Statutes Annotated (1977): Sec. 503:1 (amount).
DOLLAR LIMIT: $500.
WHERE TO SUE: District (or city or town for Municipal Court) in which plaintiff or the defendant resides.
SERVICE OF PROCESS: Sheriff or registered mail.
TRANSFER: No provision.
ATTORNEYS: Allowed.
APPEALS: Allowed only on questions of law, to N.H. Supreme Court in rare cases.

NEW JERSEY Small Claims (County District Court)

STATUTES: New Jersey Statutes Annotated (1978): Sec. 2A:6-41 through 2A:6-44, 2A:6-43 (amount), 2A:18-65 through 2A:18-71. Rules covering the courts of the state of New Jersey. Rules covering civil practice in the County District Court. Rule 6:11.
DOLLAR LIMIT: $500.
WHERE TO SUE: County in which any defendant resides. A corporation "resides" wherever it is "actually doing business."
SERVICE OF PROCESS: Constable, "sergeant-at-arms," or certified mail.
TRANSFER: Allowed to regular civil court if defendant counterclaims over dollar limit.
ATTORNEYS: Allowed.
APPEALS: Allowed by either party within 45 days to Appellate Division of Superior Court on law—not facts.
EVICTIONS: No.
NOTES: (1) The court will not hear cases involving personal injury or of property damage except those resulting from auto accidents.
(2) A jury trial may be demanded by the defendant for amounts over $50.
(3) Assignees (collection agencies) cannot sue in Small Claims Court.

NEW MEXICO Bernalillo County—Small Claims; Rural—

Magistrate Court

STATUTES: New Mexico Statutes (1976): Small Claims Sec. 16-5-1 (amount) through 16-5-13; Magistrate Court Sec. 35-3-3 (amount) through 35-3-6.
DOLLAR LIMIT: $2,000.

WHERE TO SUE: Small Claims Court: county in which the defendant can be served. Magistrate Court: magisterial district where plaintiff or defendant resides or may be found, or where act or omission occurred. But each defendant must be served within the magisterial district.

SERVICE OF PROCESS: Sheriff or disinterested adult.

TRANSFER: Small Claims: defendant can transfer case to District Court by demanding jury trial. Magistrate Court: no provision.

ATTORNEYS: Allowed.

APPEALS: Allowed by either party within 30 days to District Court on law—not facts.

EVICTIONS: No.

NOTES: (1) In Magistrate Court, the defendant must file a written answer within the time noted on the summons, or he or she will lose by default.

(2) A jury trial may be demanded by either party.

NEW YORK Small Claims (New York City Civil Court, City Courts outside of New York City, District Court in Nassau and Western Suffolk Counties, Justice Courts in rural areas)

STATUTES: McKinney's Consolidated Laws of New York Annotated (1979): Volume 29A, Sec. 1801 (amount) through 1814 of the New York City Civil Court Act and the uniform acts for district, city and justice courts.

DOLLAR LIMIT: $1,000.

WHERE TO SUE: Political subdivision in which the defendant resides, is employed, or has a business office. The types of political subdivisions are as follows: New York City Civil Court (New York City); District Court (Judicial District); City Court (County); Justice Court (Municipality).

SERVICE OF PROCESS: Disinterested adult, or certified or registered mail—valid only within the county (or New York City) in which the court is located.

TRANSFER: Allowed by defendant to regular civil court procedure only if defendant demands a jury trial. A counterclaim over the dollar limit will not cause a transfer.

ATTORNEYS: Allowed. Corporations must be represented by an attorney; the exceptions to this are that nonattorney stockholders owning one-third or more of the total shares, and nonattorney officers of corporations having ten or fewer stockholders (all of whom must be individuals) may appear on behalf of the corporation. In summary, this allows small corporations relief from the formerly very strict New York rule that corporations must be represented by attorneys.

APPEALS: Not allowed from decision by arbitrator. Allowed by defendant within 30 days to County Court or Appellate Division of the Supreme Court from decision by judge for the county, on law—not facts. Plaintiffs can appeal only on the grounds that "substantial justice has not been done . . . according to rules and principles of substantive law," and will seldom win on appeal.

EVICTIONS: No.

NOTES: (1) New York City Court sessions are held exclusively at 6:30 P.M., and are handled 85 percent of the time by arbitrators. Evening sessions are required in all other courts as well.

(2) For businesses having a record of refusing to pay three or more Small Claims judgments to winning plaintiffs, any such plaintiff who has not been paid after 30 days may sue again for three times the unpaid judgment plus attorneys fees (Sec. 1812).

(3) Business defendants can be sued in their common business names, and clerks must correct the record if told true names before trial. Judgments unpaid after 35 days by business defendants sued this way will increase liability by additional $100 plus attorneys' fees.

(4) Assignees (collection agencies), corporations, partnerships, and associations cannot sue in Small Claims Court. (An exception to this is that partnerships and associations can sue in Nassau and Suffolk County District Courts, although corporations cannot.)

NORTH CAROLINA Small Claims (District Court)

STATUTES: General Statutes of North Carolina (1979): Sec. 7A-210 (amount) through 7A-232.

DOLLAR LIMIT: $800.

WHERE TO SUE: County in which the defendant resides. A corporation "resides" where it "maintains a place of business."

SERVICE OF PROCESS: Sheriff or certified mail.

TRANSFER: Cases are originally filed as though in the regular District Court, then are "transferred" to the Small Claims docket by the judge. If the judge fails to do this within five days after the case is filed, it stays on the regular (more formal) docket! Defendants' counterclaims over the dollar limit are not allowed, and such a claim must be brought later on the regular District Court docket. But defendant can transfer case back to the regular docket.

ATTORNEYS: Allowed.

APPEALS: Allowed by either party within ten days to District Court Division of Superior Court for new trial.

EVICTIONS: Yes.

NOTE: Equitable relief is available.

NORTH DAKOTA Small Claims (County Justice or "County Court with Increased Jurisdiction")

STATUTES: North Dakota Century Code (1979): Sec. 27-08.1-01 (amount) through 27-08.1-08.

DOLLAR LIMIT: County Justice—$500; "County Court with Increased Jurisdiction—$1,000.

WHERE TO SUE: Individuals as defendant(s)—county in which the defendant resides; corporation and partnership defendants—county in which the defendant has a place of business, or act or omission occurred.

SERVICE OF PROCESS: Sheriff, disinterested adult, or certified mail.
TRANSFER: Defendant may transfer case to regular civil court procedure.
ATTORNEYS: Allowed.
APPEALS: Not allowed.
EVICTIONS: No.
NOTES: (1) Assignees (collection agencies) cannot sue in Small Claims Court. Collection of unpaid judgments is done through District Court.

(2) Equitable relief is available.

OHIO Small Claims (County or Municipal Court)

STATUTES: Ohio Revised Code Annotated (1979): Sec. 1925.01 through 1925.17, 1925.02 (amount).
DOLLAR LIMIT: $500.
WHERE TO SUE: County Court—county in which the defendant resides. If two or more defendants reside in adjacent counties, then in either of those counties. In suits against two or more defendants based on "notes or due bills," suit can only be brought in the county in which any defendant entered into the obligation.
Municipal Court—city or county in which the defendant resides. A corporation "resides" where it has an office or agent.
SERVICE OF PROCESS: Sheriff (County Court), Court Bailiff (Municipal Court), disinterested adult (with court's permission), or certified mail.
TRANSFER: Allowed to regular civil court procedure on defendant's request or counterclaim over $1,000.
ATTORNEYS: Allowed; not required for corporations, but a nonattorney who appears on behalf of a corporation may not engage in cross-examination or argument.
APPEALS: Allowed by either party within 30 days to Court of Common Pleas, on law—not facts.
EVICTIONS: No.
NOTES: (1) Assignees (collection agencies) cannot sue in Small Claims Court.

(2) A losing defendant who does not pay in 30 days can be forced to answer a mailed questionnaire revealing his or her assets. Failure to do so constitutes contempt of court.

OKLAHOMA Small Claims (District Court)

STATUTES: Oklahoma Statutes Annotated (1979): 12 Sec. 1751 (amount) through 12 Sec. 1771.
DOLLAR LIMIT: $600.
WHERE TO SUE: County in which the defendant resides, or obligation was entered into. In automobile or boat accident cases, plaintiff can sue in the county where the defendant resides or can be served, or where the accident occurred. A corporation may be sued in a county in which it is "situated" (i.e., has an office), the act or omission occurred, or where another defendant is properly sued.

SERVICE OF PROCESS: Sheriff or certified mail.

TRANSFER: Allowed to regular District Court procedure on defendant's request or counterclaim over dollar limit. After such a transfer, the plaintiff must file a written complaint within 20 days, or the lawsuit will be dismissed.

ATTORNEYS: Allowed.

APPEALS: Allowed by either party to Oklahoma Supreme Court, on law only—not facts.

EVICTIONS: No.

NOTES: (1) A jury trial may be demanded by either party.

(2) Suits to recover personal property are allowed.

OREGON Small Claims (District or Justice Court)

STATUTES: Oregon Revised Statutes (1977): Sec. 46.405 (amount) through 46.560, 55.011 (amount) through 55.140.

DOLLAR LIMIT: $700.

WHERE TO SUE: District Court S.C.C.—county in which any defendant resides or can be found, injury or property damage occurred, or obligation was to be performed.

Justice Court S.C.C.—county in which the defendant resides, or in which plaintiff resides if the defendant can be served in that county.

SERVICE OF PROCESS: Sheriff, constable (Justice Court), disinterested adult, or certified mail (on claims under $50).

TRANSFER: Allowed to regular civil court procedure on defendant's counterclaim over dollar limit.

ATTORNEYS: Not allowed without judge's consent.

APPEALS: From District Court S.C.C.—allowed by either party within 30 days to Court of Appeals, on law—not facts.

From Justice Court S.C.C.—allowed by defendant (on claims over $30) within ten days to Circuit Court for new trial.

EVICTIONS: No.

NOTES: (1) In District Court S.C.C., the defendant must demand a judge or jury trial within 14 days of service or he or she will lose by default.

(2) A jury trial may be demanded by defendant on claims over $200 in District Court S.C.C. In Justice Court S.C.C., the defendant may transfer the case to regular Justice Court procedure on claims over $200 and may then demand a jury trial.

PENNSYLVANIA Philadelphia—Philadelphia Municipal Court;

Everywhere else—District Justice

STATUTES: Purdon's Pennsylvania Statutes Annotated (1979): 42 Sec. 1515 (amount) and Rules of Civil Procedure for Justices of the Peace, Rules 301 through 325, and for Philadelphia, 42 Sec. 1123 and Pennsylvania Rules of Court (1979): Rules of the Philadelphia Municipal Court, Rules 101 (amount) through 120.

PHILADELPHIA MUNICIPAL COURT

DOLLAR LIMIT: $1,000.

WHERE TO SUE: Philadelphia County, if the defendant resides or "regularly conducts business" there, or act or omission occurred there.

SERVICE OF PROCESS: Within Philadelphia County, papers must be served by "Municipal Court Writ Servers"; outside of the county, service is by certified mail.

TRANSFER: Allowed to Court of Common Pleas only on defendant's counterclaim over the dollar limit.

ATTORNEYS: Allowed; required for corporations.

APPEALS: Allowed by either party within 30 days to Court of Common Pleas for new trial.

EVICTIONS: Yes.

DISTRICT JUSTICE

DOLLAR LIMIT: $2,000.

WHERE TO SUE: Magisterial district in which the defendant can be served, or the act or omission occurred. Corporations and partnerships can also be sued where they regularly do business.

SERVICE OF PROCESS: Sheriff, constable, or certified or registered mail.

TRANSFER: No provision.

ATTORNEYS: Allowed.

APPEALS: Allowed by either party within 30 days to Court of Common Pleas for new trial.

EVICTIONS: Yes.

NOTE: Pennsylvania has no "Small Claims" Court as such, but the new Justice of the Peace rules were designed to provide this function.

PUERTO RICO Small Claims (District Court)

STATUTES: Laws of Puerto Rico Annotated (1978): 32 Sec. 3031 (amount) through 32 Sec. 3034, and Title 32, Appendix II, Rule 60

DOLLAR LIMIT: $100.

WHERE TO SUE: Individuals as defendants—judicial district in which any defendant resides. Corporation, partnership, and association defendants—judicial district in which any defendant does business, or where obligation was incurred.

SERVICE OF PROCESS: "Clerk shall forthwith serve notice upon the defendant by mail, telegraph, or any other means of communication in writing."

TRANSFER: No provision.

ATTORNEYS: Allowed.

APPEALS: Allowed by either party within 10 days to Superior Court, on law—not facts.

EVICTIONS: No.

NOTE: The defendant must file a written answer at the hearing.

RHODE ISLAND Small Claims (District Court)

STATUTES: General Laws of Rhode Island (1978): Sec. 10-16-1 (amount) through 10-16-16.

DOLLAR LIMIT: $500.

WHERE TO SUE: Anywhere in the state, except that corporation plaintiffs can bring suit only in the District Court division in which the defendant resides.

SERVICE OF PROCESS: Certified or registered mail first; if that fails, then by sheriff, "town sergeant," constable, or disinterested adult (with court's permission).

TRANSFER: Allowed to regular District Court procedure on defendant's counterclaim over the dollar limit, provided the Small Claims judge decides that there is a good legal basis for the counterclaim.

ATTORNEYS: Allowed; required for corporations, except that family-owned corporations having assets of under one million dollars can be represented by a nonattorney.

APPEALS: Allowed by defendant within two days to Superior Court for new trial.

EVICTIONS: No.

NOTES: (1) Rhode Island is unusual in that it does not allow lawsuits based on injury or property damage. Only lawsuits based on an obligation or contract or "to recover the amount of any tax . . . and in all actions or suits to recover (money) resulting from a retail sale of . . . personal property to a member of the general public, or from services rendered to a member of the general public. . . . "

(2) Certified or registered mail service is binding on a defendant who refuses to accept and sign for the letter. (This is only true if it comes back from the post office marked "refused," not if it just says "unclaimed.")

SOUTH CAROLINA Magistrate's Court

STATUTES: Code of Laws of South Carolina (1978): Sec. 22-3-10 (amount) through 22-3-320.

DOLLAR LIMIT: $500.

WHERE TO SUE: County or township (subject to local laws) in which the defendant resides. A corporation "resides" where it is doing business.

SERVICE OF PROCESS: Sheriff or disinterested adult.

TRANSFER: No provision.

ATTORNEYS: Allowed.

APPEALS: Allowed by either party within ten days to County or Circuit Court, on law--not facts.

EVICTIONS: Yes.

NOTES: (1) The defendant must give an oral or written answer within 20 days of service (five days on claims under $25), or he or she will lose by default.

(2) A jury trial may be demanded by either party.

SOUTH DAKOTA Small Claims (Circuit or Magistrate Court)

STATUTES: South Dakota Compiled Laws (1979): Sec. 15-39-1 (amount) through 15-39-43.

DOLLAR LIMIT: $1,000.

WHERE TO SUE: County in which any defendant resides, or injury or property damage occurred. A corporation "resides" at its principal place of business.

SERVICE OF PROCESS: Certified or registered mail first; service this way is binding on defendant who refuses to accept and sign for the letter. If *not* refused, but still undeliverable, then service must be made by sheriff or disinterested adult (who resides in county where service made).

TRANSFER: Allowed by defendant to regular civil court procedure if he/she demands a jury trial.

ATTORNEYS: Allowed.

APPEALS: Not allowed.

EVICTIONS: No.

NOTE: The defendant must give an oral or written answer at least two days before the trial date, or he or she will lose by default. This rule also applies to plaintiffs, who must file a response to any counterclaim by a defendant.

TENNESSEE Court of General Sessions or Justice of the Peace.

STATUTES: Tennessee Code Annotated (1978): Sec. 16-1101 through 16-1118, 19-301 (amount) through 19-710.

DOLLAR LIMIT: $5,000.

WHERE TO SUE: Civil district in which the defendant resides, or adjacent district if nearer to the defendant's residence. For "collection of debt" where the defendant is a nonresident of the county, suit may be brought in the district where the plaintiff resides. In a suit against two or more defendants on notes or contracts, where one defendant has guaranteed payment by the other, the suit can be brought in the district (or adjacent district if closer) in which *any* defendant resides.

SERVICE OF PROCESS: Sheriff or constable.

TRANSFER: No provision.

ATTORNEYS: Allowed.

APPEALS: Allowed by either party within ten days to Circuit Court for new trial.

EVICTIONS: Yes.

NOTE: Tennessee has no Small Claims Court or equivalent to it. However, no formal written papers need be filed in JP or General Sessions courts, except for a simple one-page statement of the plaintiff's claim. No written or oral answer need be filed by a defendant, who need only show up in court as noted on the summons. (The sheriff or constable sets the court date within two weeks of service.) Neither party is entitled to a jury trial. In counties with both General Sessions courts and JPs, the JP has no civil court function other than issuing summons for the Court of General Sessions.

TEXAS Small Claims (Justice of the Peace)

STATUTES: Texas Statutes Annotated (1978), Civil Statutes, Articles 2460a Section 1 (amount) through 2460a Section 14.

DOLLAR LIMIT: $500.

WHERE TO SUE: Precinct in which the defendant resides or obligation was to be performed. Corporations and associations may be sued where they have agencies or representatives.

SERVICE OF PROCESS: Sheriff or constable.

TRANSFER: No provision.

ATTORNEYS: Allowed.

APPEALS: Allowed by either party within ten days (on claims over $20) to County Court or "County Court at Law" for new trial.

EVICTIONS: No.

NOTE: Assignees (collection agencies) and lenders of money at interest cannot sue in Small Claims Court. A jury trial may be demanded by either party.

UTAH Small Claims (Circuit or Justice's Court)

STATUTES: Utah Code Annotated (1979): Sec. 78-6-1 (amount) through 78-6-15.

DOLLAR LIMIT: $400.

WHERE TO SUE: Political subdivision in which the defendant resides or act or omission occurred; the type of political subdivision is as follows: County (Circuit Court); City (Justice's Court or Municipal Department of Circuit Court), Town or precinct (Justice's Court).

SERVICE OF PROCESS: Sheriff or disinterested adult.

TRANSFER: No provision.

ATTORNEYS: Allowed.

APPEALS: Allowed by defendant (or plaintiff who lost on a counterclaim) within ten days to District Court for new trial.

EVICTIONS: No.

NOTE: Assignees (collection agencies) cannot sue in Small Claims Court.

VERMONT Small Claims (District Court)

STATUTES: Vermont Statutes Annotated (1979): 12 Sec. 5531 (amount) through 12 Sec. 5535, District Court Civil Rules, Rule 80.3.

DOLLAR LIMIT: $500.

WHERE TO SUE: Territorial unit in which any defendant or *plaintiff* resides, or act or omission occurred.

SERVICE OF PROCESS: Sheriff, constable, disinterested adult (with court's permission), or registered mail.

TRANSFER: Defendant may transfer to regular District Court procedure by demanding a jury trial.

ATTORNEYS: Allowed.

APPEALS: Allowed by either party within 30 days to Vermont Supreme Court, on law only—not facts.

EVICTIONS: Yes.

NOTE: Defendant must give a written or oral answer within 20 days of service, or he or she will lose by default.

VIRGINIA General District Court

STATUTES: Code of Virginia (1978): Sec. 16.1-76 through 16.1-113, 16.1-77 (amount).

DOLLAR LIMIT: $5,000.

WHERE TO SUE: District in which any defendant resides, is employed, or "regularly and systematically conducts affairs or business activity," or act or omission occurred.

SERVICE OF PROCESS: Sheriff or disinterested adult.

TRANSFER: Allowed by defendant (except in eviction suits) to Circuit Court on claims over $1000; the defendant may file a counterclaim for $5000 or less, and can demand transfer if the counterclaim is over $1000.

ATTORNEYS: Allowed.

APPEALS: Allowed by either party within ten days (on cases over $50) to Circuit Court for new trial.

EVICTIONS: Yes.

NOTE: Virginia has no Small Claims Court or equivalent. However, no formal written "pleadings" (complicated papers) need be filed in General District Court; the defendant must, however, fill out and file an "appearance card" within the time noted on the summons or he/she will lose by default. The card merely gives notice of an intent to contest the lawsuit, is easy to fill out, and is available from the court clerk. Plaintiffs and defendants often come in without an attorney and sometimes do quite well, according to the Arlington County clerk. No jury trial is allowed.

WASHINGTON Small Claims (Justice or District Court)

STATUTES: Revised Code of Washington Annotated (1979): Sec. 12.40.010 (amount) through 12.40.120

DOLLAR LIMIT: $500 in some larger counties; $200 elsewhere.

WHERE TO SUE: City, town, or Justice of the Peace district in which any defendant resides. Suits in Justice Court S.C.C. may be brought in either of the two districts nearest defendant, or in the district located in the county seat for the county in which the defendant resides. A corporation "resides" where it "transacts business or has an office."

SERVICE OF PROCESS: Sheriff, constable, disinterested adult, or certified or registered mail.

TRANSFER: No provision. Defendant having a counterclaim over the dollar limit must sue on it later in regular civil court.

ATTORNEYS: Not allowed without judge's consent, unless the case originally began in regular civil court.

APPEALS: Allowed by defendant within 20 days (on claims over $100) to Superior Court for new trial.
EVICTIONS: No.

WEST VIRGINIA Magistrate Court

STATUTES: West Virginia Code (1979): Sec. 50-2-1 (amount) through 50-6-3.
DOLLAR LIMIT: $1,500.
WHERE TO SUE: County in which any defendant resides or can be served. If defendant is a corporation, the suit can be brought in the county where the act or omission occurred. A corporation chartered in the state "resides" at its principal office or where its chief officer resides. Corporations not chartered in the state "reside" wherever they do business.
SERVICE OF PROCESS: Sheriff or disinterested adult.
TRANSFER: Allowed by defendant to Circuit Court on claims over $300.
ATTORNEYS: Allowed.
APPEALS: Allowed by either party within 20 days (five days in eviction suits) to Circuit Court for new trial.
EVICTIONS: Yes.
NOTES: (1) A jury trial may be demanded by either party on eviction cases or any other claim over $20.
(2) The defendant must give a written or oral answer within 20 days or he or she will lose by default.

WISCONSIN Small Claims (County Court)

STATUTES: Wisconsin Statutes Annotated (1978): Sec. 299.01 (amount) through 299.45.
DOLLAR LIMIT: $1,000; no limit on eviction suits.
WHERE TO SUE: County in which any defendant resides (or can be served, if sued on an oral or written contract), or injury or property damage occurred. A corporation chartered in the state "resides" at its principal office. Other corporations "reside" wherever "substantial business activity" is conducted.
SERVICE OF PROCESS: Sheriff, disinterested adult, or mail (local court rules may require that the mail be certified or registered). No service by mail allowed at all in eviction suits.
TRANSFER: Allowed to regular County Court procedure on defendant's counterclaim over dollar limit, or by either party if a jury trial is demanded.
ATTORNEYS: Allowed; required for corporations.
APPEALS: Allowed by either party within 45 days (90 days if party received no written notice of the court's finding) to Court of Appeals, on law—not facts.
EVICTIONS: Yes.
NOTE: The defendant might (by local rule) have to file a written or oral answer or he or she will lose by default.

WYOMING "Informal Procedure" (County Court or Justice of the Peace)

STATUTES: Wyoming Statutes (1977): Sec. 5-91 (amount), 5-114.3 (amount), and Code of Civil Procedure Sec. 1-508 through 1-660, 1-562 (amount).

DOLLAR LIMIT: "Informal Procedure"—$200; with "Formal Procedure," the limit is $1000.

WHERE TO SUE: County in which the defendant resides or can be served. A corporation may be sued where it is "situated."

SERVICE OF PROCESS: Sheriff, constable (Justice of the Peace), or disinterested adult (with court's permission in JP Court).

TRANSFER: No provision.

ATTORNEYS: Allowed.

APPEALS: Allowed by either party to District Court as follows: Within fifteen days from Justice of the Peace on claims over $25 for new trial; within ten days from County Court, on law only—not facts.

EVICTIONS: Yes.

NOTES: (1) A jury trial may be demanded by either party.

(2) In the "formal procedure" (on claims between $200 and $1,000) the defendant must give a written or oral (JP Court only) answer or he or she will lose by default.

About Nolo Press

This book was created by Nolo Press in Berkeley, California. Nolo consists of a group of friends (some lawyers, some not) who have come to see much of what passes for the practice of law as meaningless mumbo jumbo and needless paper shuffling designed by lawyers to mystify and confuse. Since 1971 Nolo has published more than a dozen books designed to give ordinary people access to their legal system and, in so doing, has become one of the principal energy centers of the self-help law movement.

Resources

Self-Help Law Books Mentioned in the Text

These books deserve a place on your reference shelf:

California Tenants' Handbook—Tenants' Rights, Attorneys Myron Moskovitz, Ralph Warner, and Ed Sherman. An excellent guide to tenants' rights and responsibilities. Sound practical advice on getting deposits back, breaking a lease, getting repairs made, using Small Claims Court, dealing with obnoxious landlords, and forming a tenants' union. (Nolo Press, 5th ed., 1980) $6.95

California Debtors' Handbook—Billpayers' Rights, Attorneys Peter Jan Honigsberg and Ralph Warner. A constructive guide for those who find themselves over their heads in legal debts. Information on wage and bank account attachments, car repossession, child-support debts, student loans, bankruptcy, etc. Also, how to deal with collection agencies. (Nolo Press, 3rd ed., 1979) $5.95

Protect Your Home with a Declaration of Homestead. You can protect your home up to $40,000 from your creditors under California law. Here's how: cheaply, easily, and legally. (Nolo Press, 3rd edition, 1978) $4.95

Cluing into Legal Research, Attorney Peter Jan Honigsberg. This is the best guide for nonlawyers on how to do legal research. A readable, easy-to-use book for people who wish to "break the code" of the law library and do their own legal research. Much practical information on how to research cases, decipher code books, and make use of legal encyclopedias. (Golden Rain Press—Nolo Press, 1979) $7.95

How to Collect Your Child Support and Alimony. Step-by-step on how to collect back support, including sections on how to find people and their property and what to do when you do find them. (Nolo Press, 1977) $7.95

Bankruptcy: Do It Yourself, Attorney Janice Kosel. A complete guide on how to file bankruptcy, complete with all the forms you will need to do it. Contains comprehensive information on the exemption laws of all states. (Addison-Wesley Publishing Company, 1980)

Prices subject to change without notice. Further information on these and other books and up-to-date catalogs are available from NOLO PRESS, 950 Parker Street, Berkeley, CA 94710 or from Addison-Wesley Publishing Company, Reading, MA 01867.

Other Addison-Wesley and Nolo Press Law Books

The Peoples' Law Review, Attorney Ralph Warner (ed.), Addison-Wesley, 1980.

How to Do Your Own Divorce in Texas, Attorneys Ed Sherman and Jim Simons, Addison-Wesley, 1980.

How to Form Your Own Texas Corporation, Attorneys Anthony Mancuso and Jim Simons, Addison-Wesley, 1980.

Planning Your Estate with Wills, Probates, and Taxes, Texas Edition, Attorneys Denis Clifford and Jim Simons, Addison-Wesley, 1980.

The Texas Tenants' Handbook, Attorney Jim Simons, Addison-Wesley, 1980.

A Legal Guide for Gay and Lesbian Couples, Attorney Denis Clifford, Addison-Wesley, 1980.

The California Nonprofit Corporation Handbook, Attorney Anthony Mancuso, Nolo Press. $15.00

How to Do Your Own Divorce in California, Attorney Ed Sherman, Nolo Press. $8.95

How to Change Your Name, Nolo Press. $7.95

Planning Your Estate with Wills, Probates, Trusts, and Taxes, California Edition, Attorney Denis Clifford, Nolo Press. $15.00

How to Adopt Your Stepchild in California, Frank Zagone, Nolo Press. $10.00

How to Form Your Own California Corporation, Attorney Anthony Mancuso, Nolo Press. $15.00

The People's Guide to California Marriage and Divorce Law, Nolo Press. $6.95

Index

The letter *n* attached to page numbers means the referenced material is found in a footnote.